Speak of the devil

Tales of satanic abuse in contemporary England

J. S. La Fontaine

CAMBRIDGE
UNIVERSITY PRESS

PUBLISHED BY THE PRESS SYNDICATE OF THE UNIVERSITY OF CAMBRIDGE
The Pitt Building, Trumpington Street, Cambridge CB2 1RP, United Kingdom

CAMBRIDGE UNIVERSITY PRESS
The Edinburgh Building, Cambridge, CB2 2RU, United Kingdom
40 West 20th Street, New York, NY 10011-4211, USA
10 Stamford Road, Oakleigh, Melbourne 3166, Australia

© J. S. La Fontaine 1998

First published 1998

Typeset in Plantin 10/12

A catalogue record for this book is available from the British Library

Library of Congress Cataloguing in Publication data

La Fontaine, J. S. (Jean Sybil), 1931–
  Speak of the Devil: tales of satanic abuse in contemporary England /
J. S. La Fontaine.
    p.   cm.
  ISBN 0 521 62082 1 (hb) – ISBN 0 521 62934 9 (pb)
  1. Ritual abuse – Great Britain.   2. Satanism – Great Britain.
3. Occult crime – Great Britain.   4. Occult crime investigation –
Great Britain.   I. Title.
HV6626.54.G7L3   1997
364.15'554'0941 – dc21   97-9822   CIP

ISBN 0 521 62082 1 hardback
ISBN 0 521 62934 9 paperback

Transferred to digital printing 1999

CE

Allegations of satanic child abuse became widespread in north America in the early 1980s. In Britain shortly afterwards there were similar claims that sexual abuse, torture and murder were taking place as part of rites of witchcraft and devil worship. Jean La Fontaine, a senior British anthropologist, was funded by the Department of Health to undertake research into the allegations and found that there was no independent corroboration of these allegations in the many cases she studied. The problem then was to explain why they continued to be believed. Professor La Fontaine draws parallels with witchcraft accusations in the classic literature of anthropology and also with the witch-hunts in sixteenth- and seventeenth-century Europe, showing how this contemporary social movement drew on different elements in British society and was fostered by the climate of socio- economic change and insecurity.

Persuasively argued, this is an authoritative and scholarly account of a controversial, emotive issue.

Speak of the devil

Contents

Tables

Acknowledgements

This book has taken several years from the first research proposal to the final product. During this time a large number of people have helped me in different ways and at different times. It is a pleasure to be able to thank them publicly.

The research was funded by the Secretary of State for Health. For seven months I also had a personal grant from the Nuffield Foundation. I am very grateful to both organisations. However, the book is of course solely my own work and the views and ideas expressed in it mine alone. I must also thank the Steering Group set up by the Department of Health to assist me and assure them in the same way. I am indebted to the Lord Chancellor's Department for permission to study case files in the Official Solicitor's office and to David Venables, the Official Solicitor at the time, and his staff, including the invaluable archivist, Clare Brennan, for hospitality and help during the time I was working there. The Association of Directors of Social Services and the Association of Chief Police Officers gave their support to the proposal for a national survey, and the NSPCC, joining in rather later, was heroically successful in getting its teams to complete questionnaires in record time. I received help in devising these questionnaires from my colleague in the London School of Economics, Dr C. O'Muircheartaigh of the Methods Unit – my grateful thanks and my assurance that he cannot be blamed for the end product! The survey was conducted jointly with a team from the Department of Social Policy and Social Work of Manchester University who were studying organised and institutional abuse. My regular contact with the director of the team, Bernard Gallagher, was very helpful and I hope he found our discussions as fruitful as I did. The survey would have been impossible without the input of many men and women of the social services, police forces and the NSPCC who took the time to fill in the questionnaires; I am extremely grateful to them and to those who also spent time with me talking about their cases.

At the very early stages of the project I received two very valuable suggestions: Alan MacFarlane lent me his copy of Gustav Henningsen's book, *The Witches' Advocate*, which gave me a new perspective on the early modern witch-hunts; and Conrad Dehn, QC, wrote to ask why social scientists did not make use of the material available in legal documents. I replied with alacrity that I was more than happy to do so, and thanks to his good offices and the kind support of Sir Stephen Brown, President of the Family Court, I was able to obtain permission from the Lord Chancellor's Office to study the Official Solicitor's files. Without those two pieces of good fortune this book would probably not have been written.

My research grant was administered by INFORM, a charity based in the London School of Economics that aims to document, fairly and in as much detail as possible, all new religions in order to ensure better public understanding of them. The different staff members were all endlessly helpful to me in a lot of little ways that made a big difference to my morale and my ability to work. The Obscene Publications Squad of the Metropolitan Police at New Scotland Yard, under its then head, Superintendant Mike Hames, were very generous in sharing information with me and I am particularly grateful to Detective Sergeant Keith Driver for his help.

I am also happy to record the valuable work of Fiona Dunne and Mark Dunn; the former was my research assistant for seven months and undertook the essential but tedious tasks of collating information and indexing notes on cases, while Mark, at the enlightened suggestion of his social service boss (to whom I am indebted), was my collaborator on a case study of a fascinating large case. It was a pleasure to work with them both. Members of the occult community supplied me with information and some of them – Chris Bray, Leonora James, Gareth Medway and Elen Williams – were good enough to read the manuscript of chapter 3 and correct my errors. James Nice and Peter Ward were generous in sharing their research data with me, and Peter was always ready to help with queries; I thank them both.

Some early drafts of chapters were read as papers at seminars. I would like to thank the members of the Anthropology Department seminars at University College London, the School of Oriental and African Studies London, the University of London interdepartmental seminar, and the Department of Child Studies in Linköping, Sweden, for useful discussions. Part of chapter 9 was given in a slightly different version at a conference in Berkeley California in 1996; my thanks to Professor Nancy Scheper-Hughes for inviting me there.

Several other people have read what I have written, in drafts or in final form. Peter Harris, the present Official Solicitor, kindly read the whole book with great speed, despite his many commitments, and

Christopher Scarles of Cambridge University Press surprised me by giving me an opinion after three weeks. I owe them my thanks, which I extend also to the anonymous reviewers, some of whom reviewed my research for the Department of Health and others who, much later on, read the book for my publishers. Their comments helped me improve the work and encouraged me to think it was worthwhile. Gustav Henningsen kindly read a draft of chapter 2 and Sylvia Lowe, Louise Armstrong and Sherrill Mulhern undertook even greater labours for the sake of friendship. Philippa Youngman tactfully and with great skill improved the accuracy and style of the book, for which I am greatly indebted to her. Professor Schapera kindly proof read the manuscript for me. Amanda Sackur was always willing to discuss my analysis, evaluate my historical comparisons, lend me books and search for references; I am very grateful for her unselfish generosity with her very scarce time. Throughout the whole period of the research, my sister Hilary (who also read a draft and assured me that it was quite intelligible) and my family were a constant source of support when I needed it. I cannot thank them adequately but I do thank them very warmly indeed.

I can assure all these people that although the book would probably not have been written without their help, I alone am responsible for its contents and any errors that remain.

1 Introduction: the problem

During 1988 the national newspapers of Britain began to carry allegations that children were being sexually abused and murdered by secret organisations during rituals variously described as witchcraft, black magic or satanism. Television and radio programmes, national, local and weekly papers all carried stories linking the sexual abuse of children to witchcraft, 'the occult' and devil worship. Alarming indications of the nature of the rituals and their incidence were quoted: at an international conference in 1988, the founder of a British children's charity expressed her belief that 'at least 4,000 children were being sacrificed a year in Great Britain alone' (Core 1988). A British psychiatrist, Norman Vaughton, was reported as saying that there were 10,000 cases a year in the United States.[1] A little later, early in 1989, another newspaper article had stated that the Adam Walsh Centre in the United States claimed there were 10,000 young American children involved in demonic cult activities, 200 unsolved murders by satanic cults and 'thousands of similar cults in Britain'.[2] Extreme versions of the allegations asserted the existence of an international conspiracy and were even reported in *The Times* (Gledhill 1990).

Children taken from their parents by the social services in a number of Midland towns were said to have been rescued from such cults. They were victims of 'satanic abuse', a shorthand phrase which became a label for the new allegations. It implied the most depraved rites, whether or not these were directed at the devil and whether or not the person using the label believed in the devil. 'Ritual abuse' was used as a synonym for 'satanic abuse' and sometimes the two labels were combined as 'satanic ritual abuse'. There was considerable confusion over the meanings of the terms and the exact nature of what was said to be happening, which contributed to public alarm. Evidence for anything other than sexual abuse, neglect and deprivation was not forthcoming, but the conviction that there was a new and terrible threat to children became widespread as the last decade of the millennium began.

A controversy in the United States, over whether or not children had been sexually abused in the course of the rituals of some occult or satanic cult, preceded that in Britain. Although the two phenomena have been treated as independent by some observers,[3] there are obvious connections between them. American writing on the subject circulated in Britain (Marrs 1989 is a late example) and American personnel visited Britain, attended conferences or gave seminars there. The author of the first book on the subject of the British scare, Philip Jenkins, pointed out that all the terms used as labels were American or influenced by American usage (1992: 220) but still rejected the view that the problem was a 'direct imitation of American concerns, disseminated by way of US cultural and political hegemony' (1992: 220). It is true that the traffic was, to some extent at least, two-way: British evangelicals, journalists and child protection workers also visited the United States; British books on the threat of satanism were also published (e.g. Anderson 1988). Lists of 'indicators', that could be used to tell whether a case was likely to reveal ritual or satanic elements, were widely circulated. Many of these originated in the United States and some were distributed by the American 'experts' who presented their cases at conferences or acted as 'consultants' in cases of child protection around the country. Accounts of apparently similar cases were widely publicised during this period and were referred to as proof of a continuing and widespread threat to children.

The allegations made in Britain resembled in broad outline the allegations made in the earlier cases in the United States: they indicated gatherings of robed and masked people abusing children and engaging in forced abortions, bestiality, human sacrifice and cannibalism. As in the United States, it was suggested that the lack of corroborative material evidence for the allegations was an indication that the perpetrators of ritual abuse, or satan-worshippers as some felt them to be, were either very clever or were protected by powerful members of society. Nevertheless, there are differences in the British allegations, which demonstrate that the outbreak was not simply a product of the American concern. As the sociologist Jenkins remarks, despite Britain's ever-increasing social and cultural resemblance to the United States, American material would only find acceptance in Britain if circumstances there made it seem appropriate (Jenkins 1992: 225–30). Nevertheless, American influence was, and continues to be, an important factor that cannot be ignored in the search for the origins of the events in Britain (see pp. 156–170).

The source of allegations

There have been two different sources of allegations of satanic abuse: one derived from the work of child protection and the other from therapy and counselling. The first, which was the more publicised to begin with, was what children were believed to be saying, the second depended on stories told by adults, mostly women. Social workers, police, foster-parents and therapists were responsible for telling the public about the cases involving children. In the second type of case, adults have claimed that they were involved in witchcraft or satanic cults as children or adolescents; the stories resemble those told by the older children in the cases of child protection that provided data for this book. In the United States those adults who had been sexually abused as children came to be called 'survivors', by analogy with the Jews who survived the Holocaust.[4] This term has also been adopted by those who allege that their sexual abuse was part of the ritual of a satanic cult. They describe rituals directed to the worship of Satan, children bred to be sacrificed, either as aborted foetuses or as new-born babies, human sacrifice, cannibalism, torture and the administration of drugs to children, and perverted sexual orgies including the transport of the children to various places where men and women sexually abused them. The accounts include references to rich and powerful participants, to perpetrators dressed in robes and masks and to paraphernalia such as candles and altars, symbols such as the pentagram and the number 666. The use of urine, faeces and blood in the rituals is also a feature of allegations. Some survivors confess to having participated in the abuse, not merely as victims but as perpetrators. Some even refer to very recent murders in which they say they took part (Davies n.d.; *Guardian* 3 October 1990; Dawson 1990; Coleman 1994).

Survivors tell their stories to therapists and counsellors but may also speak directly to social workers or the press or on television. It is rare for them to tell the police. Those who believe that both survivors and children have had similar experiences take the existence of adult survivors as showing that satanism has been established for many years. None of the allegations made by adult survivors has been tested in the courts to date, and some stories have been proved false. Even so, survivors' accounts have been said to explain and corroborate the evidence of children. In fact, the dates of the cases show that adult stories came into the public domain before the children's cases. The survivors must therefore be seen as creating the mental climate in which what children are alleged to be saying is accepted as truth. Now that children's cases are no longer given the credence they formerly had, the cases of adults are once again being said to be the key to understanding what is happening.

The extreme accounts in both the United States and Britain have come from adults – Christian fundamentalists, or survivors and their therapists, some of them Christians themselves, but others agnostic or even atheist. Some campaigners and consultants have become well known and gained prestige through their claim to have specialist knowledge of ritual abuse. Most are convinced of the existence of a large conspiratorial satanistic organisation, which is powerful enough to protect and conceal its members. The minutest details of the rites are described to their audiences, even where they seem of little relevance to the subject under discussion; they appear to have a strong rhetorical effect, inducing belief in the audience by the sheer emotional experience of hearing the horrors recounted.

There are also less extreme views of the ritual abuse of children (see the definition by Finkelhor cited below) whose holders do not subscribe to beliefs in large and powerful satanic organisations, and who are open-minded about whether the rituals are the main focus of activities or whether they merely facilitate the sexual abuse. The whole range of views depends on an uncritical reliance on what professionals or other adults allege that children have said; criticisms of this are seen either as 'denial', an unwillingness to accept reality, or as rejection of the victims in refusing to believe what they say. As Nathan has pointed out the secular versions all provide reinforcement for the more extreme religious version; by providing alternatives for those who are unable to accept the idea of a satanist conspiracy, they discourage consideration of the evidence and inhibit any questioning of underlying assumptions (Nathan 1991: 77).

The development of controversy

The allegations have not been accepted uncritically. Scepticism in general and over certain cases in particular, has been expressed by a variety of individuals including members of police forces, lawyers and academics, some of whom have begun to study what has been happening (Carlson and LaRue 1989; Hicks 1991; Langone and Blood 1990; Richardson et al. 1991). In the United States, the only self-confessed satanic abuser has been the subject of a detailed study that has convincingly demonstrated how suggestible people are liable to construct entirely false accounts of satanic rituals under pressure from interviewers (Ofshe 1992). Such revelations have damaged the credibility of statements of belief in the existence of satanism but have not prevented them from being disseminated more widely. One book on the subject, even though largely accepting the idea of satanistic abuse, refers to 'The hysteria, for that is what it became . . . ' (Parker 1993: 287).

It was first pointed out in the United States that no material evidence of ritual or satanic practices had been forthcoming in any of the cases in which they had been alleged (Richardson 1991). In Britain the position has been substantially the same as far as allegations of satan-worshipping rituals are concerned (La Fontaine 1994). As one journalist put it, in a phrase that has become well-known: 'Investigations have produced no bodies, no bones, no bloodstains, nothing.' (Waterhouse 1990). In the United States, the only adult witness to corroborate the testimony of children in a case has continued to claim that her evidence was given 'to get it all over with' and was the result of plea-bargaining (Hollingsworth, 1986: 424, cited in Nathan 1991). An FBI agent, Kenneth Lanning, has reported that he has been unable to document any satanic murders in the United States (Lanning 1989). While this book was being written, a report of a very large study carried out by Gail Goodman and associates in the United States claimed that none of the cases reported to them produced any evidence of the existence of organised satanic worship that included sexually abusing children (Bottoms et al. 1996).

The controversy in Britain deepened with criticism of the investigators' techniques: using leading and suggestive questions, putting pressure on very young children to answer questions, and refusing to accept denials but offering inducements to encourage 'disclosures' were all alleged to have caused the children to construct bizarre accounts of what had happened. The report of a judicial inquiry into the Orkney case (Clyde 1992) lent substance to the accusations; the collapse of many cases against the accused were also cited as evidence of false accusations. Two opposing camps, who might be labelled 'believers' and 'sceptics', are now firmly entrenched.

The believers

Christianity forms the basis of belief for many of those who are convinced of the existence of a cult of satanists. A firm belief in the reality of Satan and his activities in the human world enables belief in the existence of groups of his worshippers, dedicated to carrying out his ambition to dominate the world. The secret and cunning nature of the Prince of Darkness allows his followers to remain hidden and recognisable only in the evil actions they have performed. Features of the contemporary world, such as abortion and sexual permissiveness may thus be seen as evidence of the presence of the devil and his agents. Observers have pointed out that the killing and sexual abuse of children are particularly suited to representing the quintessence of evil, the presence of the devil himself (La Fontaine 1992; Comaroff 1994; Cotton 1995).

The approach of the end of the millennium has revived the beliefs of certain Christian churches in the end of the world that is preceded by the triumph of Satan. An increasingly evangelistic, even militant stance is taken by many fundamentalist Christians belonging to the many small churches competing with one another in what appears to be a religious revival, now taking place both in the United States and Britain. The New Christians emphasise original sin and the power of God to save through faith; they expect miracles and the descent of the Holy Spirit or visions of God. They stress faith rather than reason, belief rather than argument. There has been a marked increase in concern with exorcising demons, and even the Church of England now has clergy appointed to advise and assist in 'deliverance' as exorcism is now usually called. They have become increasingly militant in attacking all that they perceive to be evil and publicising their views.

A popular account of the new, charismatic Christianity described the exorcism of a new recruit to the faith and emphasised how she said she was 'cleansed' and experienced 'the deepest, most sublime experience of peace' (Cotton 1995: 131). The author goes on to compare charismatic Christianity with new therapies, such as regression and primal scream therapy, that produce a similar result (Cotton 1995: 133–50). His point is important. Many of those who believe in the reality of the satanic rituals are not Christians; attitudes encouraging belief rather than scepticism may appear outside the new Christianity. Many believers are therapists or those, like social workers, who are trained in similar disciplines. Others are feminists, or campaigners on behalf of those they define as victims. Anyone in these categories may believe that the acceptance of the stories of victims as true, even or perhaps especially when they seem incredible, is a demonstration of support and may be experienced by the teller as healing. Therapists may assert that the only form of knowledge is that of clinical (that is, personal), experience and thereby deny the necessity of corroborative evidence. The position is well illustrated in the rejoinder made to an appeal from FBI Special Agent Ken Lanning for a study of the processes of investigation and disclosure in cases of alleged satanic abuse: 'I'm not a law enforcement person, thank God! I'm a psychology person, so I don't need the evidence, I come from a very different place, *I don't need to see evidence to believe . . .'* (Dan Sexton 1989, cited in Mulhern 1991: 146; my italics).

Believers in satanic abuse may say, reasonably enough, that they themselves do not believe in Satan or practice witchcraft but other people do. They may point to beliefs in ghosts and monsters, to the popularity of cults and to celebrations like Halloween as evidence of surviving folk beliefs in evil forces. The fact that there are people who practise witchcraft or who call themselves satanists makes it seem plausible that some of them might be involved. However, as we shall see later this is too simple an argument.

The sceptics

The sceptical position appeals to those for whom reason and evidence form the only acceptable basis of understanding. Academics, lawyers and the police are the main professionals whose training leads them to require evidential support for the conclusions they draw, but other individuals may take a rationalist standpoint, for many different reasons (Victor 1993: 248). Rationalists are appalled by the easy credence given to unsubstantiated and bizarre allegations and by the acceptance of conclusions that are based on no independent evidence. Pocock (1985: 50–51) has pointed out the difference in attitudes to explicability between those who are prepared to characterise an act, and hence the perpetrator of it, as evil and a minority who regard 'evil' as a term so strong that it is inappropriate if there is a chance that explanation might be possible. For the majority, by contrast, explanation could not be separated from excuse and so to judge something to be evil was to proclaim that it could not be explained or excused. Hence attempts at explaining how allegations of satanic abuse had come about might be dubbed apologias for the abuse itself (Victor 1993: 213).

However, there are varying degrees of scepticism about the claims of anti-satanists, just as there are degrees of 'belief'. The most extreme sceptics say that the whole problem is the result of mass hysteria. The allegations may be dismissed as fabrications; the children's evidence may be labelled fantasies or lies. The inability of the police to find evidence showing that sacrifices, whether animal or human, have taken place, is taken to mean that the accounts of ritual, including the sexual abuse of children, were inventions. The most thorough-going sceptics emphasise the wilder claims which by association discredit the less lurid ones; in some cases, doubt has even been cast on the existence of any cases of the sexual abuse of children. This extreme position seems to owe as much to hostility to the proponents of the idea of satanic abuse, particularly social workers, as to knowledge of the cases themselves.

The ranks of the sceptics in Britain are also swelled by those who are concerned, less with the ritual abuse of children, than with the protection of an ideal of society from attack. The fact that most of the cases involve the removal of children from their homes is felt to be deeply significant. Intervention by the state in what is seen as the 'private' domain of the family is considered illegitimate and state employees who do this are believed to be guilty of attempts to undermine a 'traditional way of life'. In particular there is concern among some people to deny that children are ever sexually abused within their own homes. For a large number of people parental care is assumed to be both natural and altruistic, so that to accuse parents of inhuman acts such as sexual abuse appears not merely a malicious lie but evidence of a dangerous conspiracy to undermine the family (La Fontaine 1990). By reversing cause and effect, social workers can be seen as part of a movement responsible for the manifest changes in domestic organisation and movement away from 'traditional' ways of life. Attacks on social workers are also popular among those who traditionally have most to fear from them and who tend to be readers of the tabloid newspapers that regularly publish tales of wicked social workers.

The most extreme scepticism denies the reality of *any* form of the sexual abuse of children; holders of such views may claim that children lie to get adults into trouble and deny the need for child protection. The believers, on the other hand, argue that the scepticism about ritual or satanic abuse mirrors the earlier unwillingness to believe that children were sexually abused. Those who have been personally involved in this earlier issue are persuaded to feel sympathy for their colleagues 'on the front line'. The fear of being accused of damaging the credibility of children's disclosures by encouraging scepticism has probably induced some people to keep quiet about their doubts or to stifle them. Attitudes have polarised. Few, having changed their minds as the evidence has built up, have had the courage to make this changed view known.

The terms in which the public discussion of these allegations have been couched are confused. Discussion has been obscured by the use of terms in very different ways, so that one authority on the subject has frequently remarked that people say that they believe in it, without saying what 'it' is (Sherrill Mulhern, personal communication). Before going any further some clarification of terms is essential.

Definitions and labels

The terms used for what is alleged to have happened in these cases – 'satanic abuse' and 'ritual abuse' – have been used in a variety of different ways. The use of the labels 'satanic', 'satanist' or 'satanic ritual abuse' implies that the perpetrators of it are engaged in devil-worship or are the devil's agents. This is what some campaigners, in Britain and in the United States, do indeed mean by the term. Yet many of those who are convinced of the reality of a new form of sexual abuse of children are not prepared to use terms which seem to imply Christian convictions of a rather extreme fundamentalist nature. They prefer to use 'ritual abuse' as an alternative, implying merely that the children are sexually abused during, and as part of, rituals (McFadyen, Hanks & James 1993: 37); in this sense it means sexual abuse in the context of practices that a more fundamentalist religious view might still label devil-worship or witchcraft. A recent book prefers to use the term 'satanist' or 'satanistic', arguing that 'satanic abuse' implies a belief that the devil himself is involved, whereas 'satanist' does not. The most commonly cited definition is that used by Finkelhor and his associates: sexual abuse that took place 'in contexts linked to some symbols or group that have a religious, magical or supernatural connotation, and where the invocation of these symbols or activities, repeated over time, is used to frighten and intimidate the children' (Finkelhor, Williams & Burns 1988: 59). This definition leaves open the possibility that ritual abuse could be a strategy used by the abusers of children and not an involvement in satanism. Other definitions make clear that the ritual is linked to beliefs in witchcraft or satanism. For example, Sakheim and Devine use the term 'ritual abuse' as a generic term but characterise it as taking place in a context which is justified by the perpetrators' religious beliefs; these are 'usually satanic in nature' (Sakheim & Devine 1992: xii).

The use of 'ritual abuse' as an alternative to 'satanic abuse' still leaves an area of ambiguity. The term 'ritual' has more than one meaning: in the lay sense it may be used to refer to any behaviour regularly repeated in certain circumstances such as 'bedtime ritual'. In a technical psychological sense, which also has some general currency, it refers to compulsive and repetitive behaviour often associated with sexual gratification; sexual abuse which appears to follow a set pattern may be described as ritualised or ritualistic. For the social sciences, ritual refers to practices embodying symbols that refer to fundamental social meanings and beliefs, to religion in its widest meaning. It is in this sense that the term is used in this book. It resembles the definition of McFadyen,

Hanks & James (1993) which makes the religious component clear, although the authors appear to include all forms of abuse, not merely the sexual.

What I have called the social science meaning of 'ritual' seems similar to that in common use. In the national survey of cases that was part of the study on which this book is based, the majority of respondents who were working in the field of child protection associated 'ritual abuse' with a form of religious belief or practice. Most associated the rituals with the occult, or with witchcraft or satanism. In nineteen cases respondents indicated the involvement of 'a cult'; this term refers to the small, new religious groups that grew up in the 1960s and 1970s (Beckford 1985: 1). It is also used, more commonly in the United States than in Britain, for the groups referred to in some allegations of satanic abuse. In the case of Christian campaigners, involvement in new religious movements or an interest in the occult generally are seen as leading inevitably to satanism and rituals in which every form of evil is practised (Davies n.d.; Parker 1989: 50).

Only a small minority of survey respondents used the term 'ritual' with no religious connotation. However, they did not all use the term in the same way: in one case, 'ritual abuse' was said to consist of the children's abusing (masturbating?) each other in front of the perpetrator, who had dared them to; two cases involved sadism, bestiality or the use of faeces; one concerned pornographic videos, another referred to organised prostitution, including sadistic sex and the making of videos. In two cases it was enough that one or both of the parents of a child about whom there was concern, were interested in the occult, for the case to be labelled ritual abuse. In a few of the survey cases it was not clear what the ritual was, or the allegation was recorded as having been false. Only one person used 'ritual' in the psychological sense of compulsive, repetitive routines.

The wide range of meanings contained in the term 'ritual' is characteristic of the campaign to promote recognition of it as a new threat to children. Lack of precision allows the inclusion of a correspondingly wide range of reported behaviour as 'ritual abuse' and prevents people realising how wide this is and how different the reported cases are. The identification of real cases as 'ritual abuse' seems to confirm the existence of satanic or ritual abuse in general, because of, rather than in spite of, the lack of clarity as to what exactly is entailed. People of many different professional and religious opinions can support the claim that ritual abuse exists as a distinct form of sexual abuse, because they can define it in the ways that they themselves find credible and acceptable. In this manner the support for the claims is widened without the disagreement about what the terms used actually mean becoming apparent. Some people may assert that they do not accept the more extreme views of what is happening, but their agreement that ritual abuse is a newly discovered form of the abuse of children lends credibility to the more extravagant claims. The religious campaigners can, and do, point to well-known professional psychiatrists, therapists and child-care experts who seem to agree with them.

Another term that has been used, with the encouragement of the British Association of Social Workers (BASW), is 'organised abuse' (La Fontaine 1993). This term was adopted to cover paedophile rings and other cases, including the well-publicised ones, in which large numbers of abusers were identified, together with cases in which satanic abuse was alleged. The Department of Health in its guidelines for child protection workers, *Working Together*, adopted this approach. By using a neutral term both organisations hoped to avoid a damaging split in their ranks between those who believed the allegations of 'satanic' or 'ritual' abuse and those who did not. Unfortunately, the term became a euphemism for satanic abuse and, by including paedophile rings which were successfully prosecuted, it lent credibility to the believers and suggested to some people that all large cases might be satanic. However, it too has suffered from an enlargement of its meaning, and it has recently been argued that all cases that show a systematic and planned set of actions leading to abuse should be called organised (Bibby 1994; La Fontaine 1993).

In this book I shall refer both to 'satanic' and to 'ritual' abuse. In undertaking the survey that was part of the study on which it is based, we used the less specific term, 'ritual abuse', in order to encourage reports of as many cases as possible. Subsequently it became clear that the bulk of cases involved allegations that were unsubstantiated; these I relabelled satanic abuse cases, by analogy with the accusations in the early witch-hunts, in which the witches were perceived as followers of Satan. In three cases there was evidence to corroborate the allegations that the sexual abuse of the children had taken place in the context of invented rituals; these I have called ritual abuse, but it is important to remember that they did not involve a witches' sabbath or a cult of devil worship. I shall continue to make the distinction in this way, although the unsubstantiated allegations do not always include the idea that the devil, or devil-worshippers, may be involved. The term is chosen to reflect the connotations of extreme evil that most believers give to it.

The problem

If the allegations of satanic abuse are not accepted as descriptions of actual events, they still present a number of different characteristics that need explanation. One of these consists of their extraordinary range: they have national and international dimensions. Jenkins, whose study of the British epidemic was the first to appear (Jenkins 1992), has analysed it as a national phenomenon, an approach also taken in this book, but it has an international dimension as well. The allegations show uniformities of content over great geographical distances and across national frontiers. This fact has been used to argue the validity of attributing satanic ritual to an international organisation. Cases have occurred not only in the United States and Britain, but in Canada, Australia, New Zealand, the Netherlands and the Scandinavian countries. This international manifestation of the problem requires a study of its own; its manifestations in England and Wales will be reflected in this study. All that can be said of it here is to point to the way in which it resembles the early European witch-hunts. These too crossed national frontiers and are now considered as a single phenomenon (Ankarloo & Henningsen 1990: 9); their international dimension has been attributed to a pan-European Christian crusade against superstition (Clark 1993: 46). It was also the Church that provided an international common language, Latin, that adherents, at least those with some education, could use to communicate with each other. The twentieth-century spread of allegations of satanic abuse seems to have also reflected the use of an international language: English. New cases have appeared most rapidly in countries where writing in English would be read and English-speaking experts could easily obtain an audience. Since historically the allegations began in the United States, it could also be said that their spread has reflected the dominant role of the United States in an international culture whose medium is English. However, the allegations also reflect the culture and politics of distinct nations and religions. Any analysis must attempt to remain aware of these various levels of significance.

Another equally important aspect for analysis consists of the meaning of the claims. What is the significance of the images that are projected by the allegations and how are they related to other aspects of the cultural life of the society in which they have appeared? How are we to explain the phenomenon of believing in a version of the witches' sabbath in the late twentieth century when, at least in the West, medicine has eliminated many of the diseases that killed people in the past and where scientific technology is part of everyone's life? There are moral and symbolic dimensions to the epidemic that feature in what has been written in many accounts, although in different ways. Any explanation must take account of this.

However, the allegations are not *just* ideas or symbols to be understood as bearers of meaning. They are closely connected with a variety of actions. First, they may form part of a campaign, that is, of public action. There has been activity of this sort whose aims, as we shall see, are multiple and complex, but clearly one objective has been to influence public policy, with respect to a number of objectives, some moral, some of them concerned with policy and others with administrative decisions. Secondly, particular cases among the many that concern the protection of children have been identified as different and claims that they involved satanic rituals have been made and investigated by the police. Adults have claimed that they were victimised in similar ways in their childhood. The allegations in this epidemic referred to particular cases, not to the ill-treatment of children in the abstract or in the distant past. Where the source of the alleged disclosures consisted of children, further action inevitably followed; the accounts of adults might remain uninvestigated, even if published in the national media, but they had their effect on public opinion. Any explanation of the allegations must consider the actions that were both precipitated by the ideas and affected their continual elaboration. As Muchembled wrote of attempts to explain witch beliefs in early modern Europe, 'Any myth in fact, is subject to precise sociological forms and does not exist as a mere category of the mind. This is true of the sabbath myth, which creates realities and chains of events which may affect its own consequences' (1990: 142). Specifying the link between the ideas and the actions is no simple matter, but to reduce the epidemic either to ideas or to action is to build in distortion from the beginning.

My approach derives from social anthropology and specifically from the social anthropology of witchcraft. From the first, it has emphasised the explanation of beliefs. Witchcraft is a form of mystical evil-doing and comparable ideas appear in many societies; it is also an explanation for events that have no other explanation within the intellectual framework provided by a particular culture.[5] Traditionally,[6] anthropology used a dual focus: on the meaning of the ideas and images of witchcraft and on the social context in which such ideas are activated as particular accusations. The social context in which beliefs in evil are brought into play are often situations of conflict in which accusations are made and countered; it is in the interplay of these actual situations that the particular meanings of evil are displayed. In analysing the concepts of other societies it is all too easy to impose one's own interpretations; a consideration of the way in which the ideas are mobilised in action provides a salutory check on this. Hence a truly anthropological approach will include both aspects.

The allegations we are concerned with here seemed to imply a belief in witchcraft, evil magic and the devil, although witchcraft and magic were more frequently mentioned at the start of the epidemic and allegations of devil-worshipping or satanism took over as it developed. To this extent the similarity between them and accusations of witchcraft elsewhere is immediately apparent. However, the notion that ideas developed in the study of small-scale societies in Africa, north America and elsewhere can be relevant to the understanding of late twentieth-century Britain may seem unlikely, so some justification of it is necessary.

Witchcraft in other parts of the world

The beliefs in witchcraft that have been studied by anthropologists provide an image of evil and a picture of the evil being (Parkin 1985: 1; La Fontaine 1992). In most of the societies anthropologists have traditionally studied, inhuman evil is personified in the figure of the witch. Whatever the local term that is translated 'witch' by anthropologists, it refers to those who commit acts perceived as transgressing the fundamental moral axioms on which human nature, and hence social life, is based. The sins attributed to witches may vary somewhat in their detail and emphasis according to the culture in question, but they commonly concern sex, food and killing and represent the epitome of evil (La Fontaine 1963: 214; La Fontaine 1992; Parkin 1985: 1; Pocock 1985: 47). The witches and their world reflect social life in an inverted form and are often believed to reverse human characteristics. Since a common manifestation of these inverted habits is being active at night when human beings sleep, they are often referred to as night-witches. Similarly, what Cohn has called the myth of Satan's human servants (1970) displays the violation of all the fundamental social rules that constituted early modern society: the secret gatherings at night to worship Satan, the acts of sexual perversion, murder and cannibalism together create a nightmare anti-world that resembles that of the night-witches (Rowland 1993: 166 [1990]).

In modern England evil inheres in similar acts: in the sexual abuse, ill-treatment and murder of children, in cannibalism and human sacrifice (La Fontaine 1992). Sex offenders, serial killers and other extreme offenders may all be labelled 'animals', an epithet which carries the same connotation of inhuman conduct as 'witch' (Parkin 1985;

Pocock 1985). To some people abortion belongs in the same category of acts which violate human morality. Satanic ritual abuse, which includes all the forbidden acts, serves as the quintessence of evil in twentieth-century Western society. The satanic rituals of the allegations do resemble the witchcraft of the night-witch quite closely.

Harm may be inflicted by the use of material objects and verbal formulae (spells), acts that may also be referred to as black magic or sorcery. Anthropologists used to use these terms to distinguish this kind of attack from 'witchcraft', a label used for the witch's mystical powers, and for the evil acts motivated by hatred, jealousy or the desire for revenge. In many societies, however, no such distinctions are made and the term witchcraft is now commonly used for any form of mystical evil. Human beings may be thought capable of using witchcraft on occasion without being night-witches, so that harm to persons and their property may be believed to be caused by the witchcraft of ordinary people, particularly in the course of quarrels. Alternatively the damage may be attributed to night-witches, whose motive is a love of evil for its own sake.

In modern Africa human beings are not often accused of being night-witches, although the fact that witchcraft is believed to have been used offers 'proof' of its reality and hence of the existence of night-witches. In such systems of thought, human witchcraft is always tainted with the possibility that the human appearance of the accused masks a night-witch. The lesser evils of malice and revenge are not completely separate from the supreme evil of the witch who undertakes evil for its own sake. The distinctions drawn between the night-witch and the human being who uses witchcraft are not clear-cut, and the two conceptions reinforce each other. In a subtle and complex manner beliefs in witchcraft also reinforce social controls and help to maintain appropriate behaviour by associating disruptive human emotions such as jealousy, greed or malice with the figure of the witch. Accusations of using witchcraft and sorcery may be hurled at an opponent and used to justify attacks on people who should be close allies. The emphasis in the beliefs of any one people may differ from those of its neighbours but they are always closely associated with the framework of social life.

Witches are not generally sought out in simple societies unless some event occurs that is thought to indicate the work of a witch; that is, witchcraft is generally diagnosed retrospectively. Exceptions to this were found in southern Africa, where the use of sorcery was a crime and accusations were brought before the chiefs, even where no harm had yet transpired (Schapera 1969). Witch-hunts are quite different from everyday accusations in that they do not seek out the witch responsible for a particular sickness or misfortune, but promise to cleanse the whole community of witches altogether. The witch-hunts may be described equally accurately, as 'witch-cleansing' movements or cults, since they attempt to rid society of misfortune by removing the evil that is its source. There is usually a new technique for identifying witches and new ritual experts who operate it, and these start the general witch-finding movement that ensues. They resemble the campaigns of witch-finders such as Matthew Hopkins and John Stearne, whose activities in Essex in 1645 caused a sudden rise in prosecutions in certain communities (Macfarlane 1970: 30, 135–142).

Witch-hunting, as distinct from the accusations of witchcraft that occur in everyday 'normal' life, have attracted less attention from anthropologists (but see Richards 1935; Morton-Williams 1956; Bohannan 1958; Tait 1963). In 1970 Willis summarised what was then known about witch-finding cults. The anti-witchcraft movements share basic social characteristics: there is no formal organisational structure, although the movement may be named for the person that inaugurated it; the secret knowledge that enables witches to be identified is handed on from person to person; a movement crosses cultural boundaries, adapting its ideas and practices to the traditional beliefs and practices of each area (Redmayne 1970; Willis 1968). It is triggered by the representatives of the cult who travel the country offering to detect witches. The local authorities are under considerable pressure to accept these offers, because a refusal may be interpreted as an attempt to shield the witches and hence as sympathy with them. Similarly, Willis notes that for those identified as witches 'The moral pressure to confess is enormous' (Willis 1970: 130).

Witch-finding movements seem to arise from a general sense of social unease, a public view that there is an escalation of misfortune, indicating that witches are increasing in number and that their actions are affecting everyone (Willis 1970: 131). This can be recurrent, as appears to have been the case in central Africa where movements of witch-finding arose periodically, increased to a peak and died down, to begin again after a period of calm. Or they have been interpreted as reflecting the fundamental upheavals in the religious, economic and social structures of societies affected by colonial rule. It has been pointed out that similar movements appear to have occurred before colonial rule (Douglas 1963; Goody 1957), and, as Willis remarks, witch-finding takes place in areas 'relatively remote from the centres of urbanization and direct Western influence'. But these areas were not so remote that they had not been affected by the changes set in train by European colonisation.

The witch-finders in late twentieth-century Africa emerge from a

Christian background and like their analogues in early modern Europe their targets are pagan magical practices, although these now have very up-to-date aims of accumulation (Meyer 1995). Over half a century has passed since the first study of beliefs in witchcraft but clearly witch-beliefs have not disappeared as it was once believed they would. Other recent studies of witch-finding movements show their adaptability to changing postcolonial worlds, and interpret their role as trying 'to pin down seemingly random, ramifying and impersonal forces, to give them visible faces and explicable human motives' (Comaroff & Comaroff 1994: 8). The changing referent of these nightmares reflects fears and anxieties aroused by the stresses of the contemporary world. The inexplicability of one man's success and another's failure, the uncertainty of achievement despite the effort invested, these sustain belief in unseen powers. But Meyer makes clear that it is Christianity, particularly in its charismatic and pentecostal forms, that promotes the particular form of these ideas in Ghana. While it will be important to consider the meanings contained in allegations of satanic abuse and devil worship, their social context cannot be neglected either.

Like the persisting witch-beliefs in Africa, the allegations of satanic abuse also represent a modern variant of ancient cultural themes. Thus, both anthropological and historical theories may be helpful to our understanding of them. It must be borne in mind however, that there are also differences that distinguish these allegations from those with which they have been compared. Particular social meanings and specific socio-economic conditions influence the form of allegations. Despite the many similarities between the witch-hunts in early modern Europe and the epidemic of allegations of satanism, and the resemblances between Europe, past and present and other twentieth-century societies, the allegations of satanism in twentieth-century Britain have distinctive features that will have to be explained in the context of late twentieth-century British society.

2 The personification of evil: a comparative perspective

Various explanations have been offered for the outbreak of allegations of satanic abuse. It was argued at an early stage that the allegations were part of a campaign mounted by fundamentalist Christians, who saw Satan's hand in the degeneration of society at the end of the millennium. The existence of a campaign has been demonstrated (Jenkins 1992; Victor 1993) but this explanation does not account for the acceptance of these allegations among non-Christians. Journalists such as Tate (1991) and Boyd (1991) reject the suggestion that they have been led to believe in the allegations because they are Christian fundamentalists, although they acknowledge their Christian beliefs.[1] Other campaigners point out that they are not Christian at all. There is no doubt that many of those who are firmly convinced that Satan-worshipping groups are abusing children in their rituals are not just blindly following Christian views.

It has frequently been pointed out that satanic abuse allegations started in the United States (La Fontaine 1994). There is ample proof that Americans have addressed conferences in Britain, distributed their papers and on a few occasions acted as consultants in particular cases. There have also been unproved allegations that British campaigns have been sustained by funds from the United States. Yet postulating an American origin does not explain how and why the ideas gained acceptance in Britain. It is possible to argue that having accepted the idea of children being sexually abused, which was also first canvassed in the United States, then the English public would be more prepared to accept another American 'discovery' of the same kind. In fact, the allegations of ritual abuse overlapped a major controversy over sexual abuse, in which the hostility of the public to the idea that children might be abused by their fathers was made clear (Campbell 1989; La Fontaine 1990). This was the Cleveland affair, which heavily influenced the actions of social workers in at least one major case of satanic abuse.

One observer of the British scene, the folklorist Bill Ellis, argues that all the ingredients of the allegations of satanic abuse were already present in England and were in fact imported into the United States; the epidemic of allegations in Britain was therefore nothing to do with the United States (Ellis 1993). It is true that if we wish to explain the British cases as a copycat version of the American ones, there are basic differences between the American and British cases that would have to be glossed over. However, it was the combination of these features that constituted a new threat and the first cases involving this were undoubtedly reported in the United States. Even if we do not accept Ellis' view in its entirety, events in north America probably should be regarded as a precipitating factor, rather than a cause, of the British epidemic. His point that the allegations mobilise elements of English folklore is important nonetheless and we shall come back to it later in this chapter.

Other explanations, such as that it was an attempt by social workers to obtain more standing and better financing for their work have also been suggested by sceptics. Like most of the explanations, they are couched in terms of individual motivation and belief. This leaves unanswered several important questions: why do these accounts resemble each other? Why are allegations put forward by Christians very similar to those recounted by non-believers in the threat of satanism? The epidemic is limited to what is known as the Christian world so far but why are individuals in different parts of it, not all of whom are Christians and who are presumably motivated by different beliefs and a variety of attitudes, reporting similar cases? The extent and similarity of allegations are features used by believers to argue that the allegations must therefore be true. A similar argument about confessions of witchcraft during the early modern witch-hunts was criticised and discredited by the nineteenth-century scholar, Charles Mackay. He pointed out that 'the same questions were put to them all and torture never failed to educe the answer required by the inquisitors' (Mackay 1841: 481). Mackay regarded the belief in witchcraft as a popular delusion, but 150 years later, social scientists do not dismiss it so lightly. The distribution and similarity of allegations are indications that they represent a significant social phenomenon. If this is so, then all explanations that are couched solely in terms of individual beliefs and motivation are bound to be inadequate.

Sociologists have explained the allegations, in both the United States and Britain, as a 'moral panic'. This is not, as some people seem to think, a way of talking about mass hysteria, but a technical term coined by sociologists to refer to social movements that define actions, groups or persons as threats to fundamental social values. A moral panic is the construction of a social problem as something more serious than a routine issue of social control. As Jenkins points out (1992: 6–8), since its formulation in the 1970s this approach has made it possible to understand how the panics are generated and perceived, to consider the role of the media and of interest groups in promoting the various views and to analyse the relationship between both of them and the making and implementation of public policy. Using this approach on the British epidemic of satanic abuse cases, Jenkins concludes: 'The ritual abuse panic . . . appears to have owed much to the exchange of ideas and materials among a tiny handful of well-placed activists. This suggests that the essential context of a problem is defined by broad social trends, but the specific manifestation and impact of that issue can in large measure be determined by a relatively small number of activists, either acting in small groups and even as individuals' (Jenkins 1992: 231). He identifies the social context as concern over changes in the nuclear family and over the sharp rise in crime rates and in domestic and sexual violence. As the cases show, social factors more fundamental than the public concern reflected in the media, also seem to be involved (see chapter 9).

This approach is helpful in that it lays bare the development of social movements and identifies the way in which public conflicts and ambitions are reflected in the struggle to define the public attitude to a problem, and influence policy in dealing with it. In this particular case it allows Jenkins to demonstrate the interdependence of ritual abuse allegations with other, earlier panics about violent sexual predators who targeted women and children. Jenkins also shows how shifting attention to the safety of children allowed other campaigns, such as the campaign against pornography or sexual assault to gain support by association with campaigns for the protection of children, as well as themselves contributing support to the joint endeavour. One might say, though Jenkins himself does not put it that way, that the satanic abuse allegations provided a way to absorb many earlier concerns into a single terrifying image of unimaginable danger to children.

To refer to a moral panic does not mean that there was no factual reason for public concern. The approach merely emphasises the social construction of certain events as a danger that is out of proportion to the actual threat offered (Jenkins 1992: 7). However, in the case of the panic about satanic abuse the allegations were not based on any known or witnessed events, but on allegations that such events had happened.[2] As later chapters will show, contrary to what was said, in most cases the children were not responsible for descriptions of either the activities of a secret satanic cult or the rituals such cults performed. The allegations were based on concepts of evil-doing that seemed to be entirely mythical but which entailed the most fervent and unshakeable commitment. As will be shown, men have used claims of magical powers to seduce children into participating in sexual activities, but such cases are not proof of sexual abuse in satanic rituals. Unlike other moral panics analysed by Jenkins and others, the kernel of truth underlying the allegations of satanism as a widespread threat to children has not yet been demonstrated, despite vigorous claims to the contrary.

Using the concept of a moral panic to consider the epidemic of allegations of satanic abuse also has some weaknesses. The first is that there is no theoretical determination of the links between panics; they seem to be chosen retrospectively as contributory to the panic which is the central focus of the analysis. This use of hindsight is somewhat suspect as a method, since it leaves each individual scholar free to indulge his/her intuition. This may leave one with the impression that other selections might just as well have been made. For example, in Jenkins' view the prior moral panics that set the scene for the appearance of allegations of satanic abuse concerned threats to children, and he lists events of sexual violence, paedophilia and child abuse (both physical and sexual), referring also to homosexuality and pornography. However, the content of allegations suggests that campaigns like that against abortion or evangelical campaigns against the celebration of Halloween, rock music, and any pastime that smacked of the occult, political movements like radical feminism, and finally the revelations of corruption in some police forces, are all equally relevant to the creation of the public attitudes that made the ideas plausible in Britain.

An analysis in terms of a moral panic does not deal well with the political dimension of the issues. While Jenkins notes some party political resonance stemming from the panic, there is no room in his analysis for recognition that allegations of satanic abuse were designed to initiate action on the part of the authorities; the allegations entailed legal and political consequences. When they began to arise in actual cases concerning children, it was certain that they would not just remain media stories; they would have to be investigated. Sceptics contested the allegations from the beginning. The result of the investigations was not merely a major controversy, but political struggles within child protection work and, later, within psychotherapy. Jenkins suggests that 'the hostile stereotype of the social worker provides a better-accepted and more powerful folk-devil than the altogether more speculative satanic ring' (1992: 22), but the two were not alternatives. On the contrary, they represented opposing images, mobilised by mutually hostile factions supporting or denouncing the allegations, not merely as a matter of 'symbolic politics', but in order to influence public policy.

Finally, the approach leaves the *meaning* of allegations relatively unanalysed. While their content serves to define the focus of one moral panic, its cultural significance is not the centre of interest for the analysis. The extreme nature of the allegations in the case of satanic abuse, and the absence of corroborative evidence to indicate that what was being alleged had actually happened, requires more explanation than the explanation in terms of moral panics can give it. Jenkins argues that the reference to satanism started within Christian fundamentalism, but that, once disseminated to social workers, it became an issue for social work and criminal investigation. This begs several questions. The first is the reasons for its acceptance among social workers and others who were at pains to make public their status as non-Christians. The acceptance of the ideas requires some explanation other than suggestions, with very little evidence, that the social workers concerned were crypto-fundamentalist Christians and that their statements that they were not were false. In addition, these cases were distinguished from other cases of children's sexual abuse discovered during the same period by the claim that satanists were alleged to be the perpetrators, which was not made in all cases. Why were certain cases seen as satanic and not others? The meaning of the allegations is the source of answers for both questions and will have to be taken into account.

Fundamentalist tales of satanic rituals draw on deep-seated cultural images of evil, that show continuity with the ideas underlying the witch-hunts of early modern Europe (La Fontaine 1992). Further, the ideas are comparable (though not identical) to witch-beliefs in other parts of the world, described in this century. The rest of this chapter will be concerned to establish these comparisons.

The allegations and the past

Believers themselves point to a similarity with the past, which they interpret as showing that satanism has been long established. Thus Tate states categorically: 'Satanic ritual crime, abuse and murder have been reported, investigated, proven and recorded for more than 500 years' (Tate 1991: 58; see also Boyd 1991: 108–20; J. Parker 1993: 243–7). Such claims repeat earlier statements of the same kind in the work of Montague Summers (1926) and other Christian writing about satanism and witchcraft. The satanists in the past are named as some or all of the following: heretics, particularly the Cathars and the Order of the Templars; Gilles de Rais, Marshal of France and Joan of Arc's loyal follower who was convicted of practising sorcery and subjecting children to torture and perverted sexual rites, finally murdering them; Mme de

Montespan; and the Abbé Guibourg. The modern occultist, Aleister Crowley, may be brought in to link this rather distant past with the present. The *Malleus Maleficarum*, a manual for Inquisitors written to encourage the hunting down of witches, and other writings are cited as proof that in the past Satan was worshipped with human sacrifices, that his worshippers drank the blood and ate the flesh of babies and other human beings who were killed as sacrifice, and that their secret meetings included perverted sexual orgies. These allegations against the accused are reported as facts, without historical context or indication that the accusations were made by the political enemies of the supposed witches or devil-worshippers. In the absence of proof of satanist activities in the late twentieth century, they offer a long list of apparently 'proven cases' in past times.[3]

Historians, examining the primary evidence and setting the events in historical context, have shown the unreliable nature of such folk-histories. They can best be seen as setting out a Christian myth, constructed from a chain of stories associated with historical persons. It is a widespread feature of religious and political strife that allegations of extreme evil are thrown at opponents. The general use of allegations of sorcery to justify an attack on a political rival is a noted feature of the period preceding the great witch-hunts. As with similar ideas in some modern African societies, these notions of sorcery might be difficult to distinguish from poisoning (Schapera 1969: 21; Thomas 1973: 520 fn. [1971]). Writings such as the *Malleus Maleficarum* cannot be taken at face-value and certainly not as a description of what witches were actually doing. The common factor is not the satanism of the convicted but the Church membership of the accusers (Cavendish 1975: 20). The long history of 'proven' satanism and witchcraft is largely the history of the Church's fight against its enemies.

There is no doubt, however, of the similarity of the late twentieth-century allegations to those made against people hunted down as witches across Europe during the sixteenth and seventeenth centuries (Hill & Goodwin 1989). There are differences: in today's allegations the ingestion of urine and faeces plays a considerable part but this does not, as far as I know, feature among the accusations or confessions of the early period; witches no longer fly to the sabbaths nor does the devil appear in person to have intercourse with the attendant witches as often in the twentieth century as he did in the sixteenth or seventeenth; animal sacrifice shocks the twentieth century hearer but does not seem to have formed part of the satanic rituals of early modern Europe. Otherwise, the main features: the secret rites held at night, the human sacrifice, vampirism (drinking blood) and cannibalism with orgies of perverse sexuality, seem to have survived intact the passage of three centuries. There is probably more than one reason for this stability. Henningsen sees the continuity as owing a good deal to the preservation of these ideas in folklore (private communication). Ginzburg prefers to see the origin of some of these ideas in folk beliefs that he claims represent an original European religion (Ginzburg 1990: 121, 133–5 [1983]). In my view it seems likely that Church mythology is at least as responsible as folklore. The Egyptologist, Margaret Murray, using the theoretical approach of the nineteenth-century anthropologist, Sir James Frazer, author of *The Golden Bough* (1922 [1890]; 1936), argued that the witches were in fact pagans, practising a pre-Christian religion (1921). Despite numerous refutations, the idea remains a powerful one. Like Margaret Murray, Ginzburg can produce no evidence to sustain his belief that the witches' sabbath includes survivals from the earliest European religion. However, whatever the reason for them, the similarities between the past and the present suggest that we should consider how far the comparison with the witch-hunts of early modern Europe can be helpful in understanding the modern phenomenon.

The witch-hunts of early modern Europe

The antecedents to the witch-hunts of the fifteenth to seventeenth centuries can be roughly divided into four categories: the attitude of the church to folk beliefs; the nature of those beliefs; social conceptualisations of evil; and, finally, spontaneous 'confessions' of having taken part in witchcraft and devil worship. For three of these, parallels can be found in the late twentieth century.

With regard to the first, the change in the Church's attitude to magic, the early Church Fathers had seen all belief in magic as a survival of paganism and condemned it as such, as did many later Christian missionaries in Africa and elsewhere. But by the Middle Ages a distinction was being made between 'demonic' and 'natural' magic. According to Kieckhefer, 'Demonic magic involves evil spirits and rests upon a network of religious beliefs and practices, while natural magic exploits "occult" powers within nature and is essentially a branch of mediaeval science' (Kieckhefer 1989: 1). This division roughly paralleled a moral distinction between good (white) and evil (black) magic. However, the question of where to draw the line was under constant dispute and revision. Demonic magic, the conjuring of demons to perform one's will, was generally condemned both morally and legally, but since there was no general agreement on what was demonic and what natural, one man's natural magic might be another's association with demons. The distinction might be generally recognised but its application in particular cases might be a matter of dispute. The right to make the final judgement on the matter both in a particular case and in general lay with the Church. By the second half of the fifteenth century the reformers had condemned all magic, attributing it all to association with demons. The traditional magic of healing and protection against harm, practised among the common folk, was tarred with the same brush as learned magic. According to Kieckhefer, that condemnation and the prosecutions that followed were major causes of the rise of the great witch-hunts of the early modern period (1989: 184).

The label 'occult', whose literal meaning is 'concealed, hidden' referred to knowledge that was secret or forbidden, as opposed to the publicly proclaimed doctrine of the Christian Church (Ginzburg 1976: 32). While aspects of Christianity were also considered mysterious and occult, the reformers' main targets were necromancy (divination using demons or the spirits of the dead), alchemy and astrology (Kieckhefer 1989: 176). These practices and ideas, that aimed to study and influence the natural world and could be seen as the foundations of modern science, were attacked as ungodly. The historian Keith Thomas has shown in detail how in England there was a determined attempt to end all such practices, whether or not they seemed harmless (Thomas 1971). They mainly involved the study of ancient books, many of them in Latin or Greek, and so were restricted to those with a classical education, who were largely the clergy and the elite whom they taught. The translation of Arabic treatises in the twelfth century had made available Islamic astral magic and revealed ancient Greek sources hitherto lost to the Western world (Kieckhefer 1989). These new sources of knowledge stimulated an interest in ideas condemned by the Church as unchristian and hence dangerous and suspect, even satanic. A similar antagonism to the beliefs and practices deriving from other religions and from the movement known as the 'New Age' is evinced by evangelising fundamentalists today.

The doctrines of the Church proclaimed those who were not God's followers to be his enemies, though actual prosecutions were pursued with more or less vigour according to the political circumstances of the times. Heretics and Moslems as enemies of the True Faith, and Jews as apostates, were all allies of Satan and might be said to be his servants. In later centuries such views have been associated with Protestant Christianity, which after the split with the Roman Church, has represented it as a satanic institution with the Pope as the Anti-Christ. In some descriptions of the sabbath the dress and rituals of the Catholic Church appear (see below p. 53). Christian anti-Semitism has also been fuelled by the libel of human sacrifice through many centuries (Dundes 1989; 1991).

In the twentieth century the spread of Buddhism and Islam and the establishment in the 1960s of new religions constituted a threat to traditional forms of Christianity. Whether these new religions were variant forms of Christianity, like the Jesus Army, or pagan like the occult groups discussed in the next chapter, they were seen as dangerous. Some fundamentalist Protestants claimed that they were satanic in origin, even if their members did not explicitly acknowledge their allegiance to Satan; the derogatory label 'cult' was often attached to them. The fundamentalist campaign against modern 'superstition' and 'magic' included as its targets 'occult lore' such as astrology and the practices of ungodly adolescents whose music was advertised with magic symbols. The use of tarot cards to tell fortunes or the ouija board to summon spirits have both been castigated as the first steps on a path that leads inexorably to satanism. Like the interest in learned magic in early modern Europe, these practices are not the folk beliefs in witchcraft of the uneducated, but a form of esoteric knowledge for which its practitioners have been condemned by some Christians in both periods of history.

A second antecedent consisted of beliefs in the power of witches. They are usually characterised as folk beliefs, although others besides the 'peasants' held them. As has been pointed out (Rowland 1990: 182), to try and discover what the original village beliefs were through the medium of trials and confessions induced by torture is almost impossible, but peasant ideas do seem to have reflected the differences in local culture characteristic of a much more parochial Europe than today's.[4] In general though, witchcraft was held responsible in early modern Europe for a wide range of misfortunes; witches were thought to damage property, harm livestock or cause sickness, especially to children. This might also be called black magic or sorcery and was known by the educated by the Latin term *maleficia* – 'evil-doing' or 'doing harm'. In this same world 'wise' men and women, or 'cunning folk' as they were also called in England (Thomas 1971: 210; Macfarlane 1970: 115–30), used white magic to cure ailments, to find missing property and persons (an activity that might reveal theft) and also to determine the source of harm, identifying the witch. Some of them were inevitably suspected of using their powers for evil as well as good. Villagers were denounced as witches because their neighbours believed they were the cause of particular incidents of suffering. There was little interest in the origins of their powers; there was much more concern with the manifest effects of witchcraft. The popular fear of *maleficia* was mobilised in the witch-hunts and lay behind denunciations of individuals as witches.

The early modern Church's reforms were aimed at the peasants, whose recourse to the 'cunning folk' for help with their illnesses and other problems, sustained the practice of magic and undermined the Church's pastoral influence. These 'wise' men and women who were suspected of practising witchcraft had their parallels in African societies. The charms and fetishes of magicians and curers were derided or even burnt by early missionaries and later, witch-cleansing movements also demanded that magical paraphernalia be destroyed and usually also required the rooting out of practices that were now said to conceal evil potential under claims to heal and help (Willis 1970; MacGaffey 1994). Today the evangelising church also aims to sweep away popular superstition; its members assert that practices which seem relatively harmless to most people, such as telling fortunes or celebrating Halloween, lead inexorably to entanglement in the devil's snares.

Another concept of evil-doing, one where witches also figured, was held more often by the educated, especially the Christian clergy. By contrast with beliefs in magic and witches, it showed a remarkable uniformity across wide areas, since it was spread through clerical writing that circulated among the educated. In it Satan was the powerful adversary of God, the essence of evil, whose aim was to take over the world. It was the literate elite, which largely meant the clergy, among whom these ideas of devil-worship developed (Trevor-Roper 1990 [1967]). They conceived of the Devil's followers as an evil conspiracy that performed secret rites. The characteristic features of the ritual were murder, cannibalism and incest and other unimaginable sexual depravities. According to the historian Norman Cohn, the origins of the idea predate Christianity (Cohn 1975). In the second century AD similar accusations had actually been made against the Christians (Lane Fox 1986: 427), culminating in episodes of dreadful persecution and killings in Lyons, in France, at the end of that century. Even then, Cohn argues, the allegations made use of earlier myths: of conspirators sealing their compacts with each other by a cannibalistic feast and the accusations, as reported by Livy, of holding licentious orgies that were made against the followers of Bacchus by a Roman consul (Cohn 1975: 10). Cohn's classic work shows how other ideas became associated with these core notions, adding details, shedding others and changing in emphasis over the centuries.

It is not that the concept remained exactly the same over the nine centuries since its inception, but that certain core images were retained. The witch-hunts also effected a certain amount of education of the populace in the Church's view of witches, superimposing it on traditional ideas. A simplified idea of the coven of witches flying to the sabbath, together with vague notions of ghosts, vampires and other monsters became part of European folk culture. Ideas of conjuring up the devil by reciting the Lord's Prayer backwards were recorded by the Opies among the school children they studied in the 1950s, long before allegations of satanic abuse were current (Opie 1967: 1 [1959]).

It is generally agreed by historians that popular belief did not associate witchcraft with the devil (Cohn 1975: 251–3; Kieckhefer 1976: 48–56; Macfarlane 1970: 189; Thomas 1970: 49–50) and was little concerned with its origin or nature. It was the Church that linked elite ideas of the devil to folk beliefs by asserting that the power of witches derived from a compact with the devil, and by elaborating the concept of the witches' sabbath, the gathering of witches in which Satan was worshipped. Witches, like the earlier heretics whom the Church had fought, were enemies of God and His true religion and so must be servants of Satan. Christina Larner has argued that the two aspects of witches' believed connection with Satan must be distinguished from one another because, as she rightly points out: 'Witches' sabbaths or meetings also occur in non-Christian primitive cultures where pacts with one personalized devil are unknown.' It was this idea of the pact with the devil that turned all magic into witchcraft (Larner 1984: 80). The magic of healing and fortune-telling was also declared to have its origin in a Faustian pact with the devil.

The Church's aim was to extend true religion among the people, eradicating superstition and extending its control of peripheral areas (Ankarloo & Henningsen 1990: 10–11; Thomas 1973: 307, 330–2 [1971]). It encouraged denunciation of the old ideas in order to root out what the Church perceived as heresy and satanism. The effect was to provide legitimacy for the great witch-hunts of the early modern period and in effect, if not intentionally, set them in motion.

Aspects of Christianity in the late twentieth century show some close similarities with this earlier movement of reform. Stuart Clark argues that a cause of the early modern hunt was 'a common (to Catholics and Protestants) missionary determination to impose the fundamentals of Christian belief and practice on ordinary people. One component of this new evangelism was a campaign . . . to discredit and eradicate a wide range of popular cultural forms as "superstitions"' (Clark 1993: 46 [1990]). This seems a valid description of what has happened in the late twentieth century as well. The current campaign against satanism is part of a broader attack on such popular 'superstitions' as fortune telling, the interest in occultism and the foundation of new religions and a crusade to spread their version of Christianity. The evangelical movement within the Church is a movement of proselytisation (Cotton 1995). It is directed at revitalising the Church, but also at bringing into the fold people who are not Christians or whose faith has lapsed. It overlaps with a resurgence of Christian fundamentalism that is concerned to wipe out what is seen as false accretions to the faith. At their most extreme, fundamentalists insist on the literal truth of the Bible, denying the validity of an evolutionary perspective in understanding the history of humanity. Both streams encourage the denunciation of Satan and all his works.

The devil's works include other faiths. Since the sixties new religious groups, either offshoots of established religions like the Jehovah's Witnesses, or inventions of their founders such as the Unification Church founded by the Reverend Moon, have proliferated. There has long been Christian opposition to these groups, but sustained campaigns against them have started relatively recently (Beckford 1985: 222–48). These new 'cults', as they were usually termed, were seen as enemies of the true religion and therefore as doing the devil's work. Some of them were said to involve devil worship (Baskin 1972; Kahaner 1988), others were described as witchcraft (Irvine 1973). Extreme stories about their activities have been circulated by individuals who said they had escaped them; former cult members have been on lecture tours and written books to disseminate the message about their experiences.

The cults were accused of kidnapping young people, of peddling and using drugs, and of engaging in sexual orgies. Some of the cults stand in the same relation to the reforming evangelical church of today, as the heretics did to the pre-Reformation Church that, in the distant past, accused them of worshipping Satan. The most famous of the heretics, the Cathars and the Templars, figure prominently in stories about the antiquity of devil-worship (Boyd 1991: 111; Tate 1991: 62). Those whose beliefs represent a repudiation of Christianity, rather than a deviant version of it are less prominent in these accounts, although the Jews have been persecuted for centuries and elements of the accusations made against the Jews – that they killed and ate Christian babies in secret rituals – reappear in allegations about witches and satanists (Newall 1973). The most recent suspects are the members of the new 'alternative' religions, who call themselves witches or satanists and who practise magic and explicitly declare themselves to be pagan. The term 'cult' makes all of them equally suspect to the mainstream fundamentalist Christian; any or all of them may also be called satanic. A senior member of the FBI Academy has listed thirty-four groups and practices he has heard referred to as satanism; the list includes several non-

Christian world religions, the Roman Catholic and Orthodox Christian churches and rock music (Lanning 1989: 2).

Historians today, more than twenty years after Norman Cohn's classic work was published, present a reformulation of Cohn's view, arguing that the witch-hunts represented the imposition of ideas formulated in the centre, by the elite of the emerging nation-states, on the illiterate people of the periphery. (The term 'periphery' appears to mean both the remote countryside and the cultural fringes of Europe.) It is, according to Ankarloo & Henningsen (1993: 10 [1990]), 'a violent and painful innovation process', a form of control over the peasantry which is exercised to change what happens among them. Muchembled argues that 'witch-hunting is fundamentally not a religious but a political phenomenon, and it is only one aspect of the penetration and opening-up of the countryside' (Muchembled 1990). It showed an uneven spread, being less well-established in the periphery such as in England, where witch-hunting was much less virulent than on Continental Europe. Not surprisingly the idea of the sabbath was largely lacking there, except among professional witch-finders such as Matthew Hopkins (Macfarlane 1970). Rowland argues that two different social levels involved in the witch-hunts can be related to these two levels of belief: 'the supra-national level of the churches and of the demonological treatises, and the community level to which acts and accusations of malefice (evil-doing) relate. European witch-beliefs, in so far as they reflect both Christian demonology and the local contexts of witchcraft accusations, correspond to the complexity of early modern European society' (Rowland 1990: 177–81).

The witch-craze was sustained by local beliefs in the prevalence of witches, although both the initial spark and the subsequent blaze were fuelled by information communicated by priests and other religious figures. Rose asserts that 'the discovery of any evidence of this depravity was preceded in both countries (Scotland and England), by a long period of Puritan agitation against it' (1989 [1962]). Henningsen, the historian of the outbreak in north-western Spain in the early seventeenth century, blames the preaching crusade launched in the autumn of 1610 for the recrudescence of the witch scare which had begun to die down. He records that in Spain the Bishop of Pamplona carried out his own personal investigation 'a few months after the outbreak of the persecution' in the Basque area in 1610 and established that 'there had been no mention of witches before the persecutions had started on the other side of the border' and that 'the priests in sermons against witches described very precisely what had been said by witches in France' (Henningsen 1980: 128–30). Christian campaigners, from the authors of the *Malleus*

Maleficarum to the parish priests George Gifford and Robert Holland, appear at many times and places during the witch-hunts (Clark 1993: 57 [1990]). The authority of the Church has always ensured that priests have been widely believed, but in the late twentieth century, when the Church is much less powerful, it must wield power indirectly by influencing the authorities in an essentially secular state.

A final similarity between the early modern period and the late twentieth century is the appearance in both periods of individuals, mostly women, who accuse themselves of being witches. They are not accused by others or forced to confess; they make what appear to be spontaneous unforced confessions. Explaining such confessions in the early modern period has been one of the major problems for the historians. It remains unresolved. Trevor-Roper writes in amazement of Jean Bodin 'the Aristotle, the Montesquieu of the sixteenth century, the prophet of comparative history, of political theory, of the philosophy of law, of the quantitative theory of money, and of so much else, who yet, in 1580, wrote the book which, more than any other reanimated the witch-fires throughout Europe' (Trevor-Roper 1990: 47 [1967]). According to Trevor-Roper, Bodin makes clear in his treatise that he was 'converted to the science of demonology' by the confession of a woman. It had been given without her being either questioned or tortured and it had been 'remarkably circumstantial' (1990: 49 [1967]). Spontaneous confessions not only affected the thinking of influential persons such as Bodin; when publicised, as they often were, they also served to confirm the reality of the witches' sabbath and the truthfulness of the confessions extracted under torture.

Similarly, in the late twentieth century, the stories of adult 'survivors' who claim to have been sexually abused in satanic rituals as children, have encouraged belief in the existence of the devil-worshipping cults. The publication of their accounts preceded the epidemic of allegations of the abuse of children in secret rituals. However, where in Spain in the early seventeenth century or England in the sixteenth no-one would have sheltered a witch, shielding her from justice, in the United States, Canada and England 'survivors' are not denounced to the authorities but are protected by those to whom they have confessed. Some may even state that they are still members of these groups; one British woman told a journalist that she had taken part in human sacrifices, killing small children; she confided that she had seen six human sacrifices at one meeting in 1989 (Boyd 1991: 325–9). If neither her therapist, described as a consultant psychiatrist, or the journalist, both of whom believed what she said, informed the police, the result was not recorded. In a recent account of satanist practices derived partly from self-confessed satanists, the writer states that all her patients had also victimised other children (Coleman 1994a: 250). But far from being hunted down, these women are protected as victims.

In the latest historiography of the witch-hunts, attention has been paid to the development and spread of the craze, nationally and internationally (Henningsen 1980; Levack 1987; Ankarloo and Henningsen 1993 [1990]). This makes clear the way in which witch-hunts spread: not, as Ankarloo remarks (1993: 301 [1990]), as fast as epidemics, but along the lines of communication between settlements and villages. The centre is affected earlier than the periphery but within local areas signs of the spread of accusations can be seen. The effect of witch-hunters on the distribution of cases could also be perceived. The historian Alan Macfarlane had noted that for most of the period in which he was interested, 1560 to 1660, witchcraft accusations in Essex were regular and widely scattered. There seemed little connection between them, and Macfarlane concluded that 'There are no grounds for using terms like epidemic to describe the growth of accusations.' There are, however, two exceptions, in 1582 and 1645, when the prosecutions occurred 'in a small group of neighbouring villages. Here it would be justifiable to look for some outside agent; in both . . . there was present a man of more than ordinary energy, skill and interest in finding witches' (Macfarlane1970: 30). Similar people could be found in Britain at the end of the 1980s.

The sermons of the priests also circulated in gossip and were published in pamphlets. Descriptions of trials and other information about the witches' sabbath were not only disseminated in sermons, but the witch-hunters reproduced them quite cheaply, thanks to the new technology of printing, and distributed them widely. In the same way in the twentieth century campaigners against satanism not only give lectures and speak at conferences but they distribute published papers that serve, not merely as a record of what has been said, but, by including 'indicators' of satanic abuse, encourage the identification of further cases. The new information technology of the twentieth century, particularly television, has been used to similar effect, particularly in the United States, where a multiplicity of religious channels and national chat-shows have disseminated the stories of survivors as well as the warnings of specialists. Videos made by professionals can use their skills to create an emotional atmosphere that enhances the impact of the message. Telephones allow rapid consultations. The international spread of what has been dubbed the satanism scare (Richardson et al. 1991) is less surprising than it seems at first sight.

If there are similarities between past and present, there are also differences. The most important is that in the late twentieth century no-one is put to death for being a witch;[5] nor, as yet, are witches sought out or hunted down. The allegations of satanic conspiracy have been linked with cases of the maltreatment of children that have often emerged independently. The cases of satanic abuse thus resemble the cases of *maleficia* in that they arise retrospectively from cases of harm already done. While finding out who is responsible for the satanic abuse is a major preoccupation in such cases, perpetrators of other forms of harm or of harm *in general* have not been hunted out or denounced as such.

Scepticism may be more widespread in the late twentieth century than it was in early modern Europe, although it would be a mistake to think that everyone in Europe believed in the witches, even at the height of the witch-scare. Alonso de Salazar Frias, the Spanish Inquisitor who was responsible for stopping the hunt among the Spanish Basques, wrote in 1612 that 'There were neither witches nor bewitched until they were talked about and written about.' However, Salazar certainly believed in the possibility of witchcraft and the existence of the devil; it was the particular circumstances of the cases he had to consider that he felt were unreliable.

On balance, the similarities between the allegations of satanic abuse and the accusations of the witches' sabbath, are sufficient to treat the two as similar social phenomena, despite being separated by three centuries. Enshrined in folklore and in Christian myths of the fight against evil, the idea of the witches' sabbath as a ritual directed at the worship of Satan and constructed out of the negation of humanity's most basic rules of life, remains a potent image. Given that the sexual abuse of children is the most potent representation of human evil in the late twentieth century, linking the sexual abuse of children with 'satanic ritual' is quite intelligible. The old myth refurbished has apparently lost none of its impact.

The early modern Christian campaign was based on a common agreement that witchcraft flourished because the world was in a state of terminal decline (Clark 1993: 47). Ideas that resemble these lie behind the evangelical campaign of the late twentieth century, with its millenialist perception that the end of the world is approaching. The sense of a prevalence of evil has been recorded as a factor in witch-cleansing movements as well. In all these cases the political and economic upheavals of the time were profoundly changing the structure of society. The old certainties were being destroyed and former obligations with them. The sense of painful change was not an illusion. In Britain over the last generation social hierarchy has increased in a remarkable fashion, the distance between the rich and the poor having widened massively; unemployment and the uncertainties of most forms of employment mean a greater insecurity than at any time in this century. If these are indeed the social features that underlie European witch-finding movements, then they are common to both periods.

An important difference, between the Europe of the sixteenth and seventeenth centuries and Western societies in the late twentieth century, is the nature of the occult community and its relationship to Christianity and to present-day knowledge of the world. Today's witch-craft and satanism are self-consciously constructed on principles that distinguish their ideas both from secular knowledge and from other religions. They represent a distinct moral stance and claim to be religions whose critical opposition to Christianity is explicit, whereas in the past, magic and occultism had co-existed with Christianity until the Church construed as a threat the magical practices of cunning folk and learned magicians. However, then and now, they were and are in danger of being seen as embodiments of the spiritual evil of Christian fears. Of course, accusations that modern occultism is involved in satanic rituals is also partly the result of ignorance of what it involves. Hence some description of modern occultism will be necessary. Before we embark on it, however, it is necessary to consider what anthropology might add to the comparisons we have been making.

The anthropology of witchcraft

The comparison with the past has been made possible by the immense advances that have been made in the last three decades in historians' knowledge of the early witch-hunts. These achievements have been attributed to the 'successful combination of historical and social-anthropological method' which effected a major change in the late 1960s in the historiography of the witch-hunts (Ankarloo & Henningsen 1990: 3). Subsequently, there was some debate among historians over whether the witch beliefs and practices in the rest of the contemporary world can properly be compared with witchcraft in early modern Europe. It has been argued that the use of social anthropology by the English historians Macfarlane (1970) and Thomas (1974) was suc-cessful simply because the witch-hunts in England were not typical (Ankarloo & Henningsen 1993: 1). England, being on the periphery of the main hunts, did not show the influence of the concept of satan worship, except to a small degree among its witch-hunters, and it was that concept rather than folk beliefs in witchcraft that was responsible for the witch-hunts. More recently it has been admitted that this was too simple a solution; underlying the concepts of devil worship in the centre of the area affected were local beliefs that had parallels in the rest of Europe, but these had been hidden by the prominence of the demonological version of witchcraft.

The second objection to the comparative approach used by anthropology was that early modern European society was so different from the societies studied by anthropologists that comparison would not be useful (Rowland 1990: 175). However, witch beliefs and particularly witch-hunts are also found in hierarchical societies that resembled the Europe of early modern times more closely than the model of 'simple societies' allowed. Even the society in which such beliefs were first studied in detail, the Azande of the southern Sudan, was a kingdom in which the aristocracy was concerned with mystical threats distinct from the witchcraft of the peasants, which was believed not to touch them. Moreover, as Rowland notes; 'But although it is true that the societies where anthropologists have studied witch-beliefs are radically different from those of early modern Europe, this does not imply that anthropological perspectives cannot be brought to bear on European witch-beliefs' (1993: 175).

Anthropology and history in the study of witchcraft

The initial anthropological studies of beliefs in witchcraft frankly characterised them as alien to the European observer. Evans-Pritchard remarked in the course of his classic study of the Azande which formed the foundation of the anthropology of witchcraft, that 'Witchcraft is a notion so foreign to us that it is hard for us to appreciate Zande convictions about its reality.' His concern was to show that Zande thought was quite rational, although it made basic assumptions that would not be made in a society where the natural and supernatural were distinguished. Subsequent research in Africa and elsewhere built up a picture of beliefs in witchcraft as the cause of misfortune or sickness and death that showed similarities in societies throughout the world. As well as explaining the incidence of misfortune, witchcraft also provided a picture of evil. The witch or sorcerer represented the inverse of all that was good, a terrifying figure of evil, although the use of witchcraft by ordinary human beings, though culpable, was not always so alarming. There were thus two kinds of witch beliefs: one concerned the causation of misfortune and inequities of good fortune, something that was diagnosed after the event, and the other was a more unspecific belief in the existence of evil beings, representing all that was inhuman (Pocock 1985; La Fontaine 1992). Christians denigrated all such beliefs as superstitious and as paganism. In Uganda, twenty years after Evans-

Pritchard's research, Christian missionaries were teaching their flocks that to believe in witchcraft was a weakness of faith and showed that the sinner had fallen once more into the mire of pagan beliefs.

Nothing in subsequent anthropological research disturbed the basic assumptions which are the legacy of the Azande book and which seem to preclude a cross-cultural comparison with social phenomena in twentieth-century Europe. These were first, as Middleton and Winter put it nearly thirty years after the Azande book, that: 'Most Europeans no longer hold these ideas' (Middleton & Winter 1963: 1). The implication of that 'no longer' indicates the second assumption: that Europeans did hold such beliefs in the past. Thus if witchcraft were to be studied in Europe, it would require collaboration between historians and anthropologists. A completely cross-cultural study would also be a cross-disciplinary exercise. This equation of past European society with contemporary societies in the Third World might have been common-place in the 1930s, when Evans-Pritchard was studying Azande witchcraft. At that time anthropology was emerging from a phase that began in the nineteenth century, when it considered other societies as representing stages in a universal evolution. It is odd that the idea has never been reconsidered. Perhaps that was because the work of historians seems to have confirmed at least part of it. By finding anthropology useful in their studies historians implicitly confirmed the anthropological view that witchcraft in Europe was a matter of the past.

Only a few years after the publication of the book cited above, the introduction to a volume of essays dedicated to Evans-Pritchard pointed to the convergence of historians and anthropologists concerned with the subject of witchcraft (Douglas 1970). While challenging the accumulated scholarship of the time and setting out her own theory of the generation of witch-beliefs, the editor did not challenge the assumption that witchcraft beliefs belonged either to the European past or to other societies outside Europe, whose simple structures were more likely to generate the tensions and fears expressed in accusations and confessions.

To deny the relevance of comparison with other cultures is to assume that Western culture is different in kind from all others. This unique position may be believed to have been achieved by science's substitution of a rational understanding of the world for one dominated by powers of good and evil. However, the allegations of devil worship show a similarity between early modern Europe and the present that throws doubt on the notion that Western culture as a whole made a quantum leap that cut it off from the beliefs of the past. This continuity with the past indicates that where historians have found anthropology useful, observers of late-twentieth century society may also do so. The double comparison, both cross-cultural and cross-temporal or historical, will be sustained through the rest of the book, which is directed towards describing the allegations, and explaining how they arose. The final question, 'why were they accepted?', is considered before the threads can be drawn together in the final chapter.

3   Witches, satanists and the occult

The Christian campaign against witchcraft, satanism and the occult did not begin with allegations of the ritual abuse of children (Beckford 1985). As the last chapter showed, opposition to new religions, to games with an occult slant, to forms of pop music that used satanic symbolism were precursors of it. However, as has already been recognised (Jenkins 1992), the role of the Church in encouraging allegations of satanism was a powerful one. As well as the sermons that were, and are, preached, fundamentalist writing and lecturing by individuals and members of campaigning organisations like the Cult Awareness Network in the United States, the Reachout Trust and Beacon Foundation in Britain,[1] have spread the ideas of the witches' sabbath and the black mass more widely.

As far as the subsequent epidemic of allegations was concerned, personal testimonies were as important as the Church's input. There is a well-established tradition of born-again Christians testifying about their involvement with witchcraft and satanism to the congregations of churches and in lectures sponsored by Christian organisations, as demonstrations of how deeply sunk in sin they were before their salvation by Christ (e.g. Trinkle 1986). The mother of the children in one case I studied had, for several years, made a practice of approaching small fundamentalist churches with a story of how she had been a satanist and had repented. Such 'trophies of grace', as these converts may be called, have for many years encouraged the spread of the idea among fundamentalists that witchcraft and devil worship is prevalent throughout Britain. One published autobiography by an English woman, Doreen Irvine, describing her life before she became a member of the Baptist Church, is entitled 'From Witchcraft to Christ'; in it the author claims to have been involved in drugs, to have been a prostitute and finally the Queen of Black Witches (Irvine 1973). After her conversion, she appeared on television and spoke in meetings throughout Britain. By the time that the allegations of satanic abuse began to attract national attention fifteen years later, her book had been reprinted seventeen times. There is no mention of children, whether sexually abused or sacrificed, in Irvine's book.[2] Nor are they mentioned in an American book, *The Satan Seller*, published the year before, which describes drug using and selling, and sexual orgies (Warnke 1972). Nevertheless, both books have been influential and are still referred to as sources by professionals writing about satanic abuse (Katchen & Sakheim 1992; Coleman 1994a – although without mentioning this critical lacuna).

A later book by a survivor, *Michelle Remembers*, did record the sexual abuse and torture of children in rituals (Pazder & Smith 1980). This book is often credited with starting the whole 'satanism scare' in north America. Published in 1980, *Michelle Remembers* is probably the most widely cited of all published survivor stories; the authors are a Canadian woman and her therapist, whom she subsequently married. It described a year of therapy that mirrored a year of her life, when she was a five-year-old. Her abuse at the hands of satanists during rituals is told in horrifying detail including a description of young children in cages.[3] Lauren Stratford, whose book *Satan's Underground* was later exposed as a fake, was the source of the idea of a woman's being used as a 'brood-mare' to produce a baby for sacrifice which frequently appeared in the early accounts of satanism by British survivors.[4] By the time the first account by an English woman was published, the rites of initiation included the sacrifice of a baby and the drinking of its blood (Harper with Pugh 1990: 54, 73).

Stories told by survivors clothe the idea of witchcraft and devil worship with a unique air of realism. The fact that named people stand before audiences and claim to have experienced satanic rituals convinces many of those who listen to them or read their books that the accuracy of the information is beyond question. The accounts by believers of what satanism or witchcraft is, and the nature of their rituals, rely very heavily on survivors, whether their accounts are published or they are told in therapeutic sessions. Half of one of the first books about satanic abuse in Britain, by a fundamentalist journalist, consisted of the stories of such women (Boyd 1991).

There are thus two sources of believers' ideas about witchcraft and satanism: what I have called Church mythology, whose origin was discussed in the last chapter, and the autobiographical stories told by individuals. Church and individual sources overlap to a great degree. The stereotypes of the witches' sabbath and the black mass may be taken from Christian folklore and incorporated into descriptions of satanism by survivors, particularly if they belong to a fundamentalist church. Folklore may appear in Church descriptions and survivors add to their knowledge by reading books by campaigners or by other survivors. The sexual abuse of children seems to have been added to the satanic ritual and may now remain as part of the fundamentalists' teaching about devil worship. The details of individual accounts may vary considerably, but unless specific details are repeated by others, they will be dropped; for example, Harper's account of witches levitating has not been repeated and is now never mentioned. Other unusual features may also disappear in favour of a general homogenisation that allows believers to claim that they are all telling the same story.

The people in late twentieth-century Britain who describe themselves as occultists, witches or satanists are not those to whose activities the descriptions of devil worship by believers, whether campaigners or survivors, would apply. However, the fact that various forms of occultism do exist seems to support modern allegations of satanism, since if occultists really carry out magic rituals the allegations of ritual abuse are more easily accepted as possible. Some innocent individuals, including children, have suffered from a marked increase in prejudice against them because of their beliefs and the Christian campaign against them; an interest in the occult was the main evidence against parents accused of ritually abusing their children in three cases reported to my study. Their children were removed from home and kept away from them. In the United States some occultists are even reported to have been seriously harmed (Adler 1986: 130–3, 449–50).[5] Prejudice flourishes on public ignorance and there is a general lack of knowledge of the range of beliefs and practices that make up a very complex community (Luhrmann 1989; cf. Gordon Melton 1989 for America).[6]

Occultists have made efforts to reassure the public; in Britain the Pagan Federation has produced an information booklet about their practices and circulated it to departments of social services (Pengelly & Waredale 1992). A sustained campaign by an organisation of occultists under the name SAFF (Safeguarding the Right to Freedom of Belief) and a more low-profile programme of public education undertaken by the Pagan Federation has also had some effect, if only to change the terms used in the debate. Thus, in the earliest years of the allegations of satanic abuse, the terms 'witchcraft' and 'black magic' were used interchangeably with 'satanism'; by 1991 a distinction between witches and satanists was recognised, at least in public. However, the descriptions of rituals and the terminology used, such as 'covens' for the cult-groups and 'sabbats' for the days of ritual celebration, come from the terms used in witchcraft, not satanism, and perpetuate the confusion between them. For some fundamentalist Christians, of course, the distinctions are immaterial, since for them, as for their predecessors in

early modern Europe, witches are Satan's servants as much as those
who call themselves satanists.

The existence of people who call themselves witches and satanists,
like the alleged personal experiences of survivors, may seem to
demonstrate the truth of allegations of satanic abuse, although by any
normal standards the argument is flawed. Non-Christians may assert
that they personally do not believe in Satan, but that there exist modern
satanists who do, and of course they are right. However, the existence of
satanists does not prove that they abuse children in their rituals;[7] it
merely means that care must constantly be taken to emphasise that the
actual practices of occultists, witches and satanists are different from
what is being recounted as satanic abuse.

It is very difficult for outsiders to distinguish occultists from those
who pretend to have knowledge of the occult or of magic, who have a
smattering of understanding or who display occult symbols for effect.
Although there are organised groups, it is possible to follow any branch
or branches of modern occultism without joining anything. Some new
religious movements may be identified as owing allegiance to a leader or
leaders but there are no such figureheads whose followers can be
defined as occultists, although Wiccans respect the memory of Gerald
Gardner or Alex Sanders who established the two main streams of
modern witchcraft practice. Without group affiliation or adherence to a
leader to identify them as a single religion or even as a cluster of related
religions, pagans are very different from members of conventional
religions. Many are self-taught, buying books and performing their
magic or rituals, that they either take from their reading or create to suit
themselves, in private. It is also common for individuals to be interested
to read about magical ceremonies but not to perform them; others may
be involved in more than one kind of occult practice. The whole
movement emphasises the freedom of individuals to do things in the
manner they choose. There is no compulsion to join a group, to worship
particular gods or to follow a particular form of magick or ritual. There
are, however, general principles that allow occultists themselves to
identify particular practices as genuinely part of the occult tradition.
Luhrmann has described the 'remarkable toleration of diversity both in
the practice and in the views practitioners take towards the practice'
(1989: 335). This freedom may reflect the individualism of the late
twentieth century, although occultism seems always to have been
somewhat eclectic; it means that its practice does not define it to
outsiders.

The individuality and privacy of ritual magic, contrasted with the
public worship by Christian churches, makes occultists of all sorts seem

mysterious, and ignorance of their practices may make them seem sinister. However, all over the world groups define themselves by the possession of special (hidden or occult) knowledge and exclude all but initiates from the most sacred rituals. The secrecy to which members are sworn during their initiation maintains the value of the secrets to which they are then admitted, giving those who know them a source of power (Barth 1975: 217; La Fontaine 1985: 39–41). Those who do not have access to the hidden knowledge may, and often do, indulge in fantastic speculation about what it is, claiming that what is hidden must be at least shameful and probably dangerous. Freemasonry has long been regarded with suspicion because of the secrecy surrounding its proceedings and membership, and the fact that a substantial number of the police are thought to be Freemasons allowed some believers to claim that among the police were some who were protecting satanists as fellow occultists.

The occult in Britain

The number of people involved with the occult is very hard to assess. Campaigners appear to believe that there are very large numbers of them. Inflated estimates are made, both by occultists themselves and by their detractors (Luhrmann 1989: 4 f.n. 3; King 1970: 139; Harper & Pugh 1990). In the United States in 1986, there were 'probably no more than 10 thousand' in a population of about 250 million (Adler 1986: 107–8). This represents about one person in 25,000, which would yield a comparable total in Britain of just over 2,000. There has been only one attempt so far to obtain a more accurate count. The Occult Census, a private survey, is based on a very large number of questionnaires sent to the customers of the Sorcerer's Apprentice Bookshop, to other occult bookshops, to the publishers of underground magazines and to known groups of occultists (*Occult Census* 1989). One thousand completed questionnaires were returned, a number likely to represent a much larger population than that estimated by analogy with the United States. In addition, it is impossible to establish the number of people who may share the ideas, but who do not make identifiable links with others through subscriptions to publications or by participating in group activities. Whatever the real figure, it must be recognised that occultists, pagans and witches nevertheless form a very small religious minority.

Those who are interested in the occult come from a wide variety of backgrounds; according to Luhrmann, many of them are employed in the computer industry (1989: 7; cf. Adler 1986: 446). She describes them as middle-class urbanites (Luhrmann 1989: 29). The Occult Census gives an interesting profile of its respondents. They were relatively highly educated: 37 per cent had had further education and another 21 per cent had been to university (*Occult Census* 1989: 14). While the proportions were not documented, the respondents declared themselves to be engaged in all kinds of occupations. Whatever the relative figures involved it is clear that they do not include the poorest, least educated members of society, such as those who appear in cases of alleged ritual abuse. Thus if a parallel is to be drawn with the early modern period, these occultists resemble the learned magicians more than the cunning folk of the villages.

Most occultists also seem to be relatively young. They had first become interested in the occult in their teens, although there was only a small proportion of census respondents (under 5 per cent) as young as this. The largest group of respondents were in their twenties; two-thirds of them were under forty (*Occult Census* 1989: 11). The relatively small size of the youngest group might mean that interest in these ideas is waning,[8] but as the respondents were not a representative sample of occultists, no firm conclusions can be drawn from the figures, and other sources such as the Pagan Federation claim that interest among young people is continuing. In the United States, one study noted a new concern with appropriate pagan education for children, which could imply a maturing population, although it gives no other information on age (Adler 1986: 446).

The majority of occultists who responded to the Occult Census were witches and pagans rather than satanists and this accords with other estimates of the very small number of the latter. Harvey, who has studied satanists, estimates the total number in organised groups in Britain as no more than 100. More than ten times as many respondents claimed a committed interest in witchcraft (42 per cent) or paganism (46 per cent) as in satanism and three-quarters said they had no interest in satanism. Even more undermining of the popular stereotypes is the conclusion that nearly two-thirds of the respondents (64 per cent) undertake neither ritual nor spells. As the census reported, they find 'occultism a solely religious framework for their lives' (*Occult Census* 1989: 18). By 'religious' here is presumably meant an intellectual framework or set of beliefs.

Witchcraft and satanism can be said to fall at opposite ends of the broad spectrum of beliefs and practices that is referred to as occultism (House of the Goddess 1991: 1). Witchcraft can be roughly characterised as feminist, or at least as valuing the sexes equally, anti-hierarchical and ritually permissive, while satanists are hierarchical, subordinate women to men and follow the ritual prescriptions laid down by the founders of the group, who are usually also their leaders. It is relevant here that Wicca was established in the fifties and sixties while the small groups of satanists are more recent foundations. Their ideas also present a contrast, Wicca being a nature religion which denies all connection with Christianity, although some Wiccans believe that it is a relic of pre-Christian paganism. Satanists explicitly see themselves as combating Christianity, and the choice of Satan as their deity is a denial of Christianity rather than a commitment to Christian notions of evil. An examination of their beliefs and organisations in more detail will show how they differ from the popular stereotypes that figure in Christian ideas of them or in allegations of satanic abuse.

Modern witchcraft: Wicca

Modern witches speak of their religion as Wicca or the Craft and refer to themselves as Wiccans or witches. The term 'witch' is used in the sense it had in early modern England, meaning men as well as women, but they are practitioners of magic or nature-worshippers rather than witches in the common cross-cultural sense of figures of evil. Practising witches insist that the term warlock for a male witch is only used by uncomprehending outsiders; a typical Wiccan definition of warlock is: 'Deceiver: used by those who know little to mean a male witch' (Anon. 1974: 28; Shan 1986: 60).[9] 'Wizard' has a similar connotation for Wiccans. The fact that 'survivors' and Christians use these terms (e.g. Harper & Pugh 1990) indicates to Wiccans that their descriptions are not reliable; at the very least it shows ignorance of modern witchcraft.

Wiccans do not believe in the Christian God or the devil. They worship a Goddess who may be given a number of names according to the folk tradition followed by a particular coven. Her consort, the Horned God, may be identified with the stag-god of Celtic mythology or occasionally with Pan, which may encourage fundamentalist Christians in their belief that the devil in his half human-half animal form is the object of their worship. He does not appear in most feminist Wiccan ritual. Wiccan rituals have no fixed forms, although there are some regular patterns and recurring symbols within a common culture that allow the recognition of genuine forms of ritual or magic. By these criteria the rituals described in the allegations of satanic abuse are spurious, as are the acts that were actually substantiated (see Chapter 5). Magic aims to mobilise the mental power of the participants to achieve a designated result: to heal or help, in general or with reference to a particular individual. The ritual takes place within a circle that focuses and concentrates the power that is raised.[10] Some witches will say that there are covens who use this power to harm but they view the practice as evil and are afraid of the perversion of magical power. As has already been pointed out, it is very common to find that magical power is regarded as having the potential to harm as well as to do good; fear of its evil side emphasises the belief in its power (Luhrmann 1986).

None of the Wiccan rituals require large gatherings. Many witches perform their magic alone or with their partner, although some join small groups called covens. Most styles of witchcraft put a maximum of thirteen on the membership of a coven, but groups may not be as big as this (King 1970: 139; Luhrmann 1989: 47; Shan 1986: 42). Many covens like to have equal numbers of men and women members, while others have only women as members. Children do not normally participate in the rituals until they are at least adolescent; one guide to Wicca (Anon. 1974: 25–6 [1970]) indicates that children should not be allowed to participate in the rituals if these contain sexual elements. Luhrmann (personal communication) told me that during the two years of her research into a variety of groups and into participation in many rituals she did not see children at any of them. However, another informant, a former feminist witch, spoke of taking her small children into the woods for rituals outdoors with one or two other female Wiccans.

Covens are loosely organised, emphasising the personal relations of trust among members. Where personal difficulties prevent harmony, covens may split. Individuals may join more than one coven, or change from one to another if they find themselves incompatible with the members of the one they first joined. Members are ritually initiated into a coven and some covens recognise several degrees of initiation; these represent levels of knowledge, rather than positions in a hierarchy of command, although the high priestess and priest are leaders by virtue of their intimate relationship with the mystical powers. Wiccans are consciously anti-hierarchical and egalitarian, although the pre-eminence of certain experienced witches, the founders of covens, is recognised.

Coven members consider themselves to be as close to one another as members of a family, although any particular coven may not last long. Each coven is expected to have its distinctive form of magic which ideally should be handed down to the next generation; in fact, few covens last long enough for that. This analogy with the family may be linked with the belief that some witches are born not made, inheriting their 'craft' through the maternal line since pre-Christian times. This is probably the source of the allegations concerning 'generational satanists' who are allegedly born into satanism and brought up in it.

The relationships between their members and the ties retained after one coven has been established as an offshoot of another, may make links between covens but not all covens have any ties of this sort. Even if they do, they do not form part of any larger organisation, although one observer records a tradition that in the past there was a single organisation with one figure or council at its head (Holzer 1971: 80). The Pagan Federation is a loose association of Wiccan and other groups; it speaks for members and tries to represent their general interests by combating ignorance and hostility, but it does not control its constituent groups.

There are thus good grounds for thinking that the small number of professing witches in this country would be unlikely to combine in any national or international organisation. Several features of the structure of covens make their control by a single monolithic organisation extremely unlikely: the emphasis on autonomy for each coven, the deliberate limitations on numbers in one group so as to ensure intimate knowledge of one another, the shifting membership; these are all antithetical to large-scale organisation. Many of those who are interested in witchcraft join no groups, but pursue their interest independently for a time and drift away from it later. Covens may divide or disband. Most of all, the self-conscious stress laid on diversity, freedom and equality militates against Wiccans accepting uniformity of dogma or central control. The emphasis on the freedom of each individual to do as he or she wishes appears in different manifestations, as revolt against authority or as secrecy or both, but 'self-empowerment' is a basic aim of all pagans. Not merely the capacity for organisation, but the philosophy for world domination or conspiracy, seem entirely lacking.

Satanism

There is only one study of satanist groups in Britain, by Harvey (1995a).[11] It is clear from what he writes that satanists enjoy teasing and misleading the public with shocking stories that purport to be revelations about their activities, most of which are probably untrue. This makes it difficult to be sure what is accurate. There are three satanic churches mentioned in most discussions of satanism but one is probably no longer in existence. The two main churches were founded in the United States, where they are registered as religions and hold public rituals; even anti-satanist campaigners will admit that 'there is no evidence linking these groups with illegal activity' (Kahaner 1988: 63). Estimates of the size of their membership are usually exaggerated (Brierley & Hiscock 1994: 281; Logan 1994: 158). Harvey refers to six groups in Britain, with an estimated total membership of about 100 (1995a: 284), and a fringe of individuals who belong to no groups. The Occult Census indicated that there were about forty committed satanists, with a fringe of about 150 people who showed some curiosity about it, and noted that the satanist respondents were nearly all (83 per cent) men. There was also a preponderance of young men among members of the Temple of Set who completed Harvey's questionnaire (Harvey 1995a: 285), and he notes a strongly masculine cast to their beliefs. Compared with Wiccans or occultists in general, satanists form a very small group. Within Britain they are so few3 as to be insignificant.

The Church of Satan was founded in 1966 by Anton LaVey (Barker 1989:47; Langone & Blood 1990: 32; Gordon Melton 1986: 145; Carlson, Larue et al. 1989: 7–8, 11; Kahaner 1988: 67–72). His work, the Satanic Bible, contains his philosophy, which is the doctrine of the Church of Satan: man is an animal and to indulge his animal instincts is 'good'. The Church of Satan does not believe in the existence of the devil as portrayed by Christianity and the choice of its name represents its opposition to Christianity, which they see as suppressing the 'natural' pleasure-seeking side of human nature. The Church of Satan said it has a branch in Britain but Harvey claims that there is now no such 'organised group' and the evidence I collected confirms this. A British occultist magazine that tried to organise readers to protest against being associated with the sexual abuse of children and other crimes, contains a letter from a representative of the Church of Satan supporting these aims (ORCRO 1990), but the letter was written from the United States and indicates no English branch. However the writings of its founder, Anton LaVey, continue to have central significance for satanists and other occultists in Britain.

The Temple of Set is led by Michael Aquino, a former member of the Church of Satan (Langone & Blood 1990: 35; Gordon Melton 1989: 145; Carlson, Larue et al. 1989: 12; Kahaner 1988: 72–82) who broke away from it in 1975. It appears to be more highly structured than the Church of Satan, with a system of degrees through which members may progress through study. Harvey estimates its current membership at about fifty – about half of all Satanists in organised groups in Britain. However, according to one former member I spoke to who attended several meetings, they never assembled more than about twelve members, mostly young men. Their theology emphasises the human intellect and self-reliance, which is a gift from Set or Satan. The gift carries with it an obligation to use it to develop one's understanding, but faith or worship are both considered inappropriate in the Temple of Set (Harvey 1995a: 288).

The Process Church of the Final Judgement may also be referred to as a satanic church, but in its heyday its members served four gods: Jehovah, Lucifer (in the original sense of 'Light-bearer'), Christ and Satan (Bainbridge 1978; Langone & Blood 1990: 30). Founded in 1964, by 1975 the rump had only a little over forty members, all in the United States. The founder returned to London and took 'an ordinary job' (Bainbridge 1978: 245, 288). There are probably no longer any practising members, although there are frequent rumours that it is re-forming itself.

Smaller groups exist, of which two in Britain – the Order of the Nine Angles and the Dark Lily – have been described by Harvey. Both are very small groups. The former 'clearly fits the "Satanic" stereotype better than other groups. It should be said that this is almost certainly deliberate' (Harvey 1995a: 292). Harvey recorded that he had no evidence that they practised what they claimed, but they enjoyed shocking people. Harvey declares categorically that: 'In common with other satanist groups the ONA has no role for children in any of its activities.'

The main satanist groups, although small, are organised hierarchically and show a preoccupation with self-improvement, competition and the exercise of power. The leaders are clearly set apart from the general membership. While the ideology and organisation of satanist churches would be capable of supporting an international organisation, in fact they appear to have remained the followings of their founders, rather than having become well-established as organisations. The groups have been subject to splits and a considerable turnover in membership. According to Blanche Barton, an administrator of the Church of Satan and now married to its founder, the centralised, 'tightly regulated' system of grottoes and groups of which it was formerly composed was dissolved in 1975 (Barton 1990: 119, 129).

None of the satanist groups in existence can possibly be the organisations referred to in the allegations in particular cases of satanic abuse, or in writings or lectures about the threat of satanism. They are too small, insufficiently organised and lacking in the resources that would be needed for their alleged activities. Satanism may sometimes be confused with the various commercial enterprises, usually not run by occultists, that exploit the general interest in the occult as a rebellion against (Christian) society. Books, magazines and videos with satanic themes are distributed internationally by more than one company; some of the publishers are British.[12] At a meeting in Cardiff in 1990 this trade and its international nature was cited as evidence for the international organisation of satanism but the companies appear to operate strictly for commercial reasons. It has been reported as a lucrative field (Luhrmann 1989: 5 fn.8; *Time Out* 1990) as is that of the making and selling of commercial horror videos, of which there are also large numbers available. All this largely benefits non-practitioners. Certain rock groups use images drawn from satanism and display symbols, such as the pentagram and the number 666 (probably with little idea of their origin or meaning), in combination with others currently fashionable among heavy metal fans. The music disseminates knowledge of such fragments very widely and it would be quite possible for children to be familiar from this source with a range of the ideas and symbols that might be interpreted as satanic. There is no evidence that most young people who use these symbols see them as more than emblems of the bands they admire, or as symbols of rebellion against an established order that increasingly has no place for them.

There are individuals or small groups of associates who may call themselves satanists, but who do not belong to the main groups. Usually these are teenagers or young adults, and the groups concerned break up when their activities are discovered, often on the first occasion. Similar groups in Norway made the international headlines when they burned down an ancient wooden church. It was reported of such individuals in the United States that they used satanism 'as a backdrop for the (sic) primary sexual activities' (Truzzi, 1974: 643). However in Britain it is doubtful if these teenagers do more than use the symbolism or enjoy the excitement of rebelling and experimenting with the forbidden (Harvey 1995a: 294). There are also people who call themselves occultists who might not be accepted as such by the majority of the occult community. Disturbed individuals may also use the ideas and images of satanism to justify their actions, often after the event. In one case, it seems to have been thought that to claim that the accused was under the malign influence of satanism might serve as a defence against a charge of murder.

Occultists and satanic abuse

Campaigners on the issue of satanic abuse may refer to occult practices or to witchcraft or black magic as the context in which children are sexually abused. Since there are real people to whose beliefs and practices these labels may be given, the allegations seem realistic and are more easily believed. Such accusations increase the prejudice against practitioners of alternative religions. I have been told of cases in which the beliefs of their parents seem to have been the only reason for taking children into care, and one case in the study seemed to be of this sort.

A very few adults in the cases studied appeared to have occult interests, and these were of a rather minor sort: the grandmother of one child held seances, which the child described watching; the child also showed herself capable of using tarot cards and predicted the future of her foster-mother (wrongly as it turned out). Another child was given what was described as a 'voodoo doll' by her grandmother, who was also a medium. In another case a woman admitted teaching an adolescent yoga, in order, she said, to relax her and help her sleep. In one case, the paraphernalia for magic was discovered by a woman after her husband had been arrested for the sexual abuse of his step-daughter. The girl explained that he had performed magic on the new bed he had bought for her; the magic had not been the context for the abuse. People like these would probably not be considered occultists by the community of those who practise magic, and mostly there was no evidence that they were performing magic rituals either alone or with others taking part.

Occultists have denied that the practices alluded to in the allegations of satanic abuse refer to the practices of any known group. Eyewitness accounts by observers of Wiccan and satanist ritual can be drawn on to provide additional evidence and check whether the allegations refer to their rituals or to those of other occultists. They show that genuine rituals differ in a number of ways from the rituals described in allegations of satanic abuse. While there is no doubt that prejudice against occultists has been heightened by the allegations, they do not implicate them directly or as a community because there are so few points of similarity with known occult rituals (see also Harvey 1995a).

In the occult community, magick (spelt with a 'k' to distinguish it from the performances of conjurors, according to most accounts, although others may point to the fact that it was Aleister Crowley who introduced the changed spelling) is a technique used in different groups and is not the property of any one of them. Modern magick relies heavily on the creation of an appropriate atmosphere; words are important to invoke powers or aid the concentration of human imagination and will. There are no prescribed magical formulae used by all those who practise magick, although there are common themes and certain principles must be followed, nor is the use of various forms of magick restricted to any particular occult group. The characteristic feature of magick is variability (see Holzer 1971: 216; Shan 1986: 80; Anon. 1974: 7 [1970]; Luhrmann 1989: 38). Each person or group is entitled to experiment, to find the combination of symbols, words and actions that they find effective (Gordon Melton, 1989: 138–142; Luhrmann 1989: 38–42), but it is only the experienced who do so;

others mostly follow the example or written prescriptions of recognised practitioners. Magicians may study folklore to extend their knowledge and improve their magick, using a wide range of acts and symbols drawn from more than one system of thought, such as the ancient religions of Greece, Rome or Egypt, Norse and Celtic mythology, the Kabbala and alchemy. Among pagans figures like the moon-goddess and the horned god, who are central to witchcraft, come from a mixture of ancient religions. There has also been a good deal of change in recent years as groups of pagans and magicians have proliferated.

Witches consider all the trappings of magick merely as props to assist its real purpose, which is to raise and project the psychic power of the group; the objects are not important in themselves. Participants may form a circle, which is believed to concentrate the powers of all present into a single force but no practice is mandatory. Celebratory rituals are even more varied. The use of spoken words, to aid the concentration of performers' minds and wills on their objective, form a large part of the rituals of both witchcraft and satanism. Witches may use dances that resemble simplified country dances and there may be singing or incantations (Holzer 1971: 190, 203; Luhrmann 1989: 227–9; Shan 1986: 14; Anon. 1974: 76 [1970]). Chanting was only mentioned in a small minority of allegations, although it plays a much larger part in the descriptions given by campaigners against the allegations.[13]

A common feature of belief in witches all over the world (Mair 1969; J. L. Brain 1989; Schneider 1976) is that witchcraft is associated with forbidden sexual practices, such as incest or the sexual abuse of children or with indiscriminate sex. Since the regulation of sexuality is funda-mental to human society, witches, as the embodiment of anti-social evil, are seen as acknowledging no restrictions on their sexual desires. Among occultists sexuality is believed to be a potent natural force and one which should not be repressed or denied but venerated, as should the parts of the body that contain the power of fertility and generation. They consciously rebel against what they see as the puritanism of Christian society. In turn, Christian demonology associates illicit sex with witchcraft and satanism in the same way as it links witchcraft with devil worship.

Nudity is associated with sexual activities and group nudity with orgies, in popular thinking. Covens that follow the tradition of Gardner[14] perform magick naked (or sky-clad, as they call it). Practitioners take pains to assert that this practice is a representation of freedom and human equality, not an encouragement of promiscuous sexual relations (Holzer 1971: 221–2, 237–8; Anon. 1974: 3–4, 11 [1970]). A participant observer in many rituals stated that 'There are no sexual orgies, little eroticism, and in fact little behaviour that would be different if clothes were being worn' (Luhrmann 1989: 48–9). In the Church of Satan a naked woman is also required to enact the part of a living altar; she is cross-legged in most rituals but lies on a table for the black mass. Here too the intention is to represent the naked body as a symbol of good.[15] Curiously, allegations of nakedness figure hardly at all in the cases studied, perhaps because at the end of the twentieth century nakedness is no longer considered evil, merely titillating.

Accounts of sexual orgies in satanic rituals come from survivors who say they were members of satanic cults before being converted to Christianity. An early account that describes sexual intercourse on an altar, as well as sexual orgies among satanists of an unidentified group, does not mention the sexual abuse of children (Warnke et al. 1972: 111–12). A former satanist who names the group that she belonged to and is highly critical of it, declares that she never witnessed sexual orgies, although she does describe the performance of destructive magic she observed (Blood in Langone and Blood 1990: 90).

The term, sex magick, can be found in occult writings and is used in more than one sense. Sexual relations are not part of most Wiccan or satanist rituals, although the Wiccan third degree initiation seems to be a matter of some public concern; intercourse may be a rite of mystical sexuality, performed by the man and woman who incarnate the Goddess and her consort, the Horned God. The act sometimes involves 'symbolic', rather than 'actual', intercourse. The illustration to Parker is of this kind since a cloth is interposed between the two people involved (Parker 1993). Few members of a coven reach third degree initiation and for most witches, sex magick consists of sexual relations between the man and woman of an established partnership in private (Luhrmann 1989: 48). Referring to the United States, Adler reports: 'I have found very few covens that engage in explicitly sexual rituals' (Adler 1986: 110). It may have been more common in the past. Holzer's description of the coven of Alex Sanders (one of the founders of modern witchcraft) recounts the story of a man who seduced his two daughters during a ritual, making it quite clear that the acts were not only not legitimately part of the ritual, but considered a great sin. Sanders expelled him from the coven and at the next meeting mobilised the power of the group to punish him with a potent curse (Holzer 1971: 56–7).

Some individuals use a different form of sex magick, which has some resemblance to tantric yoga (Culling 1971), but it does not seem to be either common or used in rituals. The implicit attitude to intercourse and to women, who are merely objects to be used, may appear unpleasant and offensively unliberated to many people, but it is practised in private and is mainly heterosexual and explicitly adult. It is not a recipe for orgies or for the sexual abuse of children. Some exponents of this form of sex magick refuse to accept Crowley's support of homosexual intercourse as permissible in sex magic (Culling 1971: 72) but others allegedly do. Homosexuality was one of the accusations made against the Templars, as it was also against Gilles de Rais, since it had long been regarded as a mortal sin.

Postulating the use of drugs to explain the episodes of flying to the witches' sabbath and other impossible physical feats that frequently figured in the confession of witches in the early modern period began in the sixteenth century (Levack 1987: 44–5) and still continues. It is not uncommon for it to be said that the disclosures of children indicate that they have been drugged (Coleman 1994a: 248). References to flying or bodily experiences that are physically impossible, often recounted as dream experiences may be explained, by believers, as evidence of the use of drugs. The children may then be asked, repeatedly, if they were given anything unusual to eat or drink. However, there were relatively few records of this in the questionnaires. Naturally occurring drugs may be mentioned occasionally as ingredients of traditional magic, that have now apparently fallen into disuse, but the references seem insubstantial and based on hearsay (King 1970: 141; Anon. 1974: 15). Luhrmann states categorically that drugs are never used in magical ritual and rarely outside it (Luhrmann 1989: 222). Her generalisation is supported by the absence of any mention of drugs in other eyewitness accounts. Other substances such as salt, water or wine are merely used as symbols of the elements (Luhrmann 1989: Plate 15).

Witches at the sabbath in the past were not thought to wear special clothing but the idea of the black mass has become associated with the wearing of black, hooded robes. This is the garb of devil worshippers, as described in horror stories by Dennis Wheatley or authors of similar works and depicted in the film versions by which they are best known today. The original association was with the clothes of monks, for the evil power of the rite is enhanced by the perversion of the religious vocation, but modern fundamentalists may associate them with 'satanic' clergy such as Buddhist and Catholic priests. One of the commonest features of allegations of ritual abuse recorded in our survey was that the participants wore robes or strange clothing of some sort (La Fontaine 1994: 24). Masks and robes, sometimes robes with hoods concealing the face, are mentioned in allegations of satanic rituals associated with the sexual abuse of children in other countries as well. They may appear in drawings that are illustrations in writings about satanic abuse (e.g. Pamela Hudson 1991). The robes may be said to be black, white or red; masks are much less frequently mentioned, although they appeared in newspaper illustrations, television programmes or videos. A completely faceless robed figure, said to have been drawn by an American child and first published in a book by Pamela Hudson looks more like a cross between a ghost and a Ku Klux Klan figure, and although nothing like it has yet appeared in any allegations in Britain, it has been reproduced more than once there, suggesting that it is an illustration of what may be expected of all satanists.

The ritual clothing referred to in accounts of satanic abuse is all that implicates modern satanists. However, the satanists' choice of ceremonial dress may be deliberately chosen in reference to the Christian tradition. Black robes with hoods[16] worn either open or closed, are described by Anton LaVey, the founder of the Church of Satan, as 'mandatory'. The robes 'represent a formal transition between man and beast', and therefore symbolise the animal nature of human beings that he emphasises. White robes are worn only by adults being initiated as satanists and not otherwise (LaVey 1972: 208); the only red one referred to is a child's baptismal robe (Barton 1990: 19; LaVey 1972: 214). Masks in the likenesses of various animals (and) 'entire animal heads made of papier maché or other material can heighten the effectiveness' (LaVey 1972: 79). The 'masks' referred to by Anton LaVey appear in an illustration to Barton's book (Barton 1990: 106), but photographs of rituals in the Church of Satan do not show them. They resemble theatrical costumes or old illustrations of the witches' sabbath, and represent the goat's head of the man-beast Satan. In one modern account of witchcraft, masks are referred to as a 'very old aid to ritual which helps to move participants out of their everyday identities' (Shan 1986: 50). It appears from the context that the reference is to medieval mystery plays that are assumed to have been performances of ancient ritual; the author refers to 'ritual' as the origin of theatre. A photograph of a headdress with the horns of a stag, worn by the priest as the stag god (Luhrmann 1989: plate 17) resembles drawings of the performers of medieval mystery plays or Morris dancers. It is a headdress rather than a mask or a hood, since the face is clearly visible. Some witches do wear hooded robes for ritual, but most leave their heads bare. Members of the occult groups known as the Western mysteries wear formal, coloured, robes for their meetings and some wear headdresses (Luhrmann 1989: 229), but masks are not mentioned.

To sum up, the allegations of satanic ritual abuse seem at first sight to implicate modern pagans or occultists. This chapter has shown that such conclusions are not really justified. The horrifying features of the rituals that figure in the allegations are not part of pagan ritual or magick. The variety of the ritual associated with allegations of satanic abuse is not incompatible with the variety of forms of occult magic; however, there are common underlying principles in occult ritual that give them a uniformity that is absent from the rituals referred to in the allegations. Spurious ritual can be identified as such by reference to the general philosophy underlying the practice of the occult. The claim that the sexual abuse of children takes place in the rituals is quite incompatible with the normal practice of occult groups. As the last chapter showed, the most common elements in the allegations of satanic abuse resemble features of the witches' sabbath or witchcraft beliefs in other societies rather than modern magick. Such a comparison focuses attention on the allegations as expressions of the accusers' apprehension of evil; together with the material analysed in this chapter, it suggests that this approach is more likely to be fruitful than attempting to identify any alternative religion as responsible.

4   The extent of the allegations

The origins of the allegations

Allegations of satanic abuse began in north America with the claims
made by adults, not children. The most publicised is the case of
Michelle Smith. Two Canadians, Michelle Smith and her psychiatrist
Lawrence Pazder, whom she subsequently married, published an
account of her treatment in 1980. Under a form of hypnosis she had
relived her experiences of the abuse in a satanic cult that she had
suffered as a five-year-old. The book, *Michelle Remembers*, has had a
powerful influence throughout north America and in this country. It
was followed in the United States by the book by Lauren Stratford[1] for
which it may have served as a model. (The second book, *Satan's
Underground*, has already been mentioned as an acknowledged fiction.)
The first case of allegations involving children in north America
concerned the McMartin nursery school in California in 1984. There
is some indication that Lauren Stratford was consulted by some of the
parents of children there and that adult women's stories also influenced
the case (Nathan 1991: 82; Nathan & Snedeker 1995). Thereafter
there were many other cases; by 1986 Finkelhor and his associates
could identify 'at least 36 cases' where allegations of ritual abuse in
nursery schools had been made (Finkelhor, Williams and Burns 1988:
59).

The background in Britain

In Britain at this time it was being demonstrated, often by widely
publicised cases, that children, even very young children, might be
physically and sexually abused by the adults who had care of them. The
cases of children who had been abducted, sexually abused and then
killed had also been reported by the media and had prepared people to
believe in acts of violent abuse against children (Jenkins 1992: 12–14);
the tracking down, in 1987, of a large paedophile network indicated that

large numbers of men might be involved. Rumours about 'snuff movies', in which the killing of a child was filmed for video, surfaced at the same time as these established cases were reported. It was argued that it was only a matter of time before a video of this kind was found.[2] When accusations concerning the abuse and murder of children in satanic ritual appeared, they seemed to be the uncovering of yet another dimension of what had already been established.

The first allegations of satanic abuse followed directly after the eruption of a major controversy over the sexual abuse of children that had taken place in Cleveland in the north-east of England. There was no suggestion in Cleveland that the children had been abused in satanic rituals, nor that a paedophile network was responsible. Although there were a large number of children involved, they were not part of a single case, but constituted a backlog of cases where sexual abuse had been suspected that had been referred for a consultant's opinion. Social workers and police in Cleveland had been opposed in a widely publicised conflict over the reliability of the diagnoses in a large number of cases. Bitter attacks on social workers, and on their techniques of interviewing children who were suspected of having been sexually abused, appeared in the media. The report of the judicial enquiry that resulted was critical of most of those involved (Butler-Sloss 1988). The social workers in one of the first cases to reach the media, the Broxtowe case in Nottingham, were very nervous about the possibility of attracting similar criticism. More significantly as it turned out, they were also prepared to be suspicious of the police, with whom they had to co-operate, and suspected them of the same attitudes to the phenomenon of child sexual abuse that had characterised the police in Cleveland.

The history of the allegations

The first case of sexual abuse during the course of ritual, one of the three discussed later, occurred in Shropshire in 1982, before the McMartin case which initiated the eruption of allegations in the United States. There were no further cases for five years and those that followed then were very different from the first. It is these later ones with which this book is mainly concerned, although the first case is important for two reasons: first, it was unlike most later cases in that there was material evidence that rituals had taken place that included some of the sexual abuse for which the accused were later convicted, and secondly, it influenced the views of a group of social workers who were variously connected with the case. In their later careers as independent social workers, some of them were advisers in other cases, for example in Cheshire in 1987 and in Somerset in 1988, where it seems likely that their earlier experience led them to assume that they were dealing with similar cases.

In the first cases of alleged satanic abuse of children, as in others subsequently, there had been social work concerns stretching back a number of years so that it is hard to date the start of each case. Does such a case start from the first contact of social services with the child, or in some instances its parents, or merely with the immediate circumstances that produced the allegations of satanic abuse? I have chosen the latter as the point of departure, but earlier contacts were not ignored in studying each case.

The main body of allegations of ritual abuse probably started in 1987 with a case in Congleton in Cheshire; it was followed very soon afterwards by two much larger and better-known cases in Nottingham and in Rochdale, Greater Manchester, both coming to public notice in 1988. Another case in 1987, in Liverpool, received little national publicity. Local publicity was given to other cases as they occurred; some achieved national publicity, if only in the tabloids. A case in Epping Forest on the edge of London in 1991 stimulated further publicity and was followed by another in the Orkneys that led to a public enquiry. Allegations rose to a peak in 1989 and then seem to have declined (La Fontaine 1994: 7). While there are not enough cases to draw firm conclusions, the evidence would seem to show a brief epidemic[3] of cases involving children, which gradually abated. Certainly, the figures give no reason to suppose that cases are increasing in number. The searches of eight social service areas undertaken by Gallagher, Parker & Hughes identified no case starting in 1992 (B. Gallagaher, personal communication).

The amount of publicity that the allegations concerning children received was quite disproportionate to the scale of the problem they represented. A recent estimate of the incidence of such cases, based on a survey of child protection files, is about twenty-one a year (Gallagher, Parker & Hughes 1994). This constitutes under 10 per cent of all cases of organised abuse[4] which is itself a tiny minority of all cases dealt with by child protection teams. The cases of alleged satanic abuse of children are thus very uncommon and even were all the allegations true, they would not confirm the contentions made by some campaigners as to the extent of the problem (e.g. Core & Harrison 1991: 165; Tate 1991: 228–230). However, the significance of the cases lay not so much in their numbers as in the extreme nature of the acts that were being alleged and the horror they evoked.

Table 1 *Regional incidence of cases with allegations of ritual abuse 1987–92*

1. North	
(Cumbria, Northumberland, Durham, Cleveland, Tyne and Wear)	4
2. Yorkshire and Humberside	
(North, West and South Yorkshire, Humberside)	5
3. East Midlands	
(Derbyshire, Nottinghamshire, Leicestershire, Northamptonshire, Lincolnshire)	26
4. East Anglia	
(Norfolk, Suffolk, Cambridgeshire)	1
5. South East	
a) Outer Metropolitan Area	
(London, Surrey, Hertfordshire, Kent)	19
b) Outer South East	
(Hants, Oxford, Bedfordshire, Buckinghamshire, Berkshire, Sussex, Essex)	8
6. South West	
(Gloucestershire, Wiltshire, Avon, Somerset, Dorset, Devon, Cornwall)	4
7. West Midlands	
(Shropshire, Staffordshire, West Midlands, Hereford and Worcester, Warwickshire)	4
8. North West	
(Cheshire, Greater Manchester, Lancashire, Merseyside)	12
9. Wales	1

Geographical distribution of cases

According to the postal survey I carried out in collaboration with a team from Manchester University, allegations of ritual or satanic abuse appeared to be a localised problem. Large parts of England and Wales seemed not to have experienced cases at all. The cases were not distributed evenly but clustered in certain areas. The map shows a concentration of cases in one main region and two lesser ones.[5] The pattern can be more easily seen if the cases are sorted by region. Table 1 shows the distribution of all the cases in the study according to the definitions of the standard regions of England and Wales as laid down by the Registrar-General; in a slight modification Wales was considered as a single region for the purposes of this compilation.

The East Midlands contains nearly a third of all cases (twenty-six). Almost all of these are in Nottinghamshire, with only five cases in other counties of the region. The South East (Region 5) accounts for almost the same number of cases (twenty-seven, of which nineteen were in London and the immediately surrounding area). The final clusters are located in the North West (Region 8 – twelve cases), largely in the urban areas surrounding Manchester, and in Yorkshire and Humberside (Region 2 – five cases), mainly in Humberside. Clwyd's single case

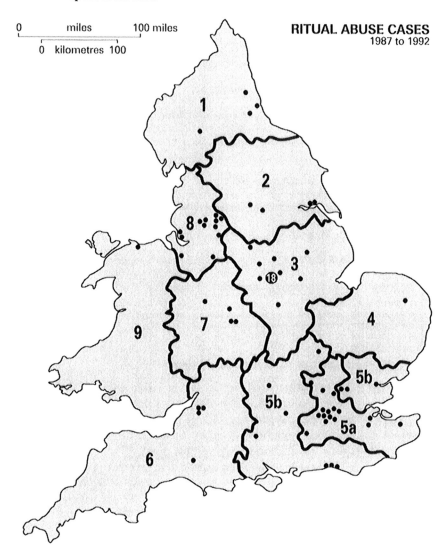

Reports of alleged ritual abuse (from La Fontaine 1994); the numbers indicate the standard regions as defined by the Registrar-General

could be considered as an outlier of this cluster, which would make it, at 18, about the same as the Metropolitan cluster.

There is more than one possible explanation for the uneven distribution of ritual abuse cases. The first is technical: an uneven pattern of reporting in the survey might explain the pattern. Critics of my conclusions have claimed that the research was invalidated by the fact that 'many' social service departments did not participate. However, the strategy of using three sources of reports seems to have avoided the worst effects of the relative lack of social service reports, which was not nearly as great as reported. In England as a whole, only one of the police forces and twelve of the NSPCC teams failed to report and, in the case of the former, informal contact indicated no case of satanic abuse. The largest number of social services departments failing to respond occurred in areas of relatively high incidence of reported cases, the North West and Inner London. By far the greatest number of cases reported was in the East Midlands, where the social services departments of three of the five counties did not respond. Plotting the distribution of cases against a map of areas where social services did not report shows no correspondence between the two.

Another interpretation of the pattern, consistent with the existence of an organisation performing satanist rituals in which children were abused, would be that the clustering of cases indicated the presence of satanic organisations in those areas. In several cases of organised abuse reported in the press and also recorded in our national survey, a spreading network of links between adults and children was uncovered. If localised covens or satanist cults were responsible for the cases in particular areas, one would expect links to be established between the cases and for there to be a general similarity in what was alleged. However, despite the fact that there were links between one or two of the cases, no such network could be discovered. Moreover, the allegations did not display the similarities that would be expected to result if a single organisation of satanists in the area were performing these rituals. In fact such few similarities as there were among these cases tended to reflect the fact that children had the same foster-parent or social workers. The children's situations after being taken into care were more relevant to the allegations than the social community from which they were taken.

The greatest concentration of cases reported to the survey was in the East Midlands. Twenty-six cases were reported to the survey, of which twenty-one came from Nottingham county and only five from the three other counties in the region together. The city of Nottingham accounted for eighteen of the twenty-one survey cases, with the remaining three coming from outside the city. The distribution of cases clearly indicates the City of Nottingham as a focus.

The focus of allegations is even more localised than these figures would suggest, since the number of cases reported to the survey do not reflect the complexity of the actual situation. Subsequent research revealed that eighteen could not be considered a final figure for Nottingham city. Different numbers of reports were sent in by the three agencies to whom questionnaires were sent; in the case of the police and social services this may be a reflection of the way in which question-naires were completed. The police, having a centralised child protection unit, delegated the work to one person who could consult with her colleagues in the unit if she needed to; the social services department had to send out to nine different areas, from which the questionnaires were returned, although it was clear that not all the files were available. Twenty-one questionnaires were completed by the police, and the NSPCC reported two of the same cases, which indicated the limited extent of their involvement there. Social services returned seven questionnaires, but too long after the survey deadline for inclusion. Fortunately all except one of the social services reports duplicated the police questionnaires. Moreover, a list prepared for me by the social services child protection manager,[6] giving brief details of twenty-two cases in the city and a further four in nearby Mansfield, had been sent to me earlier. These twenty-six cases included all the social services cases and corresponded with the police reports as far as eighteen cases were concerned, but we excluded one case as not fulfilling our criteria, which reduced the total for that list to twenty-five. The police listed four cases which were not reported to the survey by the other agencies, but only one appears actually to have been omitted from the social services list. The other three involved linked cases which the social services department had dated as beginning in 1987, outside the survey period, while the police, not having started their investigation of the allegations of satanic abuse until the beginning of 1988, included them.[7] Basing the count on the longest list, that of social services, and counting as one each case with a linked police report, the total is twenty-four cases during the four years of the study.

Nottingham had six teams of social workers, listed here under letters to preserve anonymity; collation of various sources show the cases were divided among them as shown in table 2.

Nearly three-fifths of the cases (58 per cent) involved a single team, the allegations of satanic abuse involving the 'A' team nearly five times as often as any other. Had the cases been distributed evenly across the

Table 2 *Allocation of cases among Nottingham social work teams*

A	14
B	3
C	2
D	0
E	3
F	2
Total	24

city, each team would have had about four cases. In practice, of course, a completely equal division of cases would have been very unlikely, but the imbalance represented above is unlikely to have happened by chance and does require some explanation.

The effect of energetic believers on local opinions and actions is documented in historical cases of witch-finding by historians interested in the distribution of cases. In late seventeenth-century Sweden, the witch-hunt that subsequently influenced Cotton Mather in Salem, Massachusetts, could be observed spreading. Bengt Ankerloo, who studied the Swedish hunt, wrote that the cases 'can be followed from province to province, at times even from farm to farm, in a clearly visible time/space pattern' (Ankarloo 1993: 301). A clear time pattern is harder to establish for allegations of satanic abuse in late twentieth-century England. Communications are no longer restricted to word of mouth, literacy is general and twentieth-century inventions such as television and the telephone speed the dissemination of news. However, within a small area some of the same mechanisms seem to be at work.

A consideration of the dates of the Nottingham cases in relation to the different areas where they arose shows how the problem developed. During 1988 and 1989 it seems only to have concerned area A to any great extent. Only two cases in those years arose outside it, one in C and one in B; however, by 1990 there were cases in all the other areas and outside the city, in Mansfield, but only two new cases in area A. The survey took place in 1992 and no cases from further north in the county were reported to it, but there was an indication that there had been cases in nearby Derby that had been suspected of having involved satanic abuse. This activity in Nottingham took place against further developments outside the county. Of all the cases for 1988 reported to the survey 41 percent came from Nottingham city, but by the next year that proportion had dropped to 24 per cent as cases were reported from all over the country.

In his monograph on witchcraft in Tudor and Stuart Essex, Alan
Macfarlane argued that there was no sign there of any 'epidemic' of
witch-hunting in the sense that the ideas and actions spread from place
to place. The two exceptions to this generalisation involved the same
cluster of villages. Macfarlane's Map X shows that at the 1645 Assizes
all but one of the cases came from a small area in north-eastern Essex;
the same incidence had occurred earlier, in 1582. 'Here it would be
justifiable,' writes Macfarlane, 'to look for some outside agent; in both
(clusters of cases) . . . there was present a man of more than ordinary
energy, skill and interest in finding witches' (Macfarlane 1970: 30).
These were Justice Darcy and Matthew Hopkins in 1582 and 1645
respectively. But 'Only during the year 1645, when the witch-finder
Matthew Hopkins was active, do the Essex trials bear a resemblance to
the more sensational descriptions of French or German witchcraft
trials.' (1970: 6). The accusations provoked by Hopkins' activities show
up the more clearly against the normal pattern of accusations against
neighbours which were 'widespread and regular' (1970: 30.) Something
similar can be seen in Nottingham. Children were taken into care for a
variety of different reasons: neglect, non-accidental injury and indecent
assault or incest. In eight cases there was no allegation of sexual abuse at
any stage. This was the regular and expected routine of child protection,
the 'normal pattern' against which allegations of satanic abuse appeared
alien and terrifying.

The area of Nottingham covered by the 'A' team is the area where
one of the earliest and most notorious cases, the Broxtowe case, took
place. This case earned massive publicity for several months. Serious
conflict between police and social services arose over the investigation of
allegations of satanic/ritual abuse that had been made after a successful
prosecution of several adults of a large extended family for sexually
abusing, neglecting and ill-treating their children. The first part of the
case occasioned the then Prime Minister, Margaret Thatcher, to
congratulate members both of the police and of social services. The
children were said to have made allegations to their foster-mothers and
social workers that indicated a bizarre ritualistic context to the neglect
and physical and sexual abuse that they had undoubtedly suffered. The
police investigated and found no evidence to support the allegations of a
group of satanists or devil worshippers sexually abusing children in
strange rituals. It was agreed to exclude these details from the
prosecutions so as not to prejudice the outcome of the trial, but the
agreement between police and social workers, already strained, broke
down completely after the trials. The police argued that the lack of
evidence meant there was nothing further to investigate. The social

workers did not accept this, and their views were published in journal articles (Campbell 1990a; Dawson 1990).

Newspapers and television programmes took the side of one or the other, either arguing for the truth of what the children were said to have disclosed, or arguing that the allegations were the result of a campaign by evangelical Christians who saw the devil everywhere. The leader of the social work team that had been established to deal with the case and its line manager clearly felt that they were martyrs for a cause, which they presented very widely as one of 'believing the children'. Arguing that they were not evangelical Christians and that some of the team were not Christians at all, they lectured at conferences,[8] were interviewed by the press and wrote articles themselves for the social work press and other newspapers. The feminist journalist, Bea Campbell, wrote at least six articles drawing on their material and supporting them, four in 1990 and another two in 1991. Once this work had reached its public, the two social workers were consulted very widely. Although they were not witch-hunters in the historical sense, their activities seem to have had a similar effect in provoking more cases. In particular they felt convinced that the police had failed to investigate the cases sufficiently to discover the satanist group and in 1995 their dissatisfaction was reiterated.[9]

An examination of the Nottingham cases does show connections between some of them. However, these connections are not those of membership of a cult but mostly links of blood-ties or marriage or partnership. The Broxtowe case concerned a large extended family in which it is certain that members of two successive generations had been maltreated and sexually abused as children. The parents of the children taken into care were victims of earlier sexual abuse, which they then perpetrated on their own children, nephews and nieces. The grandfather had been convicted of incest with his daughter and was said to have sexually abused all his children. Several of his children's spouses and partners seem to have come from similar families. An additional case, involving allegations against a brother of the grandfather in the main case, indicates that both were abusers of their children. This is unlikely to be coincidence and suggests that the two of them might have been sexually abused themselves, or, at the very least, suffered a childhood that was partly to blame for their subsequent behaviour. This does not represent a religious cult but the perpetuation of sexual abuse, unchecked or treated, from one generation to the next. It is a clear demonstration of how important it is to diagnose and treat children's sexual abuse.

This was not the only instance. In another pair of Nottingham cases a network of relatives, many of whom suffer mental disabilities, was involved in the neglect and maltreatment of the children who have been taken into care. It seems that friends of the adults concerned may also have been involved and there are two or three other cases where it is suggested that this occurred, a situation that is displayed in other cases reported to the survey where friends and neighbours of the parents of the victims were drawn into a network of abusing adults. While it might have been the case that this had happened in some of the Nottingham cases, the evidence provided is not of cults, satanist or otherwise. One woman who kept an occult bookshop there declared she had been harassed by social workers for years, but the tapping of her telephone (discovered by British Telecom) was believed by the police to have been the work of journalists.

The existence of a cluster of households forming part of an extended family in which abuse is endemic is not unique to Nottingham. If we now widen the focus to consider information reported to the survey, it will show how common this is. The survey asked respondents to report cases of organised sexual abuse as well as cases in which there were allegations of ritual. The three main types of such abuse, besides the cases where ritual (satanic) abuse was alleged, were paedophile rings (of which there were forty-three cases), sexual abuse in institutions or organisations catering for children (forty-five cases), and family-based cases, of which there were twenty-eight (La Fontaine 1994: 32). The relationships between the perpetrators of the sexual abuse and the children in the cases classified as involving allegations of initial abuse indicated that they too were family-based. Nearly half of them (48 per cent) involved parents and none involve strangers (La Fontaine 1994: 11).

Table 3 shows that the largest single category of satanic/ritual abuse cases was that of large extended families. These are not necessarily living together but maintain close relations between their separate households. The children may spend time in houses other than those of their own parents and if there is sexual abuse then it is not uncommon for the whole group to be involved, or at least to know what is going on. The next largest category of cases also concerns a household but here they are not known to be linked into a wider network of kin. In a group of eight cases the children were taken into care for neglect or non-accidental injury, and there was no evidence of sexual abuse, either medical or in a child's disclosure. In another seven cases the child has been abused, not merely by a parent but also by friends of the parents or neighbours. Outside the child's own household there are relatives, foster-parents or other well-known adults who may also be abusers; in six of the cases in which ritual abuse was alleged this was the situation.

Table 3 *Characteristics of cases of alleged satanic abuse*

Relationships among participants	
Paedophile 'ring'	8
Large extended family	18
Small domestic group	12
Parents and others	7
Relative or known adult	6
Domestic but no sexual abuse of the child (ren)	8
Unclassified	
Anti-satanists involved	6
Mother's allegation	6
Unclear/insufficient information	6
Other	7
Total	84

Given the allegations of cult involvement, there are remarkably few cases which show signs of an organised group being behind the abuse. There are only eight cases (fewer than 10 per cent of the total) in which it appears that a paedophile ring or network might have been in operation and in some of the cases the evidence for that is somewhat dubious. There are also twelve cases in which either the allegation comes from the mother of the child allegedly involved or the allegations seem to derive from the influence of a prominent anti-satanist campaigner. In one or two cases a social work consultant takes this role, claiming that the list of indicators shows that the case involves satanic abuse, or conducting interviews with the child that result in apparent disclosures of horrific rituals. In these cases there may be no good indications that the child has been sexually abused at all. It is not surprising that the eight cases in which children were taken into care for reasons other than sexual abuse came from Nottingham, where belief in the presence of satanists in the area was strong.

An unexpected result of the survey was the large proportion of cases where there were allegations of satanic abuse but no evidence of organised sexual abuse, that is of multiple abusers. In fifty-one of the sixty-two cases there was information on the perpetrators and in nearly a quarter of these (twelve) a single perpetrator was accused. Four more involved a single person outside the household, such as a baby-sitter or uncle. Even when there was evidence of organised abuse, the numbers were not large, especially when compared with the paedophile rings reported. Twenty-eight cases concerned one household. Small cases like these constituted nearly half the cases (48 per cent) in the study. In several cases there were allegations that large numbers of unidentified people had been involved, but these people remained shadowy figures, unlike those involved in the large paedophile networks reported, most of whom were identified by police enquiries.

The three substantiated cases of ritual abuse that will be discussed in the next chapter, only one of which was reported as part of the survey, also involved small numbers of abusers. In each there was one man who was convicted of abusing the children. There were two children in one case but more in the others, possibly as many as twenty in one of them. In that case the abuser acted alone, but in the other cases other adults (one in one case and two in another) participated in the ritual, though mostly not in the sexual abuse. In one case the perpetrator got to know a single mother, but kept her in ignorance of what he was doing; in another the father of two children was befriended and persuaded of the mystical powers of the instigator of the activities he became involved in. In the third case, the man involved his wife and her sister in his activities with girls who were asked to baby-sit. He also abused his wife's nieces, who quite independently were being subjected to incestuous intercourse by their father, who did not take part in the other activities. In this case the women were convicted for aiding and abetting the abuse, but in none of the three cases was there any larger organisation mentioned by either the victims or the abusers.

The sociological patterns

The allegations of satanic abuse made in Britain resembled in broad outline the allegations made in the early cases in the United States: they indicated gatherings of robed and masked people abusing children and committing murder, bestiality and cannibalism. As in the United States, it was suggested that the relative lack of corroborative evidence for the allegations was an indication that the perpetrators of ritual abuse, or satan-worshippers as some felt them to be, were either very clever or were protected by powerful members of society. One psychiatrist wrote 'those high in authority (in the cults) are prominent also in their ordinary lives and include doctors, lawyers, teachers, clergy, police, politicians, ambassadors and aristocrats' (Coleman 1994a: 243), and subsequently argued that 'Some of these methods (of disposal of the bodies of sacrificed victims) seem incredible until one remembers the wide variety of occupations of cult members' (Coleman 1994a: 246).

There are also some marked sociological differences between cases in the two countries that have not been properly considered, despite their considerable significance. Until 1994 none of the British cases of alleged ritual abuse referred to nursery schools or child-care centres, the 'day care' or 'preschool' institutions in which most of the United States cases have taken place. An article on 'Ritualistic Child Abuse' in a paediatric journal refers almost entirely to abuse in nursery schools (Kelley 1989), although there were cases involving older children (see Nathan & Snedeker 1995). In 1994 a single case of abuse in a British nursery school that was investigated and the abuser indicted involved some parents worrying about ritual abuse but no full-blown allegations were made public. There is one survey case in which a child made strange allegations after being left in a creche in a shopping centre. The only other case at all similar to those in the United States concerned two men moving in to live with an unregistered child-minder, but although they abused the children in her charge there were no allegations of ritual abuse.

The first consequence of this difference between the two sets of cases is that the victims' parents are not the more affluent two-salary couples of the United States (see Kelley 1989: 39); on the contrary, many are among the most deprived in Britain. Secondly, in the United States these parents may act as a pressure group urging prosecution (Finkelhor, Williams & Burns 1988: 240–3). The first allegations of abuse in the McMartin case came from a parent and another parent in the same case claimed to have been the first to suggest that the children had been the victims of a devil-worshipping cult. By contrast, parents are among the accused in most British cases; it is consistent with that fact that parents' groups in Britain are to be found among the sceptics. Finally, while Finkelhor could make the very young age of the victims a defining element of ritual abuse in the United States, in Britain older children may be involved. This is not to say that teenagers were not involved in panics in the United States; they might well start them, but they figured much less often as victims (see Eve & Roy n.d.; Balch & Gilliam 1991: 251; Ellis 1991). A number of cases involve teenagers, who may resemble adults like Michelle Smith, the self-styled 'survivor' of satanic abuse, much more than they do the three–year-olds of Los Angeles. These differences indicate that what is happening is the adaptation of a construct of evil which is common across Western civilisation in general to the local conditions, fears and cultural strains of particular societies and of communities within them.

The social position of individuals who are perpetrators and victims in cases where allegations of ritual abuse are made is a significant factor. Despite the allegations of those who claim there is a conspiracy spanning all socio-economic classes, the adults and children who were identified in Britain as involved in the cases of alleged satanic abuse came from the lower end of the social spectrum. The areas in which the first cases of ritual abuse were reported in England were also areas of long-term deprivation. Each of the early cases involved people whose material circumstances were of the very lowest and who could not realistically expect any improvement in them. Social services departments had dealt with the adults and children concerned in them over many years.

The parents of the children who figure as victims were mostly recorded as long-term unemployed, except for one or two who had unskilled, casual work, occasionally and for short spells. Many of the men had police records, mostly for theft, but also, in some cases, for violence. Their homes were flats or houses in run-down urban estates. A police officer interviewed for one of the case-histories remarked that he took no pleasure in arresting people from the estate where the families in the case lived; he thought they were abused by having to live there. A representative of the Official Solicitor reported on the house of a couple in another town, whom he had interviewed, in the following terms: 'The very poor state of the house seemed to reflect not only their poverty but the despair arising from it.'

The households themselves were often said to be disorganised and, sometimes, violent. There was usually a history of broken marital relationships. In one household the children might all be the offspring of one mother but hardly ever of a single couple with whom they lived. This was not restricted to the present generation of adults. One of the women in the Rochdale case was brought up with five siblings each of which had a different father. There might have been social services concern over the children for years and many of them were taken into care before, perhaps more than once, either voluntarily surrendered when their mother could not cope, or at the instigation of the child protection agencies. Others were left with grandmothers or aunts for varying periods. One child ended up living with her mother's former partner (who was not her father), his new common-law wife and their children. Individuals, including children, moved freely between the households of their relations and the membership of a single household might go through many changes.

The children might be said to be neglected and, even if they were not, they were not brought up in a manner which is considered normal by most standards: they had few clothes and bathed infrequently, had no set times for meals or sleep, possessed few toys but watched videos (sometimes very unsuitable ones) until late at night. Residential social workers or foster-parents frequently commented on their poor eating habits and the need to train them to eat at table. In addition, they were not children who were shielded from unsuitable television programmes or adult conversations about events that might upset them, although adults did not often talk directly to them. They might live in households where ghosts were genuinely feared or where adults amused themselves by playing on the children's fears.

In such communities fear of social workers' removing children from home is common, even standard, and has been noted since the establishment of the NSPCC at the end of the nineteenth century (Lewis 1986). Threats of being taken into care may be used to control the children; children in several cases said they thought they had been taken into care because they had been bad or 'done something'. Threats to remove the children into care are also made by social workers against parents who fail to fulfil contracts with them. In a case conference over one small boy, some members of the team thought it essential to remove him from home because his mother should not be allowed to get away with breaking appointments at the family centre. One of the other children in that case revealed that they thought of being taken into care as likely to involve being shut up on a diet of bread and water. 'Being in care' is also a stigma and several children refer to it; they do not want it known at school that they are in care.

The poverty of these families is shown in their appearance, which is often said to be slovenly. One foster-mother declared to me that she knew her foster-child's parents were satanists when she saw them first in court, they were so badly dressed and sloppy, 'with dirty tee-shirts'. In her eyes, and probably in the eyes of very many members of this society, the appearance of poverty indicates moral failing. The children may be described as completely neglected-looking, dirty and unwashed. Some of them are developmentally delayed or even intellectually handicapped; a few have defects of hearing and sight which have not been noticed or treated. Many are irregular in their attendance at school and do badly there, although part of the reason for this may be chronic fatigue from a regime of poor eating and insufficient sleep. Many are shunned at school; one child remarked to her foster-mother that now she was clean and tidy the children at school could not say she smelled. There is an indication that these children are picked on and bullied, either at school or by the neighbourhood children. Children who are bullied may become truants and may also develop neurotic symptoms (Reid in Tattum & Lane 1988: 89–93). The contribution to a child's distress that is made by bullying at school is mentioned in several cases but seems not to have been taken very seriously. In the Rochdale case it appears to have caused one little boy to hide in a cupboard; his behaviour was considered 'bizarre' and the fact that the actions of other children might have contributed to it seems not to have been considered. Isolated, and subject to attack at home and at school, these children appear deprived, not merely materially, but socially, emotionally and mentally.

The children's lack of apparent reaction to being taken into care is frequently noted and adduced as evidence that children have no strong relations with their parents, but the possibility that this passivity might have causes other than lack of affection for parents is rarely canvassed. The effects of domestic instability or violence, or of having been in care before may receive scant or no attention in the case conference minutes contained in the files. In one file, comments that the children did not seem to mind leaving their parents were followed by observations from the foster-mother that one child was sick soon after arrival and did not eat normally for a week, another cried and did not want to go to bed and both wet their beds. Since these reactions might well be considered evidence that the children were disturbed at being taken away from home, the assumption that the children did not mind leaving their homes may reflect a conviction that children living under such conditions *ought* not to mind leaving them, or else a sustaining thought that acting to protect children cannot hurt them.

For very many reasons then, these are not children who can easily be compared with the stereotypes of normal childhood. Their behaviour, verbal or otherwise, could be expected to deviate from the norm and its oddity should not have caused such alarmed surprise. It was emphasised to me when discussing families of this sort that there are families equally poor who somehow manage better; their houses are clean and neat, their children do not look like waifs and strays. This failure to meet the standards of the 'respectable poor'[10] may account for the fact that it is not uncommon for the failures to be viewed with hostility in the community as well as causing consternation to social workers. The neighbours may be hostile to both adults and children. In two cases there were incidents of stones being thrown at a flat and its windows at night. One little girl was so frightened by this that she had to be moved out of her bedroom to sleep elsewhere in the flat.

The families that do not 'manage' are often subject to further handicaps. The parents may be survivors of sexual and other abuse themselves, as well as perpetrators of the abuse on their own children. Functional illiteracy is not uncommon and some parents and children are intellectually disadvantaged, and whether this is a result of genetic factors or of emotional damage is often not clear. There may be records of previous convictions for incest or sexual assault in the file, while in other cases these earlier events are disclosed when the children are taken into care. In one of the case-histories, it seemed possible that the history of abuse stretched back beyond the children's grandparents. There is no evidence that any of these adults have had therapy to help them heal from their own childhood experience. Their abuse of their children must be seen partly as a legacy from the past. As one young man said in a police interview: 'It's disgusting, but then when you've been brought up to accept that these things are quite alright . . . it was just part of normal family life'.

The children who did not come from such deprived backgrounds were not very much better off in material terms. There were very few households where the adults' occupations indicated a comfortable or middle-class life-style, and they were mostly to be found where the allegation of ritual abuse had been brought by a woman against her husband. The most prosperous of any in the eighty-four cases was a businessman with his own small company, who was wrongly accused by his wife of ritually abusing their two children. The minority of cases that could be said to involve 'ordinary' working-class or lower middle-class families showed no particular common pattern. Two of the cases where the allegations were being made by one or two teenagers belonged to the more prosperous minority of households, but the remaining adolescents were among the majority, as members of large and impoverished extended families. There was evidence among the children, whether of the minority or the majority, that many had been physically or sexually abused. Most of these were teenagers; some seemed to have compounded their problems with drugs, one or two others had abortions and all had serious emotional problems; none of this is unlikely as a consequence of sexual abuse (Bentovim et al. 1988: 31–2; Hevey & Kenward 1989).

Cases involving allegations of satanic abuse seem not to be randomly distributed across the population. In this they do not resemble cases of sexual abuse alone, which may occur anywhere in the socio-economic spectrum. By contrast, the majority of satanic abuse cases involved extended families of the poor, together with neighbours or friends of the adults. There are also smaller cases involving a few children in smaller households. While it is well-known that social work largely involves the less fortunate, the people involved in these cases are mostly deprived even by the standards of social-work cases. In a competitive, materialistic society these are the failures. That they are also failures as parents distinguishes them from their neighbours, who resemble them in other ways.

It is a long-established finding of anthropology that witchcraft accusations are not randomly distributed. They are directed at outsiders and at those who break social norms or are socially marginal in other ways. The 'outsiders' may be defined in different ways according to the culture of the particular society in question; among the Pondo of South Africa the outsiders are the women who marry into the extended households (Wilson 1951); elsewhere the outsiders are clients of the chiefs (Middleton 1963) or destitute refugees and migrants (Buxton 1963). In early modern Europe lone women, especially those with no children or grandchildren around them, were particularly marginal. Like them, the accused in these cases of alleged satanic abuse have broken the norms of parenting, to a lesser extent where the children are badly fed and clothed, and in a far worse manner where they are ill-treated or sexually abused. Some cases are failures of social work as well, in that they have been 'on the books' of social services for more than a generation but none of the actions taken seems to have had any effect. In addition, attempts to stop the abuse of children seem often to have failed. It takes little more to see the parents as unnatural human beings and hence as satanists.

Anthropologists long ago pointed out that in making accusations of witchcraft the accuser may also be justifying the denial of any obligations – of charity or kinship – that the relationships between the parties might be expected to entail (Turner 1957; Mitchell 1956). Macfarlane (1970) showed how accusations against elderly women justified their neighbours in refusing them charitable help. Defining people who are failures as parents as satanists is a step which legitimises the withdrawal both of professional compassion and of neighbourly tolerance. In a more recent reformulation of this argument, Steadman has argued persuasively that accusations of witchcraft are used to justify injuring or destroying innocent individuals (Steadman 1985–86: 121) in order to threaten the attacker's real enemies. The killing of witches is thus a political act, not against the witches but against the potential subversion of those associated with them. His hypothesis is confirmed by the evidence from Salem in the late seventeenth century, but it is harder to see which political opponents of the accusers are being threatened by recent accusations of satanism. It is rather far-fetched to argue that these allegations are real threats against those considered political enemies. However, the unidentified satanists who dispose of great power and wealth and are protected by fellow-members of the elite may symbolise the responsibility of society's leaders for the failure to find and convict paedophiles and other evil-doers. For social workers, the image thus holds considerable attractions.

Anxiety about 'the family' is widespread in late twentieth-century Britain; the statistics showing that the divorce rate is rising and that more and more children are being brought up by a single parent seem to indicate that what is perceived as the basis of normal social life, the unit of parents and children, is being destroyed. The frequency of reports of cases of sexual abuse implies that assumptions about the natural basis of parental care no longer hold and the most recent allegations of the horrific treatment of children confirm the existence of people who lack what are considered the elementary natural feelings for their children. The claim that Satan's hand can be seen in these attempts to destroy the family is easily accepted and marginal people who also fail their children can then be identified as the lowest ranks in a satanic conspiracy to destroy civilised society.

5   The question of proof

The feature that seems to distinguish cases of satanic abuse from the accusations of witchcraft with which I have compared it is that it involves sexual activities with children. While witches may be accused of forbidden sexual practices and attacks on children in many parts of the world, and descriptions of the witches' sabbath might include the killing and eating of babies, it is only in twentieth-century Western society that sexual acts with children have come to form the central focus of accusations of supreme evil. Allegations of witchcraft have shown an ability to adapt and reflect changing issues, expressing new anxieties in the present and new fears for the future in old but potent forms (Comaroff 1994; Meyer 1995). Allegations of satanism resemble accusations of witchcraft in their adaptability. The rediscovery[1] of the cruelty suffered by children at the hands not only of malevolent outsiders but of their own parents, who have long been taken for granted as their instinctive protectors, has been a growing social issue since the 1970s (La Fontaine 1990). As Jenkins puts it, 'Ritual (satanic) abuse represented a third stage in what was almost an evolutionary process', the first two stages being sexual abuse at home and the uncovering of paedophile networks (1992: 17).

Cases of satanic abuse were distinguished from other cases of the sexual abuse of children by elements seen as 'bizarre', 'sinister', and 'frightening' by the adults who reported them. They often did not represent a clear account of any ritual, but were understood as hints of or oblique and symbolic references to what had been happening. The nature of the hints and their own lack of certainty generated strong emotions in the adults concerned.

The survey provided little detail of the allegations but some elements were recorded on the questionnaires. Listing them, in the manner of many campaigners, gives the impression of a Pandora's box of horrors: children mentioned abortions and the sacrifice of foetuses; blood on themselves and other children; drinking blood; burying babies and children; inverted crosses; graveyards; killing human beings and animals; robes and masks; magic; parties; being taken to special places; and they talked of witches, devils and ghosts. A picture emerges that is not incompatible with the performance of rituals that included killings and cannibalistic practices and at which the children were sexually abused. However, the condensed listing gives a rather inaccurate picture of what the information was really like. Some excerpts from four different cases will give a better idea.

1988 Two little boys aged six and four were found by their mother simulating anal intercourse; she reported this to social services. Curious marks on their arms, ankles and elbows were seen as friction burns.[2]
These plus the following were taken as indicating ritual abuse:
One little boy showed fears of the dark, of monsters, ghosts and shadows.
Both boys resisted answering questions, though the other child finally responded to the question 'who does nasty things?' with 'frumans with ghoolies' faces'. After the video of their interview had been switched off, he demonstrated a 'mass orgy' with six anatomically correct dolls i.e. he placed them in pairs in a position of intercourse.
The boys also played dead and buried dolls in the sand-tray.

1989 Two girls aged nine and eight, with brothers of six and nearly four. The children said that witches make children disappear.
The youngest commented on a graveyard, pointed to a cross and said it was red. Was given a raspberry drink and said it was blood.
All of them were 'obsessed' with faeces and defecating; they talked about eating faeces. The youngest found a Halloween mask in the bedroom, when he put it on he appeared (according to his foster-mother) to want to terrorise the family and appeared to believe he had supernatural power over the person he was frightening. He stood silently with hands on hips; his foster-mother thought this abnormal and 'weird'.
She reported: 'He is a very strange boy and has a funny attitude to death; he believes when you die you start the world all over again.'

1990 A boy of thirteen, the youngest of five children, drew pictures: a lantern hanging from the ceiling with flames emerging from it; candles all round the walls. A circle of chalk was drawn on the floor with strange lines on it and knives all around; smoke was coming from the circle's centre. There were crosses either side with four knives between: he was on one cross and one of his brothers on the other. Two knives were crossed and another brother said they moved. His father had a devil Mask on. Red wine was drunk, 'he then smiled and said that it was blood' and his father drank it.
The thirteen-year-old's teacher added further details of devil Worship given her by him. His father read from a book: 'O the devil Worship, darkness come to the devil site'. The boy said his father had shown him videos of devil worship to prepare him. His parents were wearing masks and silk clothing with rope hanging from the shoulders. They stood on devil mats provided by X (a named person). These outfits and the mats

were buried – a wooden cross was put on top. '(He) said he knew where the things had been buried as his dog used to dig them up'.

He also told her about a dream he had had or 'he might have been drugged': he was in a churchyard where there were gravestones and he was terrified. There were candles twice as big as himself. His father said:

'Fang from the sight
You turn the night
Make it into darkness
Destroy the goodness
Into the evil of the night.'

(The account continued on the same themes at some length.)

1991   A girl of fifteen told a residential care-worker in the children's home she was living in that her parents forced her to have sex with a variety of animals; that photographs were taken of her with the animals and with the adults there. She claimed her breasts, pubic area and legs were scarred and there were internal scars on her vagina. Bottles, vibrators, scissors, knives and razor blades were used on her, she was tied up and burnt with cigarettes if she resisted. It happened in her bedroom at home.

These examples show a little of the variety in the cases; picking out the common features of a large number of cases described rather briefly, gives a spurious impression of uniformity. This is the problem with Coleman (1994a), who condenses into one account a number of different sources, including American material. Nevertheless, it is worth considering all the different allegations over the whole set of cases, even in summary form, because it is likely that the cases' most important features were those that were reported in the questionnaire. This exercise confirms a relative lack of uniformity among the cases but there are also some common themes, particularly among the older children, which is significant.

Table 4 summarises the information on the most frequent features of the satanic rituals that were alleged or said to have been suspected, from all the cases in the study. The survey provided little scope for long descriptions, although some of our respondents helpfully provided quite full summaries. The more complete accounts obviously came from the more detailed sources. Published accounts of some of the better-known cases may not always be accurate.

The table shows a mixture of folk beliefs and more orthodox Christian ideas about satanism: ghosts and monsters appear together with Satan, and graveyards figure as often as crosses. The mention of graveyards and drinking blood corroborates Ellis' claim that a folk belief in vampires is long-standing in Britain (Ellis 1993) but it is far from a universal ingredient in the mix. Reference to two relatively common forms of paraphilia (abnormal sexual practices) is made in a little more

Table 4 *Frequency of some specified ritual features in allegations of ritual abuse*[1]

Participants		Appearance		
Devil/Satan	38	Robes	38	
Witches	20	Masks	14	
The occult	3	Pentagrams	5	
Ghosts	7			
Monsters	5	Rituals		
		Crosses[2]	7	
Sacrifice		Candles	12	
Killing babies	29	Magic	14	
Killing children	9	Chants	12	
Killing adults	8			
Killing animals	20	Vampirism and cannibalism		
Abortion	6	Cannibalism		5
		Eating foetuses		5
Paraphilia		Drinking blood		24
Drinking urine	9	Blood used in ritual		13
Eating faeces	5	Graveyards	8	
		Burying people	6	
Distinctive features not shared by any other case			51	

[1] The figures refer to the numbers of cases in which a feature appeared. The allegations in each case might include several elements so the numbers cannot be totalled.
[2] In five cases this refers to inverted crosses.

than 15 per cent of cases. What is most striking, however, is that in fifty-one cases – over three-fifths of the total – there is some distinctive feature noted that is not recorded for any other case. This and the small numbers where even the commonest features were concerned, must lead to the conclusion that, in their details, the rituals in these allegations were very different from one another. They could not be rituals belonging to the same national, let alone international, satanist 'cult'.

Some common elements resemble quite closely the early modern conceptualisation of evil: human and animal sacrifice and the cannibalistic consumption of the flesh and blood of the sacrifice are features of the witches' sabbath. These elements are also found in the blood libel against the Jews and in that connection have been interpreted by Dundes as inversions of the Christian communion, where there is only a symbolic death and consumption of the body (Dundes 1991: 356–8 and see Levack 1987: 36). The rite of sacrifice has been anathematised throughout Christian history and opponents of Christianity other than the Jews have been accused of it. However, some of the first accusations to be recorded were made against the early Christians, who were said to kill and eat a child at their communion feast. The Templars notably were said to have fed their idol Baphomet with blood sacrifices, a referent perhaps to the charge that the Templars, from their long service in the East, were 'soft' on Islam (Rose 1989: 127–8 [1962]).

Human sacrifice was the most frequently mentioned act in allegations of satanic abuse, but even there it figured in fewer than half the cases and the victims varied: babies were the most often mentioned, but children and occasionally adults also figured as victims, and in some accounts of rituals there was more than one kind of human sacrifice. Interestingly, an animal was said to have been sacrificed almost as often as babies were. It is the spilling of blood that is the common theme.

As night-witches break all the normal sexual rules, so illicit sexual practices were associated with devil worship, both in the form of orgies and in practices that the 'normal' world abhorred, such as incest, homosexuality and anal eroticism. In the modern world, satanic abuse may include references to paraphilia and bestiality. Intercourse with animal familiars and the devil in his animal form as a goat was also thought to be what the witches did at the sabbath. This evil sexuality was not natural, that is reproductive, and it is not surprising to find that allegations of abortion might also be made against accused witches (Levack 1987: 38). Campaigners may claim that the present association of satanism with the sexual abuse of children has historical precedents (e.g. Tate 1991) but historians do not mention this. It seems much more likely that the sexual abuse of children is twentieth-century Western society's symbol of the most hideously evil and anti-social form of sexuality.

The witches' sabbath was a secret and conspiratorial meeting that took place at night. The darkness and secrecy of the location represented its conspiratorial nature, just as the reference to the secret places visited, often at night, give a mysterious air to the modern satanic conspiracy. The sabbath also included as a necessary act the demonstration of each witch's subordination to the devil. Kissing the devil's buttocks or anus, the 'Osculum Infame', was a political act of allegiance, the evil mirror-image of kissing the hand of a superior.[3] Satan gave instructions to these minions to further his own aims and through a pact with him they achieved power and escaped detection. Detecting the perpetrators of the sexual abuse of children is so difficult that it may, as Jenkins points out, seem that they are under the protection of a powerful hidden cabal. The threat of a national or international conspiracy of which some fundamentalist Christians have warned (e.g. Core and

Harrison 1991), and that resembles the traditional idea of Satan's imperial ambitions, is more easily accepted as an explanation of the success of evil doing.

The final major characteristic of the witches' sabbath was that witches could fly; the idea is one that retains a strong hold on folk belief and it appears in dreams and fantasies and in folk-tales. In one case, as we shall see, a man used the promise of being able to fly as a strategy to recruit children for abuse. The sensation of flying may be attributed to the use of drugs; in fact the usual reaction in the case histories to any mention of flying is to question the child closely about food or drink they were offered. It is interesting that Levack mentions the explanation of confessed witches' belief that they flew as possibly the effect of drugs and potions they used, but he warns that many of those tested have no such effects (1987: 44–5). The alleged administration of mind-altering drugs to children to produce sensations of flying is also countered by experts on drugs, who have stated categorically that it would be very difficult to produce the same effect regularly on small children. Since there have been no tests for drugs in these cases, let alone any that have found evidence of their use, the adult accounts should not be taken literally. They are attempts to explain 'bizarre' allegations that have become too quickly accepted as fact.

The question of proof

Witchcraft accusations are not always accepted at face value, however general the belief in witchcraft itself. Accused witches in early modern Europe were brought to trial in court. Evidence was required to prove the guilt of particular persons who had been accused. The Spanish Inquisitor Salazar wrote to La Suprema (the council of the Spanish Inquisition) on 3 October 1613, putting his view of the problem succinctly, if with some irritation: ' . . . nor is it useful to keep saying that the learned doctors state that the existence of witchcraft is certain. This is only a needless annoyance, since nobody doubts this . . . The real question is: are we to believe that witchcraft occurred in a given situation simply because of what the witches (he means here the self-confessed witches) claim? It is clear that the witches are not to be believed and that the judges should not pass sentence on anyone, unless the case can be proven by external and objective evidence sufficient to convince everyone who hears it' (Henningsen 1980: 350). Three hundred years later 'external and objective evidence' for witchcraft and devil worship is once again being sought.

It is implicit in most accounts of witchcraft in other societies and at other times that the existence of witches and their activities was accepted by most people in a society. Anthropologists have described beliefs in witchcraft as part of the general culture, appearing to assume that they were generally held. Accounts rarely record the existence of scepticism or idiosyncratic unbelief. Even where a belief in witchcraft is general, however, there may be disputes over particular cases, claims that other causes than witchcraft are more likely or that the wrong person has been named as the witch. Accusations of witchcraft may be as controversial as the Nottingham case in this country, rallying the kin of accuser and accused to a political contest that will decide the case or split the community (Middleton 1960; Douglas 1963; Mitchell 1956; Turner 1957). The relation between witch-beliefs and action taken against witches is nowhere a simple or straightforward matter of cause and effect.

By contrast with non-industrial societies, it was clear that even at the height of the witch-hunts in early modern Europe there were sceptics who considered that the cases were not proven. Many of these were the educated (Henningsen 1980) or they were occultists themselves and hence had little respect for the Church's picture of the witches' sabbath. For many centuries Europe has been characterised by the variety of its religious beliefs. The distinction that has been drawn by historians between the folk belief in witchcraft and the concept of devil worship that was held by the lettered and the clerics, is only one of the variations in belief at all levels that may be a particular characteristic of Western society, whether in early modern times or today.

The issue of satanic abuse is a contested issue. From the beginning sceptics have doubted the truth of the allegations. There has also been a good deal of confusion about what might constitute substantiation of satanic abuse. Three quite different positions on this issue have emerged: the Christian fundamentalist, the therapeutic and the rationalist. For the Christian who believes in the existence of the devil, there is no need of proof; scriptural authority is enough and belief is a matter of faith. If they need evidence of Satan's activities, they have only to consider rock music, the casting of horoscopes, the use of tarot cards and ouija boards and modern social problems such as sexual permissiveness, adultery and abortion (Ward 1995).

Some 'proof' offered by believers is based on conflating different types of case. The fact that networks of men who abuse children (paedophile rings) have been discovered and their members convicted may be cited in support of the allegations involving cult organisations. Some children have been murdered by the paedophiles who abused them and their cases are particularly likely to be seen as 'proof' of the allegations of satanic abuse, because they involve sexual abuse and murder. However there is no evidence that these children were either abused or killed during rituals. Forty-three cases involving such networks or paedophile rings were reported to our survey as were another sixteen cases of sexual abuse taking place in residential homes for children; none of them involved the killing of a child and in none of them was there any indication that the abuse was performed within rituals, satanic or otherwise (La Fontaine 1994: 35).

It may be argued by 'experts' (see Sinason 1994: 34; Coleman 1994a: 251) that satanic abuse is a new form of the sexual abuse of children, and as difficult to substantiate as the initial discovery was, but that in the future it is likely that proof will be easier to find as more victims come forward. This claim seems to have the objective of fusing the different elements out of which 'satanic abuse' has been constructed into a new social problem. None of the separate elements is in fact newly discovered, but like the combination of diabolism and witchcraft that fuelled the great witch-hunt, putting them together has unleashed the determination to seek out and destroy those who are accused of the new version of ultimate evil.

Some arguments in favour of believing the allegations imply that proof that sexual abuse has occurred constitutes proof of all the attendant circumstances. While it does lend credibility to the victim's statements it cannot be *proof* that human sacrifice or cannibalism took place. Some extreme sceptics have claimed the opposite: that the manifest lack of credibility of the claims dismisses the idea of sexual abuse as well. This is not tenable either. The sexual abuse of children often occurs without rituals and rituals may take place without sexual abuse being part of them. The sexual abuse and the context for it are distinct aspects that need independent corroboration.

Evidence of sexual abuse

It is well known that it is often difficult to obtain evidence to corroborate the disclosures of sexual abuse made by children. The guilty may not be prosecuted or prosecutions fail to lead to a conviction. Cases where satanic abuse is alleged frequently have problems of this sort. There are many reasons why evidence is lacking in cases where there are strong suspicions that children have been sexually abused. Some forms of sexual abuse leave no physical signs. It is clear from the Official Solicitor's files that even where sexual abuse cannot be substantiated with medical or other evidence, neglect and maltreatment of the children are not uncommon features of these cases and many of the children are very damaged. There may be grounds for strong suspicion that the children have been sexually abused; the medical evidence may be equivocal in some cases, but the children's behaviour may be sexualised and/or they may be found sexually abusing other children (Cavarola & Scheff 1988). Even so, satisfactory corroboration may not be forthcoming.

Cases where there are allegations of satanic abuse seem to constitute particularly striking examples of this difficulty. The survey questionnaire asked all respondents whether there was clear evidence of the abuse of all the children in the case, of some of them or of none. No indication of what should be included was given in order to reveal what was considered to be relevant. Respondents who indicated that there was clear evidence for the sexual abuse of all or some children were asked to state what it was. (There could, of course, be more than one type of evidence.) There were thirty-five cases of satanic abuse where there was corroborating evidence of the sexual abuse of some or all the children; in the remainder of the cases (forty-nine) there was either no clear evidence (forty-one), the evidence was disputed or there was no information. Medical (physical) evidence was cited in twenty of the corroborated cases (60 per cent), a perpetrator's admission in nineteen (57 per cent) and a witness's statement in eleven (33 per cent). These three categories cover most of the evidence that corroborates a child's disclosure of sexual abuse. There was good evidence in less than half the cases.

Clinical experience and criminal investigations alike have shown that people who sexually abuse children may take great trouble over the selection and recruitment of their victims and use any means to hand for their purposes (Howard League 1985: 52). Unlike the few who use their superior strength to rape or commit a violent sexual assault on a child, most of those who abuse children use persuasion to get them to engage in sexual activities and to keep it a secret afterwards. Probably most of those who abuse children find their victims either through living with them (fathers, stepfathers and mothers' partners, resident staff in boarding schools and residential homes) or working with them (school teachers, choir masters, staff of organisations for children's activities); these situations provide adults with a relationship with children and often a recognised authority that may be exploited. Those who do not have these relationships must find lures to attract children.

Pretending to have mystical powers or displaying a familiarity with magic is one of the means used by people who lack opportunities to get to know children to establish a relationship with some of them, either directly or through a parent. Some of these men capitalise on children's curiosity to involve them in invented rituals that either include sexual intercourse or act as a deterrent to telling anyone after it has happened. It is not easy for an outsider to show how these 'ritual' cases differ from 'genuine' occult ones. On the other hand it is often claimed that such cases 'prove' that occult rituals involve the abuse of children (Tate 1994: 186)[4] and so they must be considered carefully. They do not constitute proof of satanic abuse for two reasons. First, they provide conclusive evidence that where sexual abuse does take place in rituals, these are not genuine occult rituals that would be recognised by any of the groups discussed in Chapter 3. Secondly, they lack the essential features of the allegations of satanic abuse: human sacrifice, vampirism or cannibalism. They cannot provide proof of any organisation of satanists sexually abusing children in abhorrent rituals.

There were three cases like this in which men were convicted of sexually abusing children whom they had involved in a form of ritual action. Each was quite different. In two cases it was quite clear that the perpetrator of the abuse was not a satanist; in the third he was not recognisable to occultists as a satanist. The idea and ritual were the creation of one man in all the cases, although the involvement of other adults and the interest of one of them in the occult may have contributed in one of the cases. In two cases the rituals involved a good deal of material paraphernalia which was found, but in the third there were no rituals in the sense of a series of symbolic acts, although the victims were taught to say prayers to a named demon[5] at bedtime. The actions that accompanied the prayers were like those that accompany Moslem prayers: kneeling and first raising the hands above the head, then bringing them down in front of one. In the first two cases, other adults were also involved, in one case the father of the children, in another the wife and sister-in-law of the perpetrator.[6] The other man acted alone. The fact that two of the three men had been accused or convicted of the sexual abuse of children in cases that did not involve any ritual is a good indication that the occult trappings were a device to entrap victims and not an essential element as far as the perpetrator was concerned.

In two of the three cases the ideas and practices did not resemble any known occult beliefs or rituals. The first man claimed to have received a mandate from the Virgin Mary to fight evil, which was personified by a character taken from a novel written by the horror fiction writer Angus Hall. He appeared to believe in his mission, about which he had written letters to the Prime Minister and the Archbishop of Canterbury. He also claimed to be the reincarnation of an Egyptian high priest from the time of the Pharaohs, and his chief victim was first said to be the reincarnation of his wife, a priestess; in a later ritual she then became a goddess. The altar consisted of an eclectic collection of ritual objects, including a monstrance, and the participants dressed in pseudo-Egyptian style for the rituals. In one photograph in the file the girl is holding a catholic rosary and there is a picture of the Virgin and Child, in an Eastern European style, on the wall behind her. In this case, the 'High Priest' had intercourse with the girl during the ritual. He also had intercourse with her at other times, and also, secretly, with her brother. Everything came to light when the girl became pregnant. Her father, a rather simple man, had accepted the ritual intercourse as a means to maintain the power of the 'priest' to fight evil, but the news that his son had been abused so horrified him that he told the whole story of their involvement with the perpetrator; in his statement the boy showed himself to be still convinced to some extent of the truth of 'the mission'.

In one of the cases the abuser told the police in great detail about his activities when interviewed in custody; the transcripts of the taped interviews display his conceited opinion of himself and his attempts to demonstrate superiority to the police interviewer. He claimed to be interested in the idea of astral travel, about which he had talked to the children, but they only thought he meant flying. In this case, the 'occult' aspect of the sexual abuse was elaborated progressively, in response to the questions of the young victims and to satisfy their curiosity about witches rather than as the ritual of any cult, for which there was absolutely no evidence. To begin with, one child was offered access to magic, so she asked if that meant like 'what witches do'. She was told yes, but in this case, the witches were good. She and the other children whom she recruited at his instigation were told that the sexual activities were part of a graded series of learning and tests that would endow them with secret magical powers; these powers would obtain for them all that they wished for. They were later told that various pop stars whom they admired had undergone this training and were shown pornography that demonstrated other children undergoing 'training'.

None of the children had progressed through more than two stages, referred to as 'processes' and those who had reached the second stage were said to have been asking what the next stage would be. Asked by the police about the third process, he answered: 'I don't know yet, I've never got that far, because there's an awful lot to learn,' and he then added: 'If I'm a step ahead of them by kind of reading up . . . Most of it is, literally, made up, just I think of something I can put across . . . ' There was no ritual other than prayers, or ritual objects other than lumps of slate, picked up by the perpetrator of the abuse abroad; some of the victims were given pieces of the slate and were told these had magical properties. Two of these were recovered.

The earliest case was the one in which the perpetrator seemed most like the general idea of an occultist. It took place before the spread of allegations of satanic abuse in England but is regularly cited as proving them. In it the rituals were said by the police to have followed prescriptions set out in an occult book,[7] but there was no evidence that any of the adults had been practising members of an occult group, although two of them were allegedly interested in it. They had paraphernalia for two altars, one of which travelled in a special case and belonged to the leader's sister-in-law, mother of the two youngest children. This material evidence was listed in the police file. On one occasion another adult had been invited to participate in a minor ritual. When interviewed by the police he had commented that the perpetrator had seemed to know very little about the occult. This man had not wished to take any further part in what they were doing (although the sexual aspects of their activities were not disclosed to him) and had not met them again.

By the time that these activities were reported to the police, the main figure was claiming that he *was* Lucifer. This fact makes it certain that he was not an occultist, not even a satanist, none of whom claim to embody Satan. Moreover, although the altar paraphernalia resembled the objects used by one type of occultist group it lacked certain essential items. Many of the resemblances also reflected the general folklore of secret cults or even common understandings in the society at large. For example the candles have no particular occult significance; candles are a marker of ritual and are not restricted to occult ceremonies. Although this man[8] was probably the nearest to a self-taught occultist of all the perpetrators of abuse in these three cases, and closer than many of those who appeared in the other cases cited by Tate, the case is not one of satanic abuse in the meaning used by any of those who make the allegations.

Collateral evidence for the ritual

In these three cases there was abundant evidence to corroborate the stories told by the victims. Not only were there several victims who corroborated each other, but occult paraphernalia, garments, books and photographic evidence were also found, to support what was said. While they substantiated both the fact of the children's sexual abuse and the ritual context in which it happened, these cases did not involve the acts that define satanic abuse; they did not supply material evidence to support the extreme allegations of devil worship.

On the evidence of the table of allegations set out earlier in the chapter, the substantiation of the allegations should include evidence of blood sacrifices, the presence of the devil and cannibalism. These three features of satanic abuse must be corroborated separately; that is to say, the establishment that one of the acts took place does not serve as proof that they all did. In addition to evidence of the children's sexual abuse, material evidence that the rituals described had taken place would be needed. The three substantiated cases of ritual abuse indicated what this might be: paraphernalia such as an altar, special garments, ritual objects, a special place and writings that appeared to relate to the ritual as described. Books that guided the ritual and a notebook in which the plan of a ritual was noted were also found. In one case there were photographs of the altar and ritual dress. In these three cases there was no allegation of murder; however, where allegations of satanic abuse included human sacrifice taking place (as at least a quarter of the cases did), there should also be a missing person, a body or other forensic evidence or an eye witness to corroborate the allegation. Bestiality and animal sacrifice require evidence that animals were there and/or were killed. If photographing the children was allegedly part of the ritual, then the equipment or the results would confirm that this was so. In some cases the evidence might have been disposed of, but it was unlikely that all of it would have disappeared and in all cases.

The excerpts from case histories cited at the beginning of this chapter come from four cases where there was no material evidence to support what was alleged. The children remained in care but it was not established what, if anything had happened. There was no mention of a medical examination to establish the scars claimed by the teenager. The boy's claim to know where his parents' ritual paraphernalia was buried did not come to anything as nothing was discovered. Over the whole set of cases, material evidence was remarkable for its absence.

Ceremonial dress

The use of robes and masks to 'dress up' is one of the commonest features of the allegations of satanic abuse. Yet little evidence of their use was found. Robes have been found in only one case, although in the Orkney case (outside this study) the minister who was accused of ritually abusing the children had a cloak that was considered to resemble these garments. In the case within my study, an accused woman claimed that the robe she was said to have worn in a ritual was in fact a *djellaba* that had been brought her from North Africa by a friend. The garment was there, the term she used for the garment was consistent with her account but there was no description of it in the files, so it was impossible to say what it was. In one of the substantiated cases described earlier in the chapter, the ritual garments and 'jewellery' that were used by the main victim were photographed and the photographs and the objects themselves were found. The main garment was a thin white dress worn with jewellery and a headdress. The effect was consistent with the idea, expressed by both victims and corroborated by their father, that she was believed to be the reincarnation of an Egyptian priestess, and then a goddess. One couple in another case admitted to dressing in sheets to frighten the children by pretending to be ghosts – unpleasant but not satanic.[9] In a police raid on the house where it was suspected that satanic abuse was going on, adults dressed in 'odd costumes' (not described further) were discovered, but there were no children present. It is possible that this was an occult group performing ritual magic, but the evidence is insufficient to be sure what was happening there.

Masks figure in the accounts of some children and of survivors but they are very varied; the drawings of them may resemble the mask worn by the cartoon hero, Batman. Face masks portraying ghosts, monsters and witches or giving a generally frightening effect are frequently to be seen worn by children at Halloween and have been reported as used by men in robberies, but it is not clear whether these are the masks referred to in some of the cases. The case of the child who reacted unusually strongly when given a 'Halloween mask' to wear has already been described, but the mask was not mentioned further in the file. One allusion was clearly to the balaclava mask worn by members of the IRA as well as other terrorist groups and some criminals; this mask can frequently be seen on television news broadcasts. In general, of course, the fact of a mask is a sign that the person's identity is concealed. It may be that in other cases where children said they did not know who the participants in the satanic ritual were, it was assumed that they were wearing masks. Alternatively some children might have referred to masks to forestall questions about the identity of the people concerned. The significance of the masks cannot really be determined without better evidence.

Pornography

According to a former head of New Scotland Yard's Obscene Publications Squad, it is a 'common misconception that there is a large-scale commercial trade in the material' produced by paedophiles (Hames 1993: 276). He identifies Thailand, the Netherlands and Portugal as the places where child pornography is produced for sale. Although he agreed that individuals who sexually abuse children may film or photograph their victims, he stated unequivocally that they do this to provide themselves with mementoes and not to sell them. He also reported that individuals who make and collect this sort of material will 'rarely if ever destroy it'. It is thus likely to be found by a careful search. Such material is useful as corroboration of the sexual abuse and may even make it unnecessary for the child to go to court (Hames 1996), so it is always looked for in police searches in cases where there is suspicion that children have been sexually abused.

Little pornography of any kind was found. In eighteen survey cases the victims alleged that they had been filmed or photographed or that videos of the sexual abuse and/or the rituals had been made.[10] Material to corroborate this was not found, neither were any cameras. In some cases its absence was attributed to the police's failure to search; in a few instances this might have been the case, as believers have asserted, but it seems unlikely that in all cases where photography was alleged the absence of photographic evidence was simply the result of a failure to search or to search properly. A certain amount of pornographic material was found but it did not include pictures of the victims in the cases. In only one case was a picture of one of the child victims found and it was a portrait, fully clothed.

Two cases were reported to the survey where the police had been alerted about pornographic photographs of children by the firm processing the films, but these cases included no allegations of satanic abuse. In a third (non-satanic) case reported to the survey, photographs of the accused couple were found, but they showed the rape of an adult woman, not abuse of a child or satanic abuse. Where the victims alleged that they had been filmed or photographed or videos of the sexual abuse and/or the rituals had been made, there was no material to corroborate them and no appropriate cameras were found either. The only pictures relating to ritual that were discovered showed no actual performance but consisted of photographs of the altar and of the 'priestess' in ceremonial dress.

By contrast, there was some evidence to show that in some cases children were being exposed to pornography. In fourteen cases the children were said to have watched pornographic videos, and in three of these cases videos were found. In one case the police went to the house and found some teenagers watching a pornographic video accompanied by one of the very much younger children they were baby-sitting. Magazines of child pornography were found in the possession of the perpetrators (two cases) and the victims had been shown some of the pictures in them (one case). Sadism was reported in eight cases and a video of sado-masochistic scenes was found in another. This video was shown on television, in a Despatches programme where it was implied that the scene shown was a satanic ritual. However, the video was later revealed to be a demonstration of performance art which had been circulating in avant-garde art circles for nearly ten years. There was some evidence that the children of the central figure had been allowed to witness these scenes, but as he and his family were abroad and did not return (presumably alerted by the programme), the matter was not taken further.

Other corroborative evidence

Even evidence that these cases concern people who are interested in the occult is rare, as has already been indicated. In three of the houses, searches revealed books about the occult that might be said to confirm the interest of one or more of the residents. However in one case, on checking, the books were shown not to relate to the allegations being made in the case; they did not provide outlines of rituals, justifications for the sexual abuse of children, for animal or human sacrifice, blood drinking or any of the other actions that were said to have been part of the rituals. A book on talismans (lucky charms) figured in the allegations made by the teenagers in one case, but were not mentioned by the much younger children of the book's owner. In the other two cases there was allegedly a link between books found and the rituals, but in only one case were the rituals said to have followed directions in a book that had been found. In the last remaining case, there were two books of relevance: *To Play the Devil*, a novel by Angus Hall, and *The World's First Love* by Fulton Sheen, an American bishop.[11] The perpetrator of sexual abuse on the two children had convinced them and their father that he had been sent by God on a mission against the evil one – identified as Toombs, the name of the evil character in the novel by Angus Hall. The books in the other cases bore no relation to the descriptions of the rituals that were alleged to have been performed. Nevertheless their existence was used to support the belief that satanic rituals were being performed, despite the fact that they did not relate to the actual allegations being made.

Belief and credibility

The absence of evidence to support the allegations of satanic abuse does not shake the belief of most believers, who continue to have faith that evidence of satanism will eventually be forthcoming (Trowell 1994: 204). In fact, it is likely that many supporters of the idea that children are threatened by this new and terrible danger do not know that there is no evidence that these things are true. They accept what they are told because they accept the authority of the person who tells them. This is probably particularly the case with fundamentalist Christians who are disposed to believe the information as a matter of faith. But it is true of many therapists as well. Clinical experience or good work in one particular field may give professionals in the psychotherapeutic world a very much wider credibility. The idea that people may refuse to accept what they find to be too painful is usefully adapted to avoid discussion: the sceptics are said to be 'in denial'.

Therapists may also hold to a belief that being believed is the beginning of healing (Hale & Sinason 1994: 272) and maintain that victims have a need to be believed. This locates the authority that guarantees the truth in the patient. To start with, in the satanic abuse cases, it was the victims whose accounts were authenticated, rather than the culprit/witch who was identified. By 1994, statements that all victims are also culprits, since they are forced to become perpetrators of abuse on more recently recruited or younger children (e.g. Coleman 1994a: 250) indicate that the difference is less significant than it appeared to begin with.

The controversy over satanic abuse has underlined the existence of two quite different views on the nature of proof. The two co-exist and one is not more 'traditional' than the other; we may even operate with one in one situation and the other in another.

First, there is the proof by authoritative opinion, that bases proof on the personal authority of the experts, whether these are clinicians[12] who claim the ability to assess their patients' truthfulness, or religious figures who claim this by virtue of their knowledge of the faith, or patients who have the authority of their suffering. In these circumstances the person, not the evidence, guarantees the truth. It may be significant that those who take this attitude talk of believing rather than being convinced.

Salazar's view quoted earlier epitomises the rationalist approach; 'external and objective evidence' is required as proof before an allegation can be accepted. As this chapter has shown, so far there has been very little of it. The absence of material evidence to corroborate the allegations of satanic abuse has confirmed sceptics in their views and may have induced a more cautious attitude among some members of the public, but it has converted few believers. However, it has been seized on as a weapon by those who would dispute the fact that incest and the sexual abuse of children does occur. By reversing the argument of some believers, extreme sceptics may claim that the lack of material corroboration for cases of satanic abuse is a lack of substantiation for sexual abuse. This chapter has aimed to show that this is not so; children may be sexually abused in extremely sadistic ways without those guilty of abusing them being organised in a satanist cult. The lack of evidence undermines only the satanist element.

Most believers have not been affected by the lack of evidence but, on the contrary, buttress their faith with the nature of their explanations of it. Lack of corroborative evidence may be attributed to the power of Satan to protect his servants or, more often, to the meticulous care of the satanists to dispose of any evidence (Coleman 1994a: 245–6). Attacking the personal authority of sceptics in order to destroy their credibility rather than addressing the substantive issue is another common method. The argument that a different point of view constitutes 'denial' relies on an argument from psychiatry and thus concentrates on the sceptic's (presumed) emotions, deflecting attention from the evidence for or against the allegations. In one seminar I also heard it said that no-one who was not a clinician treating survivors could understand satanic abuse, an argument basing veracity on occupation and particular experience in it. An argument of the same type, but for belief, is the assertion discussed earlier that it is because children are said to be telling the stories of satanic abuse that these accounts must be believed (cf. Clapton 1993: 20–2).

Since Evans-Pritchard's original study of witchcraft in Africa over sixty years ago, it has been shown time and again that it is not necessary for witches to exist for the beliefs in them to persist. There is no evidence in these cases that what has been alleged to have happened has happened. There is no evidence for human or animal sacrifice, for drinking blood or cannibalism. There is evidence that children have been sexually abused and subjected to perverse treatment and there is also evidence that children's interest in magic and witches may be used to lure them into participating in sexual activities and to ensure that they keep these activities secret. However, the satanic conspirators of the satanic abuse allegations, like night-witches or the celebrants of the witches' sabbath, reflect 'the nightmares of the group' (Wilson 1951). These are shared fears of figures of evil that reflect and embody social concerns. It is because the fears are shared that belief in their reality is so tenacious.

6   Explaining belief

If, as the last chapter showed, there is no evidence to support the notion that a satanic cult is performing evil rites that involve the torture and even killing of children, then what is the basis for the belief in satanic abuse? This is the central question to which this book is addressed. In fact, there are two questions to be answered: first, what are the reasons for a generalised belief in the possibility of satanic cults, particularly as the decline in formal religion throughout most of this century has led many observers to consider society as dominated by a secular and rational outlook on life (Jenkins 1992: 44)? Chapter 2 showed that continuity in Church mythology and folk belief has provided ready acceptance for ideas that are not new but merely refurbished in modern guise. This chapter is addressed rather to the question which follows: given that people might be prepared to entertain the notion of satanic abuse in general, how did allegations arise in *particular* cases? This chapter starts to provide an answer by considering how belief in satanic abuse can provide an explanation for difficult cases of child abuse.

Difficult cases

A psychologist in the field of child protection has recorded her view that work with the victims of satanic abuse is 'experienced as significantly more complex, more difficult, more challenging and more professionally "draining" than clinical work with other client-groups.' (Youngson 1993: 259; 1994). The cases of alleged satanic abuse that were reported to the survey showed three main features that would justify describing them as 'difficult': first, although there might be strong suspicion of sexual abuse, or even allegations by the children, there was little to corroborate it; secondly, the children were often young, or intellectually disadvantaged or with delayed or impaired development; thirdly, the behaviour of the children was extreme and foster-parents found it difficult to deal with them. The cases were thus difficult to pursue to a conviction, difficult to understand and difficult to manage.

Table 5 *Evidence of sexual abuse in ritual abuse cases compared with other survey cases*

Clear evidence for	Ritual abuse cases		Other Survey cases	
	No	%	No	%
No children	41	(49)	19	(13)
Some children	18	(21)	64	(44)
All children	17	(20)	53	(37)
Conflicting reports	4	(5)	4	(3)
Missing/not known	4	(5)	4	(3)
Total	84	(100)	144	(100)

As the last chapter showed, evidence of sexual abuse is lacking in many of these cases, at once making them difficult cases for child protection agencies to deal with. The relative absence of clear evidence of sexual abuse is far more marked in the satanic abuse cases than in the other organised abuse cases reported in the survey; these were between three and four times as many of them, compared with the rest of the survey cases. Table 5 summarises the availability of evidence for sexual abuse in the 84 satanic abuse cases and compares it with other cases reported in the survey. It shows that satanic abuse cases are much less likely to afford proof of the sexual abuse of the children than the other types of case reported to the survey. In nearly half of all satanic abuse cases (49 per cent) there was no clear evidence of the sexual abuse of any children in the case, but this was only true of 13 per cent of the other cases. This striking difference does not, however, indicate that the children concerned had not been sexually abused, merely that proof was lacking and hence identification and conviction of the offenders would be more difficult. The fact that so many perpetrators of the sexual abuse of children remain unconvicted is a source of anger and frustration in the child protection field.

The detailed study of cases shows that, even where sexual abuse could not be substantiated by means of medical evidence or a confession, there might have been good grounds for suspecting it; in addition the neglect or maltreatment of the children are not uncommon features of the cases. The effects of material deprivation could also be seen in some cases. Many of the children were very disturbed and difficult to understand or communicate with. The medical evidence might have been equivocal in some cases, but the children's behaviour was suggestively sexualised and/or sometimes a child was found sexually abusing other children. More than one child may have made disclosures of sexual abuse and these may be consistent with one another. Even so, satisfactory corroboration may not be obtained. What this means for the professionals concerned with the case is that those responsible often cannot be prosecuted or even, in some cases, identified. The professionals' resultant frustration may be experienced as stress and increases the attraction of an explanation that accounts for the failure to arrest and punish offenders against children.

The children in these cases were, on average, younger than in other cases; the average age was 6.8 years (La Fontaine 1994). They therefore presented formidable problems of interviewing, management and treatment. While the survey asked for little information on individual children, evidence from the study of cases in the Official Solicitor's office showed that a third of the children in those cases were identified as having learning difficulties, showing developmental delay, including problems with their speech, and/or showing psychological disturbance.

For the diagnosis of satanic abuse, behaviour is as important as anything children have said, whether in interviews or informally in conversation with foster-parents or social workers. The children's behaviour was considered 'bizarre' when compared with other children taken into care. One much publicised characteristic was that they were terrified. In 1990 a meeting of foster-parents in one large case noted: 'Little things frightened them (the children)'. Their fear was considered extreme and was taken to indicate the strength of the threat hanging over them. In her article about the Nottingham case in *New Statesman and Society* Judith Dawson refers to this fear twice, saying first that: 'All who met the children testified to a level of fear they had never encountered before' and, later: 'The children showed an unusual degree of fear, *even for children who had only recently been received into care.*' (Dawson 1990: 13; my italics). This must indicate that some degree of fear is expected. How this 'unusual degree' is expressed is rarely described, which makes it difficult to judge. Certainly some children seemed abnormally worried about the house being secure at night and needed to be shown that it was locked up and the windows closed. But other behaviour was also interpreted as fear. Two boys, who ran riot in the play therapy room were said to be terrified, as was another child who hid under the seats when he saw a candle-lit procession in church. One little girl could not be interviewed at all, because she cried and screamed for her brother so much that the two interviews that were attempted had to be abandoned. She, like the children in the first case mentioned, seemed to be frightened of the interviewers.

This fear was seen by believers as having been induced either by the satanic ritual or by the satanists. But one foster-mother in another case said that in her experience children from deprived homes were often very frightened by new places and activities; she took care to introduce her foster-daughter to a new place before an occasion took place there, or to get her used to new experiences gradually, and found she then managed the occasion well. This was a child who had been described as terrified of everything by her previous foster-mother. In some other cases, anxiety or the tension of insecure children might have been an explanation of what was seen as manifestations of fear.

Other aspects of the children's behaviour were unusually difficult for foster-parents to deal with and they often found it very disturbing (e.g. Kelsall 1994: 89; but cf. Thornley 1989). Much of it was extreme: constant night-terrors, depriving everyone of sleep; inexplicable games being played; eating excrement or making a habit of smearing it over themselves and their surroundings. Another child stood, apparently in a trance, for twenty-four hours from Christmas Eve till the following night.[1] One very badly abused little boy attempted what was seen as 'sexual abuse' of a young foster-sister. His foster-mother had never fostered an abused child before and could not understand his behaviour. Extremely sexualised behaviour is difficult to manage within a foster-family, and where a child's sexualised behaviour includes the family dog or breaks out in public situations, it may seem to call for the sort of explanation that satanic abuse provides.

The strange behaviour of the children might be made less, rather than more, intelligible by remarks that were difficult to interpret. Some examples from a few files may serve to illustrate the problems of understanding them:

A three-year-old girl says that the clouds are (sic) an eye which watches her. She refers sometimes to 'the master'.

An eight-year-old girl was frightened of mirrors and would cover the one in her room at night (her grandmother was a medium); She said she was 'skinned alive' at night. On another occasion she was afraid that Bloody Mary would skin her alive.[2]

A four-year-old boy said to his foster-mother: 'I go up a ladder into the ceiling and open the moon and there's a wolf inside'.

These undoubted oddities cause anxiety about the child. They remain unexplained until gathered up under the rubric of an explanation in terms of satanic abuse. They then take on meaning as attempts to disclose what happened during the ritual.

Such 'difficult' children may have several placements, the moves compounding their insecurities. Apart from waking often at night and wetting the bed, practices which prevent foster-parents getting enough sleep, the children's treatment of other children or of pets, their odd remarks and the violence of their nightmares and phobias seemed to set these children apart. In some cases people come close to considering the children themselves as evil, but seeing them instead as the victims of devil-worshipping cults makes the behavioural extremes and the strange remarks intelligible and easier to tolerate, confirming the status of the children as that of victims.

The cases also shared other features that made them distinctive, whether or not these elements could be considered to add to the difficulties they presented as cases. One noticeable element was the delay before the allegations were made. Allegations of satanic ritual were made, in most cases, after the children had been taken into care, sometimes months later. Children were rarely taken into care because it was suspected that they had been the victims of satanists, unless they had been named by another child in a case that had already been diagnosed as concerned with satanic abuse. In a few cases suspicion of a parent's occult beliefs, or remarks made by children, usually older children, or by their mothers triggered action by the social services, but most often children were taken into care for a variety of reasons distinct from the issue of satanism: neglect, non-accidental injury, or emotional and sexual abuse. One set of siblings was taken into care when their mother attacked and killed her neighbour, others had been in and out of care on a voluntary basis for several years. Normally, after the children were placed in care, certain features of the cases might indicate that they were unusually difficult or particularly serious, or the children might seem especially damaged. In one famous case, however, a diagnosis of satanic abuse was already being canvassed before the interviews that were later used as evidence for the allegation had been held. Some children were interviewed explicitly to provide evidence of satanic abuse, about which another child was believed to have said something.

It may be said that this delay before children tell of ritual abuse is an indication of how terrified they are of the consequences of telling, or how deeply buried the traumatic memories were (e.g. Hudson 1991: 60). A parallel may be drawn with 'ordinary' sexual abuse cases in which some children will tell the story piecemeal over time, starting with a minor episode and finally disclosing the full story. It is said that children need time to feel safe before they dare disclose what has happened. However, not all sexually abused children are so reticent about what has happened, nor are all the children in these cases. A minority, mostly older children, make their allegations all at once. But failure to find out from the child what happened is taken as evidence of something extremely serious, requiring interviews to induce the first stage of healing: disclosure. The interval between taking children into care and their 'disclosures' of satanic abuse may be filled with a long series of 'therapeutic interviews'. Sometimes as many as eighty hours of interviews are required to obtain a 'disclosure' that may be taken as evidence of satanic abuse. One social worker in a very poor urban district suggested to me that formal interviews were not the best way to get information from children in communities like those he dealt with; he knew this because he came from one very like it himself. As Chapter 4 showed, the background of many of the children in the cases of satanic abuse resembled those he was talking about. The adults who look after them are not often qualified by their background to understand it.

Failure to disclose, denials or silence are often interpreted by believers as evidence of the deep trauma and/or intimidation the child has suffered. It might be believed that children had words implanted into their subconscious that, when spoken, would release a memory of what would happen if they made a disclosure and prevent them answering questions. These are referred to as trigger words. (Objects might also be considered 'triggers', which was why the children taken into care in the highly publicised Orkney case were not allowed to take personal toys or to receive letters from parents.) Refusal to confirm what was suspected or to answer questions at all was in some cases considered evidence of the operation of trigger words and hence of satanic abuse. Satanic abuse thus provides an explanation for the failure to establish what happened. Rather than accept the fact of not knowing and live with the uncertainty, some people prefer to adopt a view that offers them the possibility of believing that they know what happened.

Certain characteristics of the cases were stressed by the professionals who had been involved in them. In addition to, and sometimes more significant than, the fear felt by the children or their extraordinary behaviour, or the difficulty of the cases, was the stress they induced in the adults who were engaged in protecting the children. The foster-parents at the meeting referred to earlier concluded that these foster-children were 'Very, very, very (sic) hard work' and they wanted extra payments for fostering victims of satanic abuse. To an observer what leapt to the eye in files and became apparent in interviews was the level of fear felt by *adults*, the child protection workers. All those I interviewed, who had participated in cases involving allegations or suspicions of ritual abuse, agreed that they had been exceptionally difficult. An organisation was set up to help professionals working in such cases, Ritual Abuse Information Network and Support (RAINS),[3] and the first study it produced was of the stress suffered, rather than any other features of the cases themselves. It is worth considering in detail for the light it throws on the context of the cases.

The author of this study is a psychologist, who is a member of RAINS, and has personal experience of a case (Youngson 1993). She begins by reporting that she had been 'repeatedly struck by the levels of personal, interpersonal and professional stress that seem to arise in work in the area of ritual (satanic) abuse.' The study is based on its author's belief that working with ritual abuse would form a watershed in her respondents' lives, rather than that the stress of difficult cases preceded the diagnosis. It is not possible to discover from it if any of the symptoms reported had appeared before working with a case of alleged satanic abuse. However, it is at least plausible that the stress of a difficult case made the acceptance of a diagnosis of satanic abuse more likely.

Some of the sources of stress derived directly from the respondents' belief that they were dealing with unprecedented evil. Judging from the detailed case material I used in my study, this conclusion derived partly from their view that the children were more damaged than any they had dealt with before; it was a common conclusion from this that the cause must be worse than any they had encountered. Part of the stress derived from belief in the existence of evil beings in the locality: when asked if they worried more about their own safety and that of their partners, families or friends 86 per cent said they did[4] and 37 per cent (twenty-six) 'believed that they had received some form of intimidation because of their work in the field of ritual abuse' (Youngson 1993: 260). Nearly all (nineteen out of twenty-six) of those who recorded intimidation referred to silent telephone calls, which had intimidated them but which cannot, as the author noted, be proved to have been threats. Half (thirteen) reported receiving telephone calls described as 'threatening / warning /abusive' (Youngson 1993: 256–7). However, this constitutes only 18 per cent of the total number of respondents. An even smaller proportion of them had suffered actual harm: five (7 per cent) had had their cars or houses vandalised, three (4 per cent) had had their offices broken into and two (3 per cent) had been burgled. None of the respondents had been assaulted.

It is hard to assess the nature of these threats, as Youngson herself notes. One of those who reported being burgled also said that the police had told her she lived in a high risk area, so she was 'uncertain'. Where I could find records of the details, a wide variety of happenings were recorded as threats: in one case some pet rabbits were found dead in the garden; in another, traces were allegedly left on the counterpane of a bed, where there were no indications that the house had been broken into. In neither case was there any indication of what was threatened or what action would prevent it. The foster-mother of some children in a well-known case told me that she felt that a dog[5] owned by one of the children was an evil influence and when it died things improved. Some respondents merely 'wondered' about events they also considered might just be coincidences. The safety of the former victims who were telling their stories is not mentioned in this survey, but from my own qualitative data it seemed that, with a few exceptions, this was not a major concern, unlike any other situation when witnesses may have to be protected from the criminals about whom they are informing.

It is a measure of their perceptions of the level of threat to themselves that two-thirds of those who reported intimidation had taken additional safety measures. New locks were fitted in sixteen cases and six respondents bought burglar alarms. Others said they would have bought alarms if they could have afforded them. In one case the senior social worker asked for police protection for members of the social work team. There is no doubt that these respondents were afraid, though it is harder to show that there was reason to be.

There were few foster-parents in this survey but it seems likely that they suffered as much stress, if not more. Unlike social workers, foster-mothers have no training that would help them in the task of looking after these very disturbed and disturbing children. The 'diaries' of foster-mothers that were to become so well-known in the Nottingham case were started by one foster-mother, to help herself deal with the day-to-day behaviour of these particular foster-children. Another in the same case had had only two years' experience before she took on a child who was to be an important figure in the case; she had never fostered an abused child before. The foster-mother of two very damaged children in another case had also never fostered sexually abused children before. She saw one boy's sexual assault on his much younger foster-sister as evidence of the satanism to which he had been exposed rather than recognising it as a common reaction of severely abused children. Some foster-parents, who could not cope with the children's behaviour or with the idea that they had been participants in satanic rituals, rejected the children, who then had to be removed. Others seemed to find that the thought that they were involved in a fight against evil sustained them in looking after the children.

The survey of cases of alleged satanic abuse established that foster-parents were the largest single category of adults listed as having been the first to hear an allegation. This indicates their significance in identifying cases of ritual abuse. Many of them saw fostering as a way to do good, giving help to children who needed it, and even if their religious faith was not obtrusive, it was often clear that they were Christians. Some of those to whom I talked remarked that other foster-parents whom they knew 'did it for the money' but it seems unlikely that this is a common and acknowledged motivation. The general outlook that seemed characteristic was much more conducive to accepting the idea of satanic abuse than a purely mercenary outlook would be. Lacking the training of social workers, however, they were more vulnerable to stress and to the distortions of perception that their situations might produce.

Foster-parents form an important part of the system of child protection. They work closely with social services and are seen as authorities on the children they foster, about whom they have much more information than the social workers, who do not see the children daily. This makes social workers inclined to accept what they report without querying it very much. Moreover, in many parts of the country social service departments find themselves desperately short of people willing to look after children who are, by definition, difficult to manage. A factor contributing significantly to the making of the crisis in Cleveland was the shortage of foster-parents for the children who were taken into care. It may be particularly hard to find foster-parents for sexually abused children and those that are found may show their ignorance of sexual abuse and their lack of experience in their handling of problems. In many cases it was clear that social workers went to considerable lengths to support foster-parents and were influenced by what they said about the children.

Youngson's respondents were working with nearly twice as many adults as children. This is significant because, as we shall see in Chapter 8, adult and adolescent 'survivors' generally tell more complete, more elaborate and more shocking stories than young children. Moreover they are usually told by women who appeal not just to the social workers' sense of concern for their victimisation but to feminist sentiments. The reasons RAINS members gave for the difficulties they experienced were: the extreme psychological problems of the clients;[6] their ambivalence about the therapy and the therapist, which Youngson attributes to an inverted belief system but which could have other bases in the behaviour of the children (see below p. 128); the prospect of long-term treatment, described as 'a responsibility and a pressure' (1993: 259); and finally, the details of what was said were 'overwhelming', inducing 'nausea, disgust and fear, and professional helplessness and inadequacy' (1993: 260). The last reason no doubt reflects the nature of the stories told by adults, whereas foster-parents were likely to be puzzled and anxious because of their ignorance.

The state of mind which the Youngson survey depicts may not have been universal among those who work with cases of alleged satanic abuse, but it seems to have been common; two-thirds of the RAINS membership responded to the survey. The survey itself also, rather oddly, records that 42 per cent reported some minor positive effects. What these are is not specified, but it indicates that nearly half the group appears to have benefited from working with cases where satanic abuse was alleged. This gives an intriguing hint of the motivation of believers or at the least, a reward for belief. Overall, at least according to the seventy-one social workers, psychologists and therapists who filled in the questionnaires for Youngson's study, the experience of these cases was a highly emotive one. In such a state of mind people were highly receptive to interpretations that might help them to understand, and which also gave them the support of joining a crusade against evil.

Opposition may harden the determination to protect a diagnosis, once it is established. The difficulties child protection agencies found, and continue to find,[7] in working together were highlighted by the result of the judicial enquiry into events in Cleveland. It reported in 1988, at the beginning of the epidemic of satanic abuse cases, leaving social workers nervous about being publicly criticised for taking children into care and the police not much happier about their role in protecting children. The government guidelines that were issued subsequently have not been enough to counteract critical differences in the professional cultures concerned. These alone are enough to introduce strain into the process of identifying and prosecuting offenders against children. In particular the police and social workers readily exemplify the two different attitudes to proof that were identified at the end of the last chapter: the police are required to collect evidence as the basis for identifying and prosecuting offenders, while the other professionals may be prepared to judge an allegation or suspicion as well-founded, even in the absence of material evidence. Among many who work in this field, believing the victim has become an unquestioned dogma that disregards any need for corroborative evidence.

Even where those in the child protection field are not committed to this dogma, recent cases, highlighted in the media, where policemen have been found to be corrupt or inefficient have induced a loss of faith in them. In particular cases, believers have suspected that the police were protecting the offenders and one account of the supposed satanic cult states categorically that those high up in the cult 'frequently' include members of the police (Coleman 1994: 243). This belief can hardly improve relations between other professionals and the police. On their part, police may make the mistake of thinking that lack of evidence to support an allegation of satanic abuse reveals all of the complaint to be false. In some areas, the police may not have been well-trained enough to recognise the possibilities of child prostitution or paedophile rings that might underlie the allegations. Social workers may also have a mistakenly optimistic view of police powers and are frustrated at the failure to identify and arrest all perpetrators; they are likely to blame the police for failure to arrest the culprits or discover material evidence of what has happened. In one large case the social workers apparently expected the police to mount 24–hour surveillance on all those whom they suspected, ignoring the fact that they had provided no grounds for the police to obtain the necessary permission for such a costly procedure. The police may be angry when lack of evidence is taken to mean that they have not tried to find any, and frustrated at what they perceive as the slowness of social services to move. On the other hand the police may not inform their colleagues in the other agencies about what action they *have* taken, thus encouraging the belief that they have done nothing. Personal relationships of trust can overcome these divisive features and some child protection teams I interviewed worked well together, but friction over difficult cases, and in particular open conflict between the professional groups involved, exacerbating the normal stress of working in a difficult field, seems to be a contributory background factor in allegations of satanic abuse.

Similar divisions appeared within some social service departments, where those who disagreed with the diagnosis of satanic abuse might claim to have been deprived of information or left out of meetings. The pressure on one social worker induced a nervous breakdown and caused another to leave the profession. In one case a foster-mother who changed her mind about the diagnosis of satanic abuse when some people she knew were accused, claimed that all her foster-children were removed from her as a reprisal. There is no doubt that divisions might be deep and cause lasting bitterness; they also ensured that when the most influential of those involved in a child protection case had agreed that satanic abuse was involved, opposition was hard to sustain.

Direct influences

The source of the explanation offered by the hypothesis of satanic abuse is clearly religious; it derives from Christian doctrine. This does not mean that all those who promote it are fundamentalist Christians. It is also characteristic of these cases that 'experts' are consulted usually by social workers or foster-parents. The people consulted are mostly not trained for social work, or their training has not been in Britain, nor are they usually members of professions that at first sight might be relevant to the problem; instead they are journalists, American therapists, and evangelical Christians, all of whom are committed to a particular view.

They will be considered in more detail in Chapter 9, but their relevance here lies in their offering solutions to problems and explanations of events and behaviour that are not provided within normal professional knowledge or common understanding.

Consultations with those thought to be specialists in the field, whether evangelical campaigners or secular 'consultants', not only suggest satanic abuse where the people involved are worried about features of the case but in other cases may also confirm the diagnosis of satanic abuse, suggesting further elements to look for. In thirty-eight of the cases – nearly half of those I studied – 'experts' of this sort were involved and in a study by New Scotland Yard of forty-five cases there was a far higher proportion of experts reported. The 'experts' were very influential. There was only one case among those I studied in detail where the specialist consulted did not endorse the suspicion that satanic abuse had taken place, and, significantly, in that case the suspicions fizzled out without being taken further.

Conferences at which the idea of ritual abuse was canvassed were frequent during the years 1987–92[8] and spread the idea of a new threat to children; they still continue. A result of these gatherings was that specialists met the men and women involved in child protection and these relationships might be activated later when advice was needed. The first conference I attended, in 1990, was Christian in general approach, although two social workers from the controversial Nottingham case gave a presentation that was determinedly secular. The second, over a year later, was also secular. It was, however, enhanced by a certain excitement over an alleged threat of attack by occultists or satanists that created a dramatic atmosphere, stimulated by the obviously well-organised security.

Neither conference allowed for the slightest doubt that what was being presented was the literal truth. Sceptical questions were largely brushed aside. Attempts have been made to see these conferences as the source from which the allegations sprang, but this is hard to demonstrate and it is not necessary to prove the presence of social workers from X at a conference a suitably short time before a case broke. What was significant was that the conferences spread the idea that a new form of abuse had been discovered and that once this was accepted the cases would be uncovered. The prestige of being in the vanguard of such discoveries was balanced by the nervousness felt by inadequately trained workers at what was ahead of them. During the conferences and afterwards in child protection circles, papers from American 'experts' circulated. These had an undoubted influence on diagnoses of satanic abuse.

Some of the written material circulating offered assistance in diagnosing cases in which satanic abuse has occurred. Many generalised references to the features of ritual abuse are to be found, either in handouts prepared by organisations such as the Beacon Foundation or in accounts given at conferences or published in journals and books. These do not usually provide complete descriptions of the religious practices or beliefs that are said to form the context for the abuse of children. A partial exception is the pamphlet published by the Beacon Foundation, *The Rehabilitation of Satanic Cult Members* (The Beacon Foundation Rhyl 1991), which gives very brief sketches of various rituals, or the book *Satanism and the Occult* by an evangelical vicar, Kevin Logan. A much more extensive description has recently been published by Coleman (1994) but, like the others, it puts together a number of accounts without regard for differences between informants' stories, or for possible contradictions or incomplete accounts. Coleman differs from all others in describing the organisation and leadership of the satanist cults she refers to, but it seems likely that much of the information on those points reflects her interest and derives from a particular case. No children in the cases I studied gave information that was comparable, with the exception of one case, in which she was involved.

Lists of indicators

Lists of 'indicators' are regularly provided by specialists working in the field to assist in diagnosis. The material prepared for inquisitors and judges during the witch-hunts had the same function: to provide a diagnostic yardstick for new cases. Lists tend to have a powerful confirmatory effect because all items on them, even the common symptoms of emotional disturbance, appear to have equal weight, so that any set of them may confirm a diagnosis. Matching features of a case with indicators on the list of an 'expert' may be considered to legitimise classification of a case as one of satanic abuse. Given the variety and lack of specificity of many sets of indicators, it is easy to match cases with them or to interview children to provide confirmation; and thus form a powerful instrument for spreading belief in satanic abuse by identifying 'new' cases.

Most of the lists that circulate in England and Wales derive, ultimately, from lists constructed in the United States. For example, at a Reachout conference in 1990 run by Maureen Davies it was possible to obtain a 1986 list by a Californian psychologist, Catherine Gould; at the BASPCAN conference in 1991 Maureen Davies was offering a 1986 list from a project in Ohio as well as the document published by her newly founded organisation, the Beacon Foundation, which drew on the Gould list.

The assumption underlying the use of lists is that they summarise case-history experience; the paper from a children's charity discussed below explicitly states this, implying also that all the features were endorsed by the charity's experience. They do not explain the dynamics of the abuse or how and why the trauma affects children; nor do lists explain why the items cluster. Lists are not arguments to explain satanic abuse, they are means of detecting it. The assumption that a list represents experience is never queried but even if it were, it would be difficult to discover the factual basis for any item on the list, or, by the time it has passed through a few hands, what cases the items came from. Its legitimacy is guaranteed by the status of the 'expert' whose list it is.

One list, which has been widely distributed, is unusual in that it describes the source of the information it is based on, which gives it an aura of scientific reliability (Hudson 1991; see also Tate 1991: 10, 348–56). In discussing the list, the author, Pamela Hudson[9] points out that: 'An experienced child therapist will observe that all but one of the symptom clusters can generally be found in any sexually assaulted child.' Some of the symptoms occur even more widely. However, she claims that it is the combination of these symptoms with the allegations which indicates the possibility of satanic abuse. So here the definition of satanic/ritual abuse that is implied is that it consists of sexual abuse together with allegations of satanic abuse, and this is the message that has been acted on.

'The exceptional symptom' that this expert argues is present 'in ritual abuse cases is the sudden eating disorder demonstrated by these children' (Hudson 1991: 7). This is a symptom and indicator of satanic abuse alone, because it derives from the children's being forced to eat the 'body parts' of babies. Tate argues (1991: 13) that this symptom was being displayed in Britain at the time at which Hudson wrote, although he does not make it clear where, and I have been unable to find one British case in which it occurred. It appears in no case in my study which covers that period and two of Hudson's own cases are marked negative on this point. The absence of this allegedly critically diagnostic feature in British cases would logically entail some doubt as to the validity of diagnosing satanic abuse in them, but Hudson herself has claimed that satanic abuse had taken place in a British case in which this symptom was not present. Two implications of her work that appear more widely in the cases studied are that behavioural symptoms can be indicators of satanic abuse, and that children in cases of sexual abuse who are more traumatised than usual have been abused in satanic rituals, whatever they say about it.

Many of the lists of features of satanic abuse that are circulated in Britain are not based on identifiable cases at all but on another list. Those who have a case which they consider to be satanic abuse may add more points (usually without identifying the new features) to it; sometimes some original features are left out. Andrew Boyd in his book *Blasphemous Rumours* lists the 'common threads' as 'rituals with chants, costumes, and the invocation of deities; the sexual abuse of children and/or adults; ritual sacrifice of foetuses, children and adults; cannibalism; control by hypnosis, fear, blackmail, drugs and by forcing the abused to become an abuser; the production of pornography, including videos and snuff movies; prostitution; a high degree of organisation and funding; a cult membership which includes respectable and influential people, and international connections' (Boyd 1991: 54).

Boyd is a journalist, not a social worker or therapist, but his list of features is presented as a summary of a list in a document put out by some workers for a children's charity that he had described earlier (1991: 29). This document, shown below, has been withdrawn by the organisation concerned, but has been very influential and copies were still circulating during my study. It appeared, very slightly altered, together with Pamela Hudson's list in the workbooks of courses in child protection held in Liverpool at the university and the former polytechnic. A comparison with the original list shows that Boyd has added some items to his list: the invocation of deities, control by hypnosis and snuff movies. He has omitted some others such as the involvement of very young children and new-born babies, the use of farms and cellars, the involvement of women and the use of alcohol. On what basis these alterations have been made is not indicated.

The charity's discussion document itself is described as based on one published in a newsletter produced by a psychiatrist that circulated briefly in East Anglia, 'with embellishment from the experience of . . . workers in the NorthWest and workers from other parts of the country.' It gives no clue as to the numbers of adults and/or children whose cases formed the basis for their contribution to the list. The list from which the charity's list derives has fewer items; eleven 'characteristics of ritual abuse cases' are given while others are included in a preliminary description of witchcraft and satanism that conflates modern Wicca, modern satanism and the allegation made by anti-satanists. Parts of this account seem to have been turned into items on the charity's list and also into items on the one compiled by the Merseyside Training

Discussion document, dated 16 June 89

The characteristics of ritualistic abuse:

a. The involvement of very young children and very young new-born babies.
b. Large number of perpetrators including women.
c. Children being transported to special places where the abuse takes place. It has been reported that farms are used, cellars and outdoor venues. Some survivors make reference to large houses in their own grounds.
d. The use of threats to control and intimidate children. This includes threats of death and demonstrations of what appears to be magic and death to the children.
e. The occurrence of pornography and the use of drugs and alcohol as part of the abuse.
f. Very high levels of sexual abuse. This includes violence towards children and children are often scarred as a result of the abuse. The levels of sexual abuse are often unbelievable to professionals dealing with it.
g. High level of physical abuse both to intimidate the victims and as part of the abuse. Victims report they are penetrated by objects and they are subjected to bizarre forms of cruelty and mutilation.
h. There are descriptions of animals being involved in the sexual abuse and there are descriptions of animals being ritualistically killed. Survivors report animals are killed and their blood is passed to members of the network (coven) to drink.
i. Survivors report witnessing children and babies being sacrificed (murdered) or mutilated.
j. Survivors also talk of witnessing and participating in eating the flesh i.e. cannibalism, of infants and young babies. They report eating certain parts of the child's body and internal organs. They also talk about being made to drink the child's blood.
k. There are reports of children being sacrificed and women, often the child's mother's body, being used as a sacrificial altar.
l. Children talk of being tied up and being locked in cupboards and being trapped in boxes, cages, spaceships (sic, but in the Merseyside version spaceships are replaced by wheeled dustbins – wheelie bins).
m. Children and adults who have been involved in such networks talk of being scared of the power of the network.
n. Survivors, particularly children, talk of being scared of water and afraid of going to the lavatory.
o. Survivors talk of the smearing of bodies with blood or faeces and being made to drink blood and urine and often eat faeces. It is felt that this is often linked to the fear of using the lavatories by children.
p. Survivors talk of adults wearing strange costumes and masks. They provide descriptions of magic circles and pentagrams and candles and symbols being present in special ceremonies.[10]

Partnership. Other features appearing in the discussion section of the document, but which are not identified by a letter, are included in the derived versions of this list as though they were included in the original listed characteristics.

The influence of 'experts' from the United States is obvious in all versions of the lists that have just been discussed. These lists are taken at face value without any indication of the source of their information. If a new case shows different elements, the discrepancy is not taken as indicating a different type of case or a negative instance. The new element is merely added to the list of typical features, despite the fact that, by definition, it is not characteristic of the other cases on which the list is based. By the time the list has been through several of these transformations, the relation between the features listed and any documented facts is extraordinarily tenuous.

One set of files read for a case study, in which there was a copy of the charity's discussion document, gave some indication of the way the lists might be used. The list was annotated by one of the practitioners dealing with the children in the case. Elements that showed any resemblance to items on the list were written in with a tick; any item on the list that had not been manifest in the case was marked 'not yet demonstrated' (my emphasis). Some of the positive identifications of features were very strained from my reading of the case. The list was then altered slightly, which had the effect of making it a better fit with the current case, before being passed on to colleagues as evidence supporting the diagnosis of their own case as one of ritual abuse. A new list had been born.

Whatever is included in any particular list, and they do vary from one to another, it is asserted that 'There's an uncanny similarity. There are so many threads going through the cases which are the same thing . . .' (Core cited in Boyd 1991: 54). The similarity of cases from different parts of the country and from one country to another is said to show a widespread network of satanists. In Tate's words, '. . . the same points crop up in almost every known British or European case of ritual abuse' (Tate 1992: 10). The same argument was being put in during the witch-hunts, to be dismissed by Charles Mackay in 1841 in his book entitled *Extraordinary Popular Delusions and the Madness of Crowds* (1841: 481). Unlike Mackay, I am not arguing that in these cases torture has produced similar answers, but that, as he also pointed out, the definitive features were known beforehand and so the right answers could be produced. The lists were not used in all cases and the match in many cases is far from exact. While it is not inaccurate to say that the allegations may show some common features, their mutual resemblances are much less striking than is claimed, as we have seen.

In order to protect belief from being undermined by contrary evidence, it may be further elaborated by using other issues as 'corroboration'. Using the term 'organised abuse' for cases in which there were allegations of satanic abuse and those involving paedophile networks, allowed some believers to claim that the successful prosecutions of paedophiles proved the existence of 'organised abuse', implying the other sense of the term. The public concern over Freemasonry in the police forces and some well-publicised cases of corruption are used to support the idea of satanic influence in high places. This conspiracy to protect satanists explains why there is no evidence, leaving the original belief intact. Other crimes, such as particularly brutal or serial killings, can be associated with satanism: there were attempts to make the serial murders committed by Fred West into satanic killings.[11] The reasoning is identical with that recorded by anthropologists studying witchcraft, where secondary rationalisations of this sort protect the validity of the general belief in witches. Neighbours of mine in Uganda where I did research often urged me to look for evidence of witches when I visited strange villages. My failure to find any was taken as my fault: I had looked in the wrong place, at the wrong time or in the wrong village. It was never taken as casting doubt on the possibility of such evidence existing, particularly in distant villages of strangers.

To begin with, allegations of satanic abuse were said to have been made by children and were claimed as the incontrovertible truth. It had already been shown in the 1980s that children do tell the truth about being sexually abused, although the problems of obtaining that truth, especially when children are very young, were often overlooked.[12] A slogan among believers in satanic abuse is, 'We believe the children', and any scepticism about a particular case was treated as cruelly rejecting child victims who had already suffered the torments of satanism. However, as the various illustrations in this and the previous chapter have indicated, some younger children do not describe occasions when they have seen or suffered abuse during rituals. While their words may form the basis of allegations about ritual abuse, these words are not sufficient in themselves to serve as descriptions of anything. A good deal of interpretation by adults, who may be foster-parents, care-workers, police, social workers, interviewers or therapists, is necessary in order to transform them into disclosures of satanic abuse. This process is the focus of the next chapter.

7   Children's stories

The idea of satanic abuse, like that of witchcraft, provides a multi-faceted explanation for words and actions that seem unintelligible in normal terms. As the last chapter showed, it can account for the extreme state of damaged children, their odd behaviour and apparently meaningless remarks, providing an explanation of the emotional and psychological damage they seem to have suffered. It is also, as Evans-Pritchard has written of the Azande, 'a response to situations of failure' and the last chapter has also shown how these cases are extremely difficult ones where ordinary explanations seem inadequate. Explicit concerns about the difficulties, stress and local conflicts generate and exacerbate professional fears. The idea that a case involves satanic abuse may increase these fears but it also accounts for the inexplicably extreme damage suffered by many of these children and the failure of other explanations or forms of relief. Lists of indicators offer the consolation that the situation is not unique, since for the lists to be made, other cases must exist. The inclusion of some very common symptoms of disturbance ensures that the list seems immediately relevant. Also, the presentation of the idea of satanic abuse in this form, as a professional diagnosis, increases its acceptability among people who work in the field of child protection.

However, belief in satanic abuse, like beliefs in witchcraft or in the demonic origins of all evil, is not merely an idea shared by believers; it is also displayed in the identification of actual cases as examples, just as ideas about witchcraft shape accusations against witches. Cases and beliefs are mutually reinforcing: the cases 'prove' that the satanic abuse exists and the idea of satanic abuse explains the extreme nature of the cases. There are thus two dimensions to allegations of evil: on the one hand their explanatory, symbolic or rhetorical significance – their meanings, which are shaped by being part of a common culture – and on the other, representations of what is actually happening which will initiate action, whether legal, governmental or administrative, for which the allegations are a means of canvassing support. In practice the sociopolitical and the cultural dimensions are aspects of a single social process; distinguishing them is simply a device to clarify their inter-relation. The last chapter was concerned with the use of the idea of satanic abuse as an explanation for difficult cases and with the circumstances in which this idea might seem attractive. This one will consider how, given that the idea of satanic abuse had become accepted, at least as a possibility, the identification of particular cases was made.

The cases that were believed to be examples of satanic abuse involved children as victims: it was they who were said to be telling adults of the satanic rituals in which they had been involved. There is some historical precedence for this. During the early modern witch-hunts, children made allegations of witchcraft and identified those who they claimed took part in witches' sabbaths. In Pendle in the seventeenth century a boy's allegations led to the convictions of seventeen people whom he named as witches, although he later confessed to having given false testimony and they were acquitted (Levack 1987: 191). One of the most famous cases in early modern Sweden involved a large number of children giving evidence (Levack 1987: 191; Sjoberg 1995). In other parts of Europe and in Salem, Massachusetts, children made accusations of witchcraft. The fact of children's identifying witches and giving evidence against them does not seem to have given their evidence a special status, although some authors imply otherwise (Robbins 1959; Brain 1970).

By contrast with the early modern period, the effect in the twentieth century of allegations of satanism in both Britain and America was immensely enhanced by the fact that it was children who were claimed to be the source of the information on satanic rituals. Indeed it could be said that it was only when satanism and witchcraft were linked to the abuse and torture of children that the religious campaign of fundamen-talist evangelicals acquired high public visibility. The autobiographical testimonies of survivors did not arouse widespread media interest until they were said to be confirming what 'the children said'. These effects indicate that the idea of children constitutes a powerful cultural symbol (see Boas 1966, especially pp. 42–45). The slogan mentioned in the last chapter, 'we believe the children', is a potent means of inducing belief in satanic abuse.

The meanings with which childhood has been invested have been discussed widely since Ariès claimed, in his book *Centuries of Childhood*, that the idea of childhood as a special state was not universal but an invention of early modern society.[1] His argument has not gone without criticism (for examples see Cunningham 1996; Pollock 1983), but it made the point that biological immaturity is not always understood in the same way but is given a social value that may vary at different times.

It may also vary in different places (see R. Stainton Rogers 1989 for a summary of the arguments). Anthropologists would agree that in most societies children are valued for the social and cultural continuity that is assured by their existence (Robertson 1991; Comaroff 1994: 14), but this value does not have the same meaning as in Western societies, where children represent the future in themselves.[2] In European societies of the nineteenth century, the concept of progress represented the future as an improved version of the present; this idea was consistent with the economic emphasis on saving and accumulation and with the social concern with self-improvement, education and upward mobility. Under these conditions, it is easy to accept that it is the children who will benefit from the efforts of their parents; the children represent a better future. In traditional societies the emphasis is different, although the idea of continuity may still be there. In many African societies, for example, the living represent a link between the past, represented by the dead, and the future, when today's adults will also be ancestors; the birth of children ensures that the ancestors, of whatever generation, will not cease to be venerated, that tradition will continue. Whether the cultural emphasis is placed on continuity with the past or on future progress, children are seen as vital to society and any attack on them is a threat to the whole community.

Ariès' work has also usefully reminded us of the changes in attitudes to children and in children's lives since the Industrial Revolution. The modern idea of childhood is bound up with the gradual establishment through the nineteenth century of universal and non-vocational education for children and its steady prolongation past the age of puberty. Since adulthood was earlier defined by marriage[3] and work, the postponement of both these by the demand for more and more training appears to have created separate worlds for adults and children. But this is more apparent than real, a cultural distinction between categories of people, not a description of the real world. Even though most children no longer work in family enterprises, in farm or workshop, they are rarely out of worlds in which adults are present; in households or 'families' or in schools, which are *the* institutions whose function is the care of children, the authority of adults is an essential feature.[4] Children are participants in social life from birth (La Fontaine 1986). Their worlds are ones in which they are subordinate; the physical strength of adults, their superior social skills and greater knowledge make adults more powerful generally and society endows some adults with the right to exercise authority over particular children.

Children are seen in Western societies as adults-in-the-making, the raw material out of which fully social adults would be shaped.[5] It was as examples of human nature that children became the focus of scholarly attention after the Enlightenment (Jordanova 1989). The Englishman Hobbes had described human nature as self-seeking and aggressively competitive, only restrained by the controls exercised by social and, in particular, governmental institutions. In this he may have been reflecting the view, common in the England of the sixteenth and seventeenth centuries, that children needed regular beatings to subdue the inherent sinfulness of their human nature and ensure that the moral lessons given them by adults were remembered. His view was consistent with the Christian Church's doctrine of original sin, although Hobbes' solutions were political. By contrast, his near contemporary, the Frenchman Rousseau, argued that children were essentially innocent and 'good'; to him, the conflict and competitive selfishness in the adult world derived from particular social arrangements within which the child would inevitably become corrupted. The consensus among social scientists seems to be that the modern view of the child owes most to Rousseau (Jenks 1994: 114), but it is clear that the more pessimistic view of human nature has not disappeared. One retrospective view of the role of children in the witch-hunts sees them as malicious. Robbins' *Encyclopaedia of Witchcraft and Demonology* records: 'During the centuries of witch hunting, hundreds of people were sent to their death (sic) because of the wanton mischief of undisciplined youngsters. England was especially afflicted with such little monsters, and American children copied their antics' (1959: 94, cited in Spencer & Flin 1993: 309 [1990]).[6] Children who commit serious crimes such as murder are very easily seen as evil by nature, and the notion that they can never be anything other than evil lies behind the insistence that they should be locked up for ever. The willingness to attribute to children the propensity to lie to get adults into trouble, which is a weaker version of the negative view of childhood, is sufficiently common for the authors of a standard textbook to need to refute it (Spencer & Flin 1992: 318–33 [1990]). It must surely be the legacy of a Hobbesian view. However, the contrary assertion that children do not lie, which reflects a much more Rousseauesque tradition of thought, is certainly more general now; it has been powerfully instrumental in convincing people that satanic abuse is a real danger.

In contemporary non-Western societies children feature very little in cases of witchcraft, although their illnesses and deaths are often seen as caused by witchcraft and may trigger accusations. Children were also victims in Tudor and Stuart Essex but, as Macfarlane points out, attacks on children were seen as injuring their parents (1970: 162–3) as they are in modern societies. During the witch-hunts children were accused of being witches in England (Macfarlane 1970), in Germany (Walinski-Kiehl 1996) and in north-west Spain (Henningsen 1980). By contrast in non-Western societies children are very rarely believed to be capable of witchcraft. In Bugisu, Uganda, it was considered that children had too little personal force to cause harm by witchcraft (La Fontaine 1963: 202), and similar views are very general. The Bangwa of Cameroon are unusual in that they do believe that children may be witches. Even their own illnesses may be attributed to their witchcraft. Since the proper ritual and herbal remedies depend on the details of what the witch did, Bangwa children are pressured to confess. As we shall see later in the chapter, there are instructive similarities with some cases of satanic abuse.

In *The Cult of Childhood* (1990 [1966]) Boas charted the growth of the symbolic value of childhood and linked it, through a connection with the development of primitivism in various cultural fields, to the growth of anti-rationalism in recent European history. There is no doubt that, in the West, children have become the focus of adult attention in an unprecedented fashion. The interest in children has been tacitly recognised in the use of photographs of children in all forms of advertising for charitable and commercial purposes.[7] The media have used children to draw attention to their stories. Wars, famines and natural catastrophes are given popular significance by the deaths and suffering of powerless children caught up in them. The reporting of these events did not create the image of innocence and helplessness that was evoked by children and which contrasted with the evil of cruel adults, but it underlined the ideas and brought them constantly to people's attention. The image of the child in Western society is, in the words of Jean Comaroff, '*the* plausible innocent in whose name moral claims can be made' (Comaroff 1994: 14; original emphasis).

If the image of innocent children has not been much altered by the late twentieth century, the idea of parental love as based in human nature has been shaken. At intervals from the late nineteenth century onwards,[8] the publicity given in the United States and Britain to the death and injury of children at the hands of their parents has given a strong warning about the unreliability of parental instincts as a protection for children. However, the idea that parental feelings for their children were 'natural' made such warnings difficult to compre-hend, and people found it incredible that human parents would kill or injure their own children. As one of the social workers in an early, much-publicised, case in this study put it: 'It was . . . difficult to believe how evil people could be' (Dawson 1990). Notions that such people were evil, subhuman monsters unlike other people, were common.

These were judgements rather than explanations of the acts (Pocock 1986 [1985]; La Fontaine 1990: 1992), but the idea that they were the followers of Satan did provide a way of accounting for such dreadful parental failures.

Incest and the sexual abuse of children were events that made it clear that while children might be valued by society as symbols, real children were vulnerable to more powerful adults, whether in the guise of perverted strangers or at home (La Fontaine 1990). Children have become the archetypal victims of evil. Published accounts of their childhood by adults confirmed what the children were saying, and the fact of this mutual confirmation was to be brought up again and again in supporting the belief in satanic abuse. Adult autobiographies and children's accounts of being sexually abused also revealed that adults often did not wish to listen to children when they tried to get help. The public were gradually educated to accept that children who disclosed that they had been sexually abused were not lying or trying to get adults into trouble; they found it painful to reveal what had happened, would only do so piece-meal and were prone to retract their accounts under threat or for fear of what might follow. It became accepted without question that the first step in endowing children with the confidence to tell the full story was to believe what they said. Further, it was emphasised that if adults did not believe children they were denying help to innocent victims and revealing their own inability to accept the horror of what had happened. The slogan 'we believe the children' condensed all these ideas into a single potent message (cf. Best 1991: 95 et seq.; Jenkins 1992: 147).

The first article written by Judith Dawson (in the *New Statesman and Society* of 5 October 1990) about the allegations of satanic abuse in Nottingham is an early example of the rhetorical use of the image of innocent children. She refers to 'very young,[9] traumatised children . . . ' 'born into a world where good had to be destroyed, innocence perverted'. This introduces both the notion of very vulnerable victims and also the religious notion that such evil acts must represent a reversal of all that is good. Bea Campbell's article in the same issue of the magazine makes the image more violent. She writes of children whose 'struggle to survive torture (which) has been nothing less than heroic' and of women 'who at first, didn't know what these children were talking about', but now that they do: 'Together they are showing us something terrible about the oppression of children . . . '[10]

At this point we are dealing with what is claimed to be an actual case of satanic abuse. It is a step removed from the general condemnation of occultism in the evangelical campaign and it appears to be based on the words of real children. In fact, as this chapter will show, the public presentation of such cases may be as much removed from the actual words of the children as from the more general allegations of international satanic conspiracies. The aim of this chapter is to show how the unspecific allegations, that satanists were sexually abusing children in rituals that included murder, cannibalism and torture, with which the epidemic began, became translated into what purported to be evidence given by children that such things had indeed happened to them. It is also an account of how adults invested the words and actions of children with significance, in order to bridge the conceptual gap between the acceptance of satanic abuse as a general threat and the identification of particular cases as involving satanic abuse.

Children's evidence

As a result of the prosecution of cases of the abuse of children, children are increasingly called as witnesses in criminal trials; there has been considerable debate about their reliability (Ceci & Bruck 1993; Spencer & Flin 1993: 285–337 [1990]; Gudjonsson 1993: 94–5). The research done on the question seems to result in the not very surprising recognition that children, like adults, vary in their capacity to give an account of events they witnessed, but that age is an important additional variable affecting the nature and reliability of children's testimony. Distinctions of age are important in considering children as sources of allegations about satanic abuse. In the cases being considered here, small children usually offer only fragments or odd remarks which are understood by adults to refer to their experiences, but require interpretation. Older children understand much more of what is expected of them and the situation is very different. Where older children are developmentally delayed or have learning difficulties they must be considered with the younger ones, but in general the allegations in cases involving older and younger children differ markedly in one important respect: the degree of adult interpretation required. The basis of the allegations is thus very different according to the age of the children involved. This chapter is concerned with young children; the next will consider the adolescents.

That quite young children can give good evidence about their sexual abuse even in cases where the perpetrator has claimed magical powers, is shown by what happened in one of the substantiated cases. In this case, the perpetrator of the abuse confessed and gave a long account of the history of his entrapment of more than a dozen children, the youngest of whom was six years old and only one of whom was over eleven. The accounts of the children when interviewed by the police corroborated each other exactly and matched the perpetrator's account. They were also given very soon after the perpetrator was arrested; despite some initial reluctance on the part of one child who was fond of him, the children told their stories to the interviewers at the first interview. The main differences between his account of what happened and theirs are that his is longer, more detailed and embellished with a number of demonstrable lies and some special pleading; it also gives considerable insight into how he constructed the bogus 'magic' that the children thought he was teaching them. The difference between their evidence and what is presented as children's evidence in cases where satanic abuse was alleged is considerable: these children gave a coherent description of events where they took place, when, and in what context, while the others could not provide anything sufficiently coherent to be called a description of events, until after a period of time during which they were formally interviewed, either therapeutically or for information. Equally important during this period was the questioning, direct or indirect, that reflected the anguished curiosity of foster-parents and the effect of foster-parents' views.

My argument in this chapter, then, will *not* be that children are unreliable witnesses or that they lie with or without malice, but that in the *majority* of these cases the stories that are said to be those of the children are not what they are claimed to be. They are adult constructions. The extracts cited in the last chapter give some impression of the kind of odd remarks that some of these children made; given that many adults involved in these cases were already profoundly convinced of the threat of satanic abuse by what they had heard, read and seen on television, these remarks sufficed to arouse their suspicions. Once the explanation of satanic abuse has been accepted, then the behaviour and sayings of children that provoked the search for explanation in the first place can serve as evidence for it. The case material affords a picture of how the adults involved constructed their understandings of a case as one of satanic abuse, using what they knew, read, or were told of satanism in general and satanic abuse in particular.

The designation of a specific case as one of satanic abuse is not the simple result of belief in the existence of such enormities but a social process, entailing discussion and negotiation among the people concerned with it. A number of different professionals may be involved in cases of child protection: foster-parents, social workers, police, psychiatrists and the staff of child protection charities. The children's sayings and behaviour are fed into the discussion as evidence for particular conclusions. The views of 'experts', or colleagues thought to be more experienced, carry particular weight in this situation and influence the outcome. The effect of the various influences on both adults and children may go unrecognised. A range of different influences on children have been shown to operate in cases where the allegations of satanic or ritual abuse were considered by the psychiatrist to be unreliable (Weir and Wheatcroft 1995, Appendix: 500–5).

Influences on the children

In many societies adults expect to conceal the truth on occasion and their children observe and learn when to do so too (Barnes 1994: 108–111). In some societies only kinsmen have the right to be told the truth, so that questions from anyone else are invariably answered with lies and equivocations. It was pointed out to me in more than one interview that placating and misleading social workers and other officials was normal behaviour in the households from which most of their clients came. In this context, and given their likely misapprehensions about why they have been taken from home, it would be surprising if one were able to rely on what the children said in answer to questions (cf. Vizard & Tranter 1988: 89). However, as the last chapter indicated, the allegations attributed to children were often derived from reports by their foster-mothers.

This reporting may be inaccurate. One reason is that the children were hard to understand. Many of them were young, their speech might be underdeveloped for their age or they might be struggling with emotional and intellectual handicaps. There were class differences in vocabulary between social workers and children or foster-parents and children. Under these circumstances it is not surprising that what the children said might be misheard. It is not easy to find an example that shows that a child has not been heard correctly, because usually the people who listen to a child are the people who write down what is heard. However, there is some evidence. Informal conversations with children have been taped and the transcriber is not usually the adult on the tape. The transcript of one tape made by a foster-mother shows the little boy saying 'I'se big lad now', but his foster-mother responds, 'Oh, you're glad you're here are you?'. She had heard it as 'I'se be glad'. In another case there was a disagreement between two psychiatrists over whether a child had said 'ghost' or 'goat' in a therapeutic interview that was being assessed.[11] Misunderstandings may add to the impression given by the children that they are 'bizarre' and so confirm suspicions of satanic abuse.

Foster-mothers who are stressed or anxious that the children have been exposed to satanism are prone to focus on and interpret behaviour narrowly. For example, one child was believed to have attempted to sacrifice the family dog, an act which was then widely cited as the child's demonstrating what he had observed in a satanic ritual. Much later, when I was interviewing the diary writer, she described the full context of the incident: there were two family dogs, both female, one of which had recently been spayed. The child had marked the stomach of the other dog, which was lying on its back, with a line like the scar on its companion and was found holding a knife. She did not dispute my suggestion that the act might actually have been completed when she came upon the scene and that it represented an imitation of the veterinary operation rather than a ritual of sacrifice.

It is frequently said that children in a case know more about ritual or satanic abuse than they could possibly have known unless they had actually seen what they were describing. Apart from the objection that in many cases the children's remarks did not amount to a description of anything, this statement indicates a certain blindness to the children's social environment and naiveté about their awareness of it. As Brain notes for the Bangwa, children have 'plenty of opportunity' to absorb material that can be used to build a confession or a disclosure (1970: 171). In Britain pictures and information about witches and devils are to be found everywhere; together with ghosts and vampires, they are part of the general folk-lore that children absorb from their elders and peers (Weir & Wheatcroft 1995: 498). A wide variety of superstitions have been recorded by research among adults (Jahoda 1970: 17–26 [1969]); the interest in astrology that was also noted at the time has become very widespread. Among the people who figured in these cases were several families with beliefs in ghosts and spirits so that such ideas in the children were hardly to be wondered at. The warning videos prepared by Christian evangelicals promote the Christian view of satanism and the witches' sabbath with terrifying images. Dreams and nightmares can supplement the horror videos, and television supplies further ingredients.

A good deal of information on the source of some children's stories was to be found in the files. In one case a consultant psychiatrist traced many of them. In another, the fact that the mother of two girls in early adolescence had been talking in various churches about her participation in satanism for many years was completely ignored. The girls could not have failed to know a good deal about the subject as presented to fundamentalist Christians. In another case a small boy remarked that his friend at school had told him that 'you can bring the devil out of the ground'; despite his foster-mother's disagreement with this view, a fortnight later he referred to his stepfather trying to bring the devil out of the ground. One thirteen-year-old admitted to having got information from a news broadcast about another case. In yet another case a child claimed to have witnessed a murder that was being reported in the press and on television at the time.

Children also learn from one another. In one town the children involved in one large case of alleged satanic abuse were fostered in six foster-homes, in four of which children who were taken into care for reasons unconnected with the main case were also fostered. There were subsequent allegations of satanic abuse from all but one of the thirteen children fostered together with children in the main case. The only two children in eighty-four cases to have mentioned 'special singing lessons' both lived with the same foster-family.[12] A foster-mother, Mary Kelsall, has described in a published article listening to one of her foster-children explain the hierarchy of devils to another of them (Kelsall 1994: 98). Transcripts of tapes indicate foster-mothers questioning all the children together or talking to one child in the presence of others. These additional cases were seen as 'proof' of what children said, but are better understood as indications of how children can learn from each other what adults are expecting to hear from them.

As has been noted already, much of what was made public as what children had said comes from selective records. The published versions cited earlier are not first-hand accounts but rely on what foster-mothers said of their children or noted in their diaries. The effect of the mutual contamination of children's stories and of the way in which foster-mothers might obtain 'information', is particularly well illustrated in the following extract from a foster-mother's diary. (It is from a different case from the one mentioned above; names have been deleted but punctuation is as given):

14.5.89   (Report of previous evening) I felt he wanted to tell me something so I asked him about the time the man was stabbed in the kitchen I asked him if anyone else was killed and put in a box; he said 'I've got to ask (his sister), she'll remember.' I said, 'Why don't you tell me, he said I've got to ask (his sister).' So he did, she said Yes. Both said 'No' to ladies and 'Yes' to children killed.

8.6.89   After he had seen his social worker he came home and said he had got to find the key to open up his mind and remember all the things that happened. I asked him if he would like his sister and his brother to help him to remember? She was great, told him what C. did. He remembers being spanked on bare bott (sic) by C. She told him more but he said: It's locked in my head and I can't remember. Did not remember being peed on.

13.6.89   He was determined to 'talk'. 'I (foster-mo) had got to say it all out and if I went wrong then he would tell me. His sister joined in and added urine in cup; he. said 'I didn't drink it'. She seemed as if there was no holding her. Masks covered whole head and dracula teeth painted with zigzag blood on the teeth. C. had only half an ear on one side and a whole ear on the other.

I asked if they had to drink anything. She said 'C.'s wee' her brother added 'and perhaps blood'. I asked her; she said they all drank blood – didn't know where from – in cup. I asked if they had to eat anything, they said No.

It is not surprising that these two children and their brother, who does not figure in this particular passage, gave a shared account of what they said happened or, as it was put in the case file, that they corroborated each other's accounts.

Influences on adults

Attempts to get children to talk about what had happened to them had two ostensible purposes. First, the need to identify the perpetrators and obtain evidence to prosecute them was traditionally the role of the police; evidence was also required for other legal purposes: to obtain the different orders needed to place a child in care and under the protection of the state. The other aim was to help the child recover and lead a more normal life, this being the original restorative role of social workers and foster-parents. These aims were less clearly separated in practice, however. There was often considerable confusion about the purposes of the many interviews that children were subjected to. While in principle the police and social workers have different roles to play in the process of protecting a child, in practice this division of labour is difficult to maintain. Social workers and foster-parents might be very actively engaged in trying to get information; it was not always clear whether they were trying to help the police in doing this or were pursuing other aims, such as finding 'proof' of satanic abuse.

There were other, less clearly recognised, intentions: the desire to know more of what the child has witnessed, whether displayed by child protection workers, foster-mothers or therapists, is a common feature of these cases. The files revealed a great concern to obtain further information from the children, who might be questioned about details gleaned from other cases in order to see if they were similar. The interviewers in some cases drove the children round to see places that had been mentioned and reacted strongly to each new revelation. One foster-mother even went as far as to hide a tape-recorder in her jacket when she took the child for a walk, hoping to use the occasion to encourage a disclosure. Foster-parents and social workers told me openly that they became very anxious to know exactly what had happened. The children offered the only means of satisfying their curiosity and the proliferation of interviews seems, in some cases, to have reflected these adults' needs. The children were under observation and subject to informal questioning or pressure to tell for long periods of time.

The other most important expressed motive for adults to try and obtain information from the children was probably the view that 'telling' was the first step a child would take on the road to a normal life. The view that talking about their experiences is therapeutic is widely held among those dealing with the sexual abuse of children and is passed on to foster-mothers. The foster-mother of one nine-year-old recorded in her diary:

> 31.6.89   'I felt that G. needed to talk tonight as the last few nights have been really restless for him. Sleep walking and he seems really frightened.'

While child protection experts may refer to the therapeutic relief gained by children when they have spoken about having been sexually abused (Vizard & Tranter 1988: 121), the adults I am referring to are not trained nor are they clinicians; the view they express is the common-sense one which refers to all that is noxious, whether substances that have been eaten, feelings that have not been expressed, or experiences that have not been described. These are all summed up in the folk dictum: 'better out than in'. Moreover the belief that in these cases the children had been 'programmed' not to tell what had happened, reinforced the view that the children should be made to disclose it. Getting the children to talk was in effect a contest with the satanists who did not want them to. Interviewers were prepared to brook no denials in order, as they saw it, to release victims from the power of the cult. Refusal to answer questions or denials that anything had gone wrong were seen on occasion as the evidence for abuse by satanists, and in one big case a long list of words that might have been triggers to ensure the children's silence, was constructed after the interviews. The words came from questions that had been asked, but had received no answers from the children.

As long as foster-mothers and social workers shared in the general view that 'telling' was the first step in healing from the trauma of satanic abuse, the children were under pressure to tell. Like the Bangwa remedies for witchcraft that required a confession, disclosures were held to be therapeutic. This adult view seemed to have been communicated to at least some of the children. One child, who had been able to tell his social worker very little to support the general view of the case, was recorded as coming back from a visit to his social worker and saying that he 'must' remember what had happened. After one interview, the foster-mother was recorded as saying to the six-year-old:

'Why are we all happy now?'
She answers: 'Because I've told you.'

Research has shown that children are susceptible to pressure from adults, particularly those whom they see as representing authority (Moston 1990a; Spencer & Flin 1993: 305–6 [1990]; Gudjonsson 1993: 95). Questioning, particularly questioning that is repeated (Moston 1987) or takes place in repeated interviews (Ceci 1987) may cause them to doubt their memories of whether or not something took place or the details of what happened. Bangwa child-witches told Brain of a number of reasons why they confessed: some wished to please their parents and others 'to escape the pestering of elders who loom around the sick-bed' (Brain 1970: 169). Others knew that a confession was necessary to provide a cure to the illness or else they wanted the ritual meals which included meat or chicken. Still others, Brain remarks, 'seem to enjoy confessing horrible details'; he refers to them as exhibitionists playing the system (1970: 170). Similar motives can be inferred in some of the case histories of English children. Unlike Bangwa children though, the children in these cases were not always clear about what they were expected to say; however, they seemed to know that something was expected of them. As one slightly older girl, who retracted her first account, answered when asked why she had told the original, untrue, story:

You lot are into those things and the police and social workers wanted to hear them so *I thought I had to say something and I went from there.* (My emphasis)

This passage clearly illustrates both the child's awareness of the motives of the adults and the pressure she felt to comply.

Adult/child relations as a source of accounts

In many cases after a period of time and under pressure from adults, whether formal or informal, a child develops an account which is more extensive, in that it describes an occasion, and more detailed, in that it may include descriptions of people and places. Apart from the child's parents and relatives the people are never identified and if buildings are identified as locations their interiors or other features are not as described. The descriptions in the cases are very varied and differ from the witches' sabbath of folklore or the devil worship of modern Christian fundamentalists. They may refer to abusing parents and other relatives, to unusual sexual practices or to the deaths of babies and pets. Some descriptions seem to reflect adult ideas.

A small number of cases[13] shows how children can be induced to construct fictional evidence along lines indicated by an adult. In these cases satanic abuse allegations occurred as part of a custody dispute between a separated husband and wife (Jones & McGraw 1987), or were made by the mother against her own father. In one extreme case the child appeared to participate completely in her mother's view of the world and was treated more like a sister than a child. The child's lack of autonomy was so complete that her aunt found, when she took her into her own household later, that she expected to be accompanied to have a shower or to use the lavatory, although she was then about eleven years old. In two less extreme cases the mother's obsession with inducing her children to tell the story she wanted resulted in elaborate procedures. The children were 'interviewed' frequently and with great intensity over long periods until an appropriate story was produced; this was then reported to the child protection agencies as the child's 'disclosure'. In the first case, the mother hid a tape-recorder under the child's bed and talked to her at bedtime, encouraging her to talk about what happened when she visited her father. The transcript of the tapes gives the impression that this child saw the questions her mother asked her as a game. In the other case it was not so and the two children did on occasion say that they did not like doing this or that what they were being asked to say was not true. They were not allowed to persist in their resistance, however; threats and bribes, such as saying that the children could have tea when they had done some more 'work', were used to stop it.

These cases demonstrate without doubt that children can be put under pressure until they invent stories that support the allegations of adults and reflect their beliefs. The children involved were all young: the only one who was more than six years old was only just ten when the case was first reported. The cases show the methods used by the women to coach their children: the most obvious was to show anger at the 'wrong' answer and pleasure when the child produced what was wanted. Both mothers who 'interviewed' their children indicated what was expected by repeating what they accepted of what the child had said earlier and ignoring anything else. One of them also switched the tape-recorder off from time to time; by the nature of the dialogue when recording was resumed, one could only conclude that the answers to questions were rehearsed.

Children are uniquely vulnerable to pressure exerted by their mothers and the cases involving maternal coaching are distinctly unusual. However, the children in many of the other cases were in an abnormal situation: they had been removed from their normal homes and placed with strangers. It was not uncommon for the children to have more than one placement, occasionally as many as four in a year. They started going to completely different schools, which separated them from any friends they might have had and might even be separated from their siblings. Placating the new adults in their lives might well seem very important. The eagerness with which small children offer information is an indication that they are 'telling' to please, or to obtain the sympathy they have never had before and can now enjoy (Vizard & Tranter 1988: 123). It is not insignificant that some foster-mothers I interviewed said that the children always wanted to 'disclose' more of the satanic abuse at awkward moments when their foster mother was busy; in one case it happened frequently when she was bathing the younger children. The grandparents of one child remarked that if anyone was cross with him he complained that his stepfather had pulled his willy; there was evidence in the diary kept by his foster-mother that they were right. Certainly on one occasion when he was being scolded very sharply for abusing another foster-child, he desperately tried to deflect his foster-mother's anger by telling her how many people had abused him.

Foster-mothers or social workers may use similar techniques to those used by mothers in the cases of maternal influence to get children to tell their stories. One woman bought her foster-children a game involving spiders, which she thought would encourage them to talk about the horrors of ritual abuse (not surprisingly, their interviews did then include allegations about spiders); another taped discussions she held with several foster-children at once which made clear why their stories in interviews were remarkably similar. Several foster-mothers other than the one who was quoted above, indicated pleasure when children were prepared to 'talk'; some set aside a special time for a child to do so, which these neglected and abused children clearly valued and wished to encourage to continue. One of a pair of foster-mothers working with a severely neglected and abused child has published an account that shows how they had involved him in their fight against sceptics (Kelsall 1994). The article ends with a statement said to be from the child, reacting angrily to being told that there were people who did not believe him. The statement is in rather mixed language: part childish, part resembling a record in officialese. In this it resembles the written records of other foster-mothers.

Interviews

There has been a good deal of criticism of the interviewing of children in these cases (for Scotland see Clyde 1992: 254–64). At the period of this study much of the fault-finding seemed justified. The conviction that they were dealing with a case of satanic abuse encouraged interviewers to go beyond accepted guidelines in order to obtain information that they were convinced children might be brought to disclose. Repeated interviews, sometimes at short intervals and over many weeks were not uncommon. Leading questions, refusal to accept a child's denials, pressure by repeating questions and revealing information that other children have supplied are all to be found. In a few cases the interviewers have invented information they claim to have been given in order to pressure a child to speak. Children may be interviewed over and over again, as attempts are made to force them to release information and provide a coherent account.

The context of interviews also appears likely to have intimidated these children. Police officers and social workers embody the power of the state and even quite young children may know they are to be feared. One teenager thought that her young nephew might get into trouble if she did not back up what the interviewers told her he had said, so she corroborated his account. As Gudjonsson has pointed out: 'Children appear significantly more responsive than adults to expectations and instructions of people in authority' (Gudjonsson 1992: 95). Despite attempts to make interviews less frightening, they must often have been intimidating. In some cases a child was interviewed with as many as four adults present. The effects of repeated interviews were probably not recognised, since no mention was made of them in the minutes of case conference files.

To the extent that the children are not allowed to leave the room or the building where they have been taken for interview, they are under duress. In many transcripts of interviews, children are recorded as asking if they may leave or if the interview is over. Some children appear to try and resist the situation in various ways; a few react hysterically. Interviewers and therapists record difficulties in getting children to stay in the room in several cases. One child did nothing but cry and scream for her brother through two attempts to interview her; two boys in another case virtually wrecked the play therapy equipment in the room and one of them had to be restrained from climbing out of the window. In two other cases the child kept running out of the room. This evidence suggests that for some children the detention implicit in an interview is distressingly coercive. However, their behaviour may be interpreted as a refusal to talk out of fear, or as an indication that there are evil forces at work enforcing the child's silence. As has already been noted, one 'specialist' used the fact of a child's not answering questions as evidence that she had been ritually abused.

In other interviews, coercion and distress are not apparent: the children seem happy enough to be there and relaxed enough to talk. For some deprived children, the furnishings of an interview room may turn out to be the problem: more toys than they have ever had to play with before constitute a formidable distraction. In fact the interviewers may be driven to use permission to play as a reward for answering questions. The following exchange taken from my notes in one case shows some hard bargaining going on between foster-mother and child at the beginning of an interview carried out by a woman detective sergeant (FM is the foster-mother, FC her foster child):

FC 'I don't want to come again to talk about Bill.'
FM 'Well, when we've told Mary we don't have to speak about it again, do we? Then we can have a play.'
FC 'Just a play?'
FM 'But we've got to tell Mary first.'
FC 'You know while she's down there (talking of another child) can I play here on my own?'
FM 'After we've told Mary all about Bill.'

In yet another case a girl told her foster-mother that she wanted to go to her therapy sessions because she had been promised sweets. The inducement to conform to the expectations of the adults may consist of a carrot rather than a stick. Whichever it is, it is a potent factor affecting interviews and the 'information' they provide.

Unlike the substantiated case described to begin with, the interviewing of children in most satanic abuse cases is focused on certain children. The case-history material shows that when there are many child victims in one case, it is often only one or two of them who are critical for the allegations of satanic abuse. Some of the children taken into care in a case of alleged satanic abuse may have been named by another child and may themselves make no disclosures; this was the case with children taken into care in the 'dawn raids' in the Orkney Islands. As in that case, children who were prepared to 'tell' became key informants and were often interviewed more than the others. In the long interchange between a foster-mother and two children quoted above, the girl was clearly orchestrating the accounts of her brothers. In another case, one small boy appeared to relish his position as an informant and ended his interview by saying, 'Anything you want to know, just come to me.'

It was the sayings of these key children, whether reported by foster-parents or made in interviews, that were regularly quoted in support of the conclusion that this was a case of satanic abuse. Although fifteen children were taken into care in the Broxtowe case in Nottingham, accounts by journalists (e.g. Boyd 1991; Tate 1992; Campbell 1990b) and social workers (Dawson & Johnston 1989; Dawson 1990) mostly refer to the contributions of four children of whom one, a four-year-old boy, was easily the most often quoted. In one case in Rochdale the allegations were largely based on the interviews of a brother and sister, although twenty-one children had been taken into care. Other interviews in that case were attempts to explain and amplify what the two children had said, rather than to establish what each child said had happened.[14]

Distortions in the records

To be used in judicial proceedings children's evidence must be recorded and then processed in various ways. There are many types of distortions of what children have said that are introduced in the process of recording, summarising and transmitting the results of interviews. Misrecording may introduce errors and the communication of information may distort it. Affidavits prepared for court may change the sense of what has been said in summarising it. In large cases there may be so much material that it presents a problem of management, so that it is not surprising that there are errors. However, it should be noted that the errors tend to emphasise the bizarre and support the hypothesis of satanic abuse.

Interviews may be recorded but the transcripts may be faulty, and it is the latter that are used as a record. One consultant reviewing the tapes of interviews in a case remarked that she had not found one transcript that was accurate. Her list of errors included a child reported as saying 'yes' when (s)he said 'no', or vice-versa; when, in one instance 'it took considerable discussion to produce one name', the child was reported in the transcript as having produced a list of names; however, the 'list' was not a list of people involved in abuse but, as the child clearly said, a list of members of his family. This catalogue of errors was uniquely bad, but one or two of these mistakes can be found in every case; on occasion they distort the information quite seriously.

The repeated transmission of information between different people may considerably distort it. One little girl was asked by the woman police constable who was interviewing her: 'Where were you when it happened?' She answered 'In the shadow'. Asked to explain that, she said that they were 'in the trees', then indicating that she meant Christmas trees 'that are near our house but you have to walk'. Three weeks later at another interview she was told that she said that it had happened 'in the dark'. She attempted to correct this by saying that the shadows were in the trees, but to no avail. This incident was described by an expert as follows: 'The children described going to the woods at night' and was listed as a reason for considering that they had been involved in satanic abuse.

In endeavouring to manage large amounts of data or to reconcile the accounts of several children, changes may be introduced into them, wittingly or unwittingly. Itemising various features and listing them has already been identified as a technique which may seriously distort and it has this effect here. (As we have seen, lists of 'indicators' are common elements in the anti-satanist literature.) The procedure also highlights the selective way in which what children say is recorded. Items which do not figure in satanic abuse allegations are omitted from records. The early diary entries for children in one case contain many references to witches. As time went on witches were no longer listed. It was not clear whether witches were no longer mentioned by the children, or whether the absence of records related to the remark made by a social worker that at first it was thought the case involved witchcraft and only later was it realised that satanism was involved.

In one case lists of bizarre elements in the children's talk were created from the daily records of their foster-mothers. The aim was to show the amount of information and to compare one child with another. This introduced a further selection from what already was a selection of what the children said. The listing procedure cut words and phrases from the context in which they were used and in doing so removed much of their significance. The words appeared as though they were summaries or references to much more detailed accounts, particularly as the lists were referred to as 'lists of information'. In fact they were only words, taken out of what had been recorded of the children's remarks. Often several items come from the same short speech: for example, one-third of all the items listed under one girl's name for November 1987 came from one passage that consisted of five sentences. This read: 'When she (her cousin) is on about monsters (not noted on list), I can remember one. It was a *blow up shark*, kept in a cupboard. Dad used to frighten me with it. He also had some *pretend blood* and he'd put it on and *pretend* he was *dead*. It was scary.' By detaching these items from their context, they seem even more 'bizarre' than they are in context.

The lists, so far from indicating what was known, were thoroughly misleading. The failure to date the items in the list gives the impression that a good deal of information is offered, when in fact the records show that these remarks were made on only a few days. For example, January 1988 shows thirty-four items against this girl's name, giving the impression of a large amount of information. However, when they are traced to the daily records of her foster-mother, they are seen to occur on five days, 7, 15, 22, 24 and 29 January; on the first and last of these there is only one item recorded. On the first it has nothing to do with satanism: she reported that she was given a tablet to make her sleep. Her 'bizarre disclosures' refer mainly to three days in the month and one recorded remark on a fourth. On the 27 other days of January she apparently said nothing of relevance to the case. But the record does show her much more frequent accounts of serious sexual abuse amid bouts of drunkenness that were common to the adults of her extended family.

The contents of interviews may be summarised inaccurately for a case conference or an affidavit. This is particularly striking in another case where it was stated in an affidavit that a little boy had 'talked of ghosts' in an interview. Going to the transcript of the interview, I discovered that this phrase summarised an hour in which the interviewer had asked thirty-three questions on the subject of ghosts, to which the child had given some short, and apparently reluctant, answers. This was a particularly exaggerated example but similar patterns appeared in other interviews. The cases of maternal coaching, and others like them, show that children can learn what they are expected to say from what they are asked and from the reactions to their answers. It is only the trained interviewer who realises that questions convey information as well as attempting to elicit it, but most of the adults who tried to obtain information from children, whether informally or in formal interviews, showed no such sophistication in their approach. It is not surprising that when they were successful in persuading children to talk about what had happened to them, the results were stories that reflected what they expected or wanted to hear. These exchanges between adults and children are critical to understanding how the allegations came about; it was here that general beliefs in the prevalence of evil were transformed into the practical details of what particular children said and did. In the process the beliefs were greatly strengthened.

The image of very young children desperately trying to get adults to understand what they had suffered appeared frequently in the early accounts of satanic abuse. Little children, being generally seen as innocents, are likely to attract public sympathy, particularly if their stories are associated with the dogmatic and simplistic statement that 'children do not lie'. During the peak years of the epidemic, children were far more prominent in the writings and speeches of campaigners for the reality of satanic abuse than either the disturbed adolescents who were also involved or adults whose allegations at that point were merely said to 'confirm' or 'corroborate' what children said. By the end of 1994, after the collapse of several well-publicised child-protection cases involving allegations of satanic abuse, the publication of the Clyde Report on the Orkney case and my report to the Department of Health, all demonstrating the lack of evidence in cases involving children generally, children ceased to be the main centre of attention. Adult survivors' accounts were then claimed to 'explain' the children's stories and provide the main source of information about satanic rituals in which they were abused.

8   Confessions and tales of horror

Confessions have received little attention in anthropological studies of witchcraft (Douglas 1970: xxxiv), but, in the little that we know about epidemic witch-hunting in Africa, it is reported that during the cleansing rituals or the magic seeking-out of witches, men and women of the village concerned might confess to having performed witchcraft (Willis 1970: 130). Historians have had to concern themselves more with confessions, since they formed a major part of the evidence in the witch trials. It was a puzzling feature of the early modern witch-hunts that some of the accused confessed quite freely to being witches, although by doing so they might well have been signing their own death warrants. Levack argues that a small minority of the accused witches probably did practise magic, for the existence of which there was independent evidence, but confessions were the only evidence for the existence of the collective worship of the devil and such confessions almost never arose until torture was applied (Levack 1987: 11–13.) An analysis of confessions in seventeenth-century Germany by Lyndal Roper shows them to have been a mixture of private feelings, folk beliefs and the effects of torture; the narratives describing the activities of witches and their worship of the devil were built up in a series of interchanges between investigator and accused (Roper 1994: 204–6).

Despite the existence of spontaneous confessions of pacts with the devil and even of devil worship during the period of the witch-hunts, there has been no evidence that such acts ever took place. Historians have speculated about the reasons for spontaneous confessions, canvassing the possibilities of senility, mental illness or drug-induced dreams. Levack remarks that 'We also know too much today about people who confess to crimes they did not commit – and even to crimes that no one *could* commit – to dismiss the possibility that some of the individuals who made free confessions to diabolism were mythomaniacs' (Levack 1987: 15–16; original italics). His suggestion offers one interpretation of the allegations with which this chapter is concerned.

A similar view is offered in the analysis of more recent, African confessions. Meyer has described confessions of demonic involvement that appeared in the Ghanaian press and has pointed out their connection with popular pentecostalism there. She suggests that they are made by people who feel guilty about their desires for wealth and, by implication, resent the obligations to kin that seem to prevent them acquiring it. She also remarks: 'The fact that they (the confessors) say things about themselves which nobody would like to be accused of makes the confession very credible' (1995: 243). The importance of confessions, however, lies not merely in the intriguing problem of uncovering the motives for making them, but also in the way that they influence the beliefs and actions of those who hear them. The effect of one confession on the scholar Jean Bodin, as described by Trevor-Roper, has already been mentioned, but other men were moved to take action in other ways. The whole witch-hunt scare in north-western Spain in the early seventeenth century, which ultimately involved thousands of suspects, was started by the account of a young woman who had lived in France, where a witch-hunt under the leadership of Pierre de Lancre had just started. This had particularly affected the town where she lived and she claimed that she had for 18 months been a member of a coven. Worse, she said she had visited covens in Spain and she proceeded to name local witches. This provided the spark that set alight the witch-craze in that area (Henningsen 1980: 30–31).[1]

The position of older children and adults who claim to have been abused in childhood resembles that of these earlier witches in that they too tell stories of satanic rites. They may accuse themselves of having participated in killing babies and children as sacrifices and of taking part in acts of cannibalism afterwards. Some of the adult 'survivors' confess to continuing participation in the rituals; in one case the rites were said to have taken place shortly after the interview with the journalist in whose book her case is recounted (Boyd 1991: 325). However, there is one major difference in the position of these self-confessed witches or satanists that distinguishes them from those in the past, whether in Europe or more recently in Africa. The 'survivors' of satanic abuse have been treated as victims, no matter what crimes they confess to having committed.

The existence of older children involved in allegations of satanic abuse distinguishes the epidemic in England from that in the United States. In the United States there was a sharp contrast in age between the survivors and the child victims, who were mostly very young children.[2] In addition, in the United States the accused in the children's cases were mainly the owners of and workers in nursery schools, but the adult survivors accused their parents and relatives. The logical conclusion is that in the United States the satanists must have changed their tactics quite recently, turning from abusing their own children in the 1960s and 1970s (when the present adults were young), to abusing other people's children in nursery schools in the 1980s.

This discrepancy between the allegations associated with children and what adults say about their satanic abuse in childhood is absent in Britain, where in both types of case parents, and friends or neighbours of the parents, are the accused. So similar are the accounts of older children and adult survivors that in the absence of data on age, it was often very difficult to tell if a questionnaire returned for the survey related to a child or an adult. Sometimes the identity of the person hearing the first allegation is the only clue: adults do not have foster-mothers. Of course, the line that separates child from adult is not a great natural divide. Adulthood is a status decided by law, somewhat arbitrarily, as reached at eighteen, although girls reach sexual independence two years earlier. But there is no great difference between a seventeen-year-old and a nineteen-year-old. So it is not surprising that there is also similarity between the cases of teenagers alleging satanic abuse and those of the adults. In one article concerning survivors, the summary referred to five adults, although the text indicated that one of these was only fifteen years old (Coleman 1994b). Another article in the same book included a seventeen-year-old as one of three 'men' discussed. Alternatively, discussions of the material provided by survivors may refer to the survivor's story as though it were being told by the child she once was, in such a way as to leave it unclear whether the patient/client is still a child or not. Such examples show how the line dividing child victims from adult survivors may become blurred.

The significance of adult survivors has altered over the course of the epidemic. When my research began in 1992, it was being alleged that the key to the question of satanic abuse lay with the children (Tate 1991; Boyd 1991). Although Audrey Harper and other survivors had been addressing Christian groups for some years by then, there was relatively little publicity concerning other 'survivors'. In the United States, television and radio both publicised survivors to a far greater extent than has been the case in Britain. They appeared on the important chat-shows in the United States, such as those of Oprah Winfrey, Geraldo Reviera and Bob Larson (Victor 1991: 223). The effect of the publicity was to familiarise a large section of the American population with the most dramatic allegations. Lauren Stratford's book, *Satan's Underground*, has been claimed as the populariser of the idea that girls were chosen to bear children so that they could be sacrificed –

the so-called 'brood-mares'.[3] The newsletter of the evangelical Reachout Trust in Britain reported the unmasking of Stratford's book as a fake as soon as it happened in spring 1990, remarking that it was sad but that 'it does not mean to say that the sort of story she tells is untrue' (*Reachout News* 1991). Judging from the popularity of the idea of the brood-mare in the early stages of the British epidemic, Stratford's fiction continued to be accepted as fact.

In England adult survivors also helped to create the climate of belief in which the stories of children, including teenagers, could be told. However, in a different system of broadcasting with no religious channels, there was far less radio and television coverage than in the United States. Survivors had to rely on the old-fashioned means of publicity: speeches and published accounts. The 'survivor' Audrey Harper was giving lectures in various parts of England and Wales at least a year before the epidemic of cases involving children got under way. Her book records that after her baptism in March 1986, she began speaking in churches of her experiences until she was taken up by the Reachout Trust. Their first pamphlet, *Doorways to Danger*, published in 1987, included her story. This pamphlet (and a version made for video) was widely distributed; it was reprinted in 1994. The stories of others have also been published. Sue Hutchinson (*Independent on Sunday*, 12 August 1990), 'Jane' (*Observer*, 16 September 1990), and 'George' and 'Terry' (both in the *Independent*, 17 March 1990) are some of those whose stories appeared in national newspapers. Some unrealistic estimates of the numbers of adult survivors are also made. Twenty-nine people are listed by Boyd as having information collected first-hand from more than 834 victims, adults and children; 600 of them were allegedly reported by three people (Boyd 1991: 35–6).[4]

In our survey of allegations of the satanic abuse of children, twenty cases of survivors were also reported. These twenty cases resemble the published accounts (e.g. Boyd 1991; Coleman 1994), and have similarities with the cases of older children. Most of them concern young adults, who are younger than those reported in the United States (Jenkins & Maier-Katkin 1991: 127), half of those whose ages are known being in their twenties. In three cases the survivor has been telling the same or similar stories since adolescence; had the survey been undertaken a few years previously the cases would have been those of children. In eighteen of the eighty-four children's cases the main source of the allegations of satanic abuse was an older child, usually a teenager; eleven of these were cases studied in detail. While the cases of survivors do not form either a representative sample or anything like a total incidence at any point in time, together with the cases of teenagers they form a solid body of data. These thirty-eight cases will form the basis of this chapter.

The difference between the cases of survivors (using the term to include teenagers) and those of younger children seems most marked when one considers how their stories are told. The allegations of survivors are not usually constructed from heterogeneous evidence and may appear more spontaneous. Where these older children are concerned, the fact of sexual abuse in satanic rituals is not inferred by others but told by the victims themselves. Nevertheless the person who hears the story still affects what is said. Older children, like survivors, have more choice in the person to whom they tell their stories and seem to seek out someone whom they can depend on to accept the literal truth of everything that is said. The attitude among their supporters is one almost of pride in believing the impossible. Jenkins and Maier-Katkin, writing of survivors in the United States, have suggested that the attitude of their supporters resembles that of the early Christian, Tertullian, who proclaimed that he believed *because* it was impossible (1991: 131). What they are pointing to is that in such cases belief is faith, not a conclusion of fact. A similar view is not uncommon in England, but belief in the story has as much to do with a declaration of support for the person of the survivor or the need to believe them (Feldman, Ford & Reinhold 1994: 64). It may be said that disbelief is damaging to survivors (Sinason 1994: 6) but that belief is healing and that they need people to believe them. The hearer's attitude to what is said is an essential and universal factor in these cases, and it plays an essential part in the generation of stories of satanic abuse (Mulhern 1991).

Survivors may tell their stories in circumstances, such as self-help groups or Rape Crisis centres, where their hearers are committed as a matter of principle to believing whatever participants choose to tell the group. Moreover there is evidence to suggest that they seek out such listeners.

Research in the United States shows that a rather small group of psychotherapists are associated with the bulk of allegations by survivors, indicating the likelihood of input from the therapists (Mulhern 1991; Bottoms et al. 1996a). Similarly, only forty-eight of the membership of the Ritual Abuse Information Network and Support were counselling adults, but they had ninety patients (Youngson 1994). Such therapists may adopt an attitude that is distinctive: for example, it may be said that if survivors sense a testing or sceptical attitude they may refuse to speak. Hale and Sinason go further and claim that an attitude of 'irrational disbelief',[5] a phrase which they do not explain, may actually provoke survivors to fabricate (1994: 275). Untrue accounts thus appear to be neatly, but paradoxically, attributed to those who were sceptical of them in the first place. This argument is a version of the rather naïve and circular argument that people will tell the truth to those who believe what they say. Survivors, whether teenagers or adults, were likely to say that those who showed scepticism were actually satanists themselves. Two teenagers in my cases accused police and a police surgeon after they had shown scepticism of being members of the satanist groups and claimed they would be at risk if they spoke to them.

As their attitude to what is said is integral to the allegations, the listeners, the confidants, must be recognised as actively involved in the eliciting of the account of satanic abuse. The accounts that are acknowledged as the stories of teenagers and adult survivors can best be understood as the product of conversations, whether informal or designed to be therapeutic, in which narratives of satanic abuse are constructed by the developing relationship between teller and hearer (Mulhern 1991; cf. Aronsson & Nilholm 1992). As the means by which the relationship is established, the narratives also reflect the material available and meaningful to them both. That is, regardless of the personal beliefs or fantasies of either of those who construct it, a survivor's story draws on the shared culture of the society they both live in, on Christian folklore and mythology. For the same reason it is likely to resemble other accounts.

In most of these cases reported to the survey, the initial confidants were not those who were trained to handle the emotional problems involved in dealing with this sort of allegation and might have got drawn in too far. Among the adolescents in the eleven detailed cases in my study, four told staff of a children's home or teenage project that they had been satanically abused, three of them told foster-parents and two told untrained 'counsellors' who were also fundamentalist Christians. Of course more qualified professionals, such as psychiatrists or psychotherapists may also be convinced of the truth of the stories (Coleman 1994a; 1994b; Sinason 1994), but the unqualified have fewer defences against becoming involved emotionally. Only 17 per cent of the members of the Ritual Abuse Information Network and Support were clinical psychologists, but 43 per cent were counselling adults (Youngson 1993: 253).

Psychiatrists or therapists may claim that their experience as a clinician enables them to judge the truth of accounts. Their professional standing may then serve as a guarantee of the account's veracity. Other 'experts' whose experience, it is claimed, gives them the authority to decide on whether an account is the truth or not, may also serve to legitimise them. However, the ability to pronounce on the truth of a patient's story has not generally been claimed by psychotherapists; quite recently a psychiatrist wrote that 'there is nothing about a healthcare professional's training that enables them to "know" if someone is telling the truth . . . The role of the investigator is quite different from that of the therapist' (Adshead 1994). However, as we shall see in the next chapter, their perception of the nature of satanic abuse may result in believers considering themselves released from some of the rules and precepts of their profession. Other confidants are not trained professionals to begin with.

While older children are responsible for the stories they tell about satanic rituals, they may be influenced by the strong beliefs in satanism shown by the person they tell their story to. Two teenagers in cases reported to the survey were being counselled by convinced evangelical Christians, three others in the survey were being advised by campaigners. The influence of campaigners was also to be seen among the survivors, nearly half of whom had been in touch with well-known supporters of the belief in satanism and satanic abuse.

The following case of a teenage girl in my notes is typical:

A worker at the residential home has had a special relationship with a teenager since May 1990. She listens to the girl's accounts of being sexually abused; often this takes place at night. She tells her she is afraid to go to sleep and will seek her out to talk to. 'On occasions she indicates that she wants to talk by saying that she's unwell (quote from social worker's report)'. The care-worker didn't record the conversations until later when she was told to by the social worker. An untrained residential care-worker, she became the girl's key-worker because of the good relationship between them. Since then the girl has spent weekends at her house; on one occasion they went shopping and she drew the care-worker's attention to a video called Dolls. In the car on the way back she said: 'Have you got an idea now what it is?' The care-worker said: 'I have an idea but I don't know if it is the right one.' The girl then said: 'Oh no, they'll get me now – the black things.' When she was taken back to the children's home she threatened to take twenty-one paracetemols. Her care-worker took her back home where she told about watching late-night videos. Said all the family (except her youngest sister who was asleep) would be asked to do what the video showed. Her leg was cut to punish her and she was threatened with the black things and they burned her with cigarettes. She said she didn't want to live; she was shaking. (This account of the day was written afterwards from memory.)

Being the girl's confidant was a source of pride for a worker, who was singled out in this way as worthy of a damaged child's trust. Becoming her key-worker was a promotion and probably also raised her self-esteem. Such a situation was not uncommon. Since it may also be the case that this is the first time the child has appeared to want to build a relationship with anyone, the success may give the listener the prestige of succeeding where others have failed. This woman was also given the responsibility of encouraging the girl to 'disclose', also a not uncommon outcome. The status of being a chosen confidant to a survivor of satanic abuse may awaken ambitions to become a therapist or counsellor and both sides rapidly make an investment in the relationship, which ensures that the 'dislosure' will not be questioned. This helps to explain why the authenticity of the accounts given by teenagers is so often accepted by their confidants, apparently without reservations.

The closeness of the relationship between a survivor and her chosen confidant may involve considerable strain for the supporter, on whom the survivor may become heavily dependent and extremely demanding, expecting almost twenty-four-hour support. One survivor was reported as saying to her psychotherapist: 'I suppose I recognise what you have been saying – how much I want Shirley (her former supporter) to be my own possession' (Colver 1994: 133). One woman ended by having the survivor to sleep in her room to protect her from possible satanist attack and calm her after nightmares. The stress of supporting survivors of satanic abuse and the 'commitment' needed is frequently emphasised (Sinason 1994: 6; Youngson 1993, 1994; Morris 1994: 162–3; Scott & Wistrich n.d.). Cooklin and Barnes state that it is a mistake to become 'too excited or fascinated by finding the truth of what happened' (Cooklin and Gorrell Barnes 1994: 129), but in the same book Hale and Sinason claim that it is 'crucial to discover as near to the historic truth as possible and have it confirmed' (Hale & Sinason 1994: 274). A preoccupation with the subject that amounts in some cases to an obsession, seems to characterise many of those dealing with the satanic abuse of children, including the supporters of survivors. Such people give the impression of undertaking what is almost a divine mission and to the fundamentalist Christians who are 'experts' in this field, this is indeed what it is.

Supporters may become so close to the survivors they are protecting that they appear to identify with the story and become the survivors' mouthpieces. On two of the three occasions when I was invited to listen to survivors' stories, almost all of what I heard was told me by the supporter. A journalist told me that she found the therapist who introduced her to a survivor very reluctant to let her talk to the survivor alone; during the interview the survivor's answers appeared controlled by her supporter, who frequently took over the interview.

One of the survivors I spoke to was a teenager and her foster-mother effectively spoke for her, the girl herself speaking hardly at all during the hour-and-a-half that I was there. The episode effectively demonstrated the difficulties such a close relationship between supporter and survivor might introduce into the child protection process. This girl was said to have talked freely to the adults in whom she regularly confided, but when a formal interview was held to record the information for use in court, she refused to co-operate. The understandably frustrated interviewer, having been informed of what the child had been saying to others, but getting no answers himself in the formal interview, resorted to leading questions. Later, when the transcript of the interview had been presented as evidence in court, he was sharply criticised by the judge for trying to force a story from the girl. Similar episodes in other cases indicated the reluctance of teenagers to talk to people other than those they have chosen to hear them and to speak for them.

Teenagers may be particularly reluctant to talk to the police, but this reluctance is even more characteristic of adult survivors. A minute number of adults have reported their cases to the police, who have so far failed to substantiate any of the allegations. Where the abuse is alleged to have happened twenty years in the past it is understandable that it might be thought of little use to report it, although both those whom I know to have gone to the police reported satanic abuse in childhood. However, some survivors claim that the abuse is continuing, that they are still trapped in the group and even that they have recently witnessed human sacrifices (Boyd 1991: 325; Anon. 1994: 198; Coleman 1994b: 90). The apparent failure of supporters in such circumstances to report to the police is strange; can it mean that, at some level, they do not believe it?

Those who believe in the stories of survivors face two problems. The first is that survivors may allege acts and events, such as flying, that are physically impossible; this difficulty may face the believers in the satanic abuse of children as well. Unless satanists or witches are commonly believed to have mystical powers that make them able to do things no human being can do, as is the case in many societies in the Third World, these impossible features of the stories undermine the credibility of the tellers of such stories. This problem was also faced in Europe at times when belief in the existence of magic and supernatural powers was much greater than it is today. Salazar, the Spanish Inquisitor, wrote to his superiors: 'However, who can accept the following: that a person can frequently fly through the air and travel a hundred leagues in an hour; that a woman can get out through a space not big enough for a fly; that a person can make himself invisible; that he can be in a river or in the sea and not get wet; . . . or that a witch can turn herself into any shape she fancies, be it housefly or raven? Indeed, these claims go beyond all human reason and many even pass the limits permitted the devil' (quoted in Henningsen 1980: 350).

In other societies in the Third World, such tall tales merely go to prove that witches are involved, since witches, especially the dreaded night-witches, have more than human qualities (Pocock 1985). As we have seen, some people apparently perceive the story's incredible qualities as a test of their faith in the person who tells it. Other intellectual strategies may also be adopted to protect beliefs from being undermined by manifestly false allegations. The two most common are to attribute the incredible elements to the effect of drugs (Hale & Sinason 1994: 275; Coleman 1994a: 248) or perceptual disorders (Coleman 1994b: 88). Some accounts of what survivors say merely omit the incredible elements. However, where survivors' stories are told to the police or records of interviews with teenagers exist, these elements cannot be explained away or ignored so easily.

Secondly, the lack of corroborative evidence for all survivor stories so far leaves the allegations of satanist activity completely unfounded in fact. As with the children's cases, it may be claimed that proof of sexual abuse (such as a record of someone's having been convicted of the crime), indicates the truthfulness of the victim and hence it follows that everything else that is said is also true. A similar claim may be made for evidence that physical injuries are not self-inflicted. Two anonymous policemen and their woman colleague agreed that when a surveillance camera discovered a victim, who had complained of symbols being daubed on her door, painting it herself, they were still 'prepared to continue an investigation and understand the complexity of contradictory evidence', on the basis of being convinced that her allegation of being tortured was true (Anon. 1994: 195).

The tellers of tales

It is characteristic of both adolescent and adult cases that they are more likely to involve girls than boys, and women than men. There was a London group for male survivors of satanic abuse led by Nigel O'Mara (Boyd 1991: 35); three articles in Sinason's collection of essays discuss males (Beail 1994; Charleson & Corbett 1994; Norton 1994), and one male survivor was reported to the survey.[6] The vast majority of survivors, however are women. This pattern is reasonably consistent with the higher reporting rate generally of sexual abuse among girls, but it is quite inconsistent with the cases of organised and ritual abuse reported in the survey (La Fontaine 1994). In the abuse cases covered in the survey, the number of boys and girls is roughly equal (fifty-six girls to fifty-four boys). Yet all but three of the teenagers making allegations of satanic abuse are girls and all but one of the twenty survivors are women. It may be that because more women than men seek counselling or therapy for sexual abuse suffered earlier in their lives,[7] known survivors are more likely to be women. Whatever the reason, the preponderance of women and girls among survivors makes it easy to perceive as a feminist issue their need for support and belief in what they say.

Survivors are frequently described as 'disturbed' or 'damaged' individuals. Many of them injure themselves or have eating or sleep disorders (Coleman 1994b: 89). In this and in several other ways they resemble the victims of factitious disorders, most particularly in their inability to satisfy their desperate need for affection and attention (Feldman, Ford & Reinhold 1994: 222). Survivors resemble the latter also in the escalation of the dramatic features of their stories and their fear of any challenge to the truth of what they say. Pointing to the existence of survivors' problems is not intended to denigrate the individuals concerned, but to suggest possible reasons why their stories may not be factual accounts. If the resemblance of the survivors to the sufferers from factitious disorders is indeed exact, then they know that themselves.

The poor psychological state of adult survivors is mentioned in eight cases reported to the survey: three refer to drug-induced psychosis, two to hospitalisation and in the other three questionnaires various phrases are used to indicate the existence of psychological problems. Two of the survivors referred to their drug-induced psychosis as being the result of their involvement with satanists. The five patients who were Coleman's informants were described as having been variously diagnosed as suffering from personality disorder (three), schizophrenia (two), hysteria (two); all were said to be depressed (Coleman 1994b: 89). Fewer of the teenagers are described as 'disturbed' or mentally ill, and the symptoms of Coleman's teenager patient were markedly less severe than those of the adults (Coleman 1994b: 89), but the subsequent history of two teenagers in my study has included hospitalisation for mental illness. These were both teenagers whose stories were believed, not, as might be imagined by believers, two who were not listened to. Their fragile state of mental health appeared to have been worsened by the encouragement to continue making disclosures rather than the reverse.

Teenagers in ritual abuse cases may have confirmed histories of earlier sexual abuse, which sometimes include the conviction of an adult for the offence. There was corroborative evidence to support allegations of sexual abuse in nine of the eleven detailed cases involving teenagers, and six of those accused in those cases had made admissions of guilt to the police. Four of the survivors had also had proven histories of sexual abuse. In two of the substantiated cases, where the victims were in their teens when the abuse was disclosed, there was evidence of sexual abuse. But, for a variety of reasons, medical evidence of more recent abuse to corroborate allegations is mostly not available in these cases or the evidence may be equivocal. Teenagers may be sexually active whether they were previously abused or not. One girl ran away from home and admitted on her return that she had had an abortion; another, who absconded from a children's home, claimed that she had been gang raped and then involved in prostitution. Two others refused to have a medical examination that might provide evidence of their having been abused. In one case reported to the survey the medical examination indicated that the girl was a virgin, but in another, similar case, two doctors disagreed over whether the girl was sexually experienced or not. Because the medical evidence is not necessarily likely to be helpful, the search for corroborative evidence must concentrate perforce on finding evidence to substantiate other aspects of their stories and, if that is lacking, on the consistency and likelihood of the stories themselves.

The history of one child, whose sexual abuse at age seven was particularly well substantiated, suggests that the unresolved effects of sexual abuse may be connected with the satanic abuse allegations of teenagers and survivors. As a teenager, having been involved, possibly with her mother's knowledge, in inappropriate sexual activity with adult men, this girl became very disturbed. She joined an (adult) incest survivors group where she started making allegations of satanic abuse. The group had been introduced by a participant to an account of satanic abuse written by an American survivor, now an 'expert' and this may have triggered the allegations by the teenager. Much of my later information on this case is sketchy, but it was enough to allow me to conclude that the allegations she is making now about the circumstances surrounding her earlier sexual abuse are quite unlike those that were described in the trial of the abuser at the time, which were admitted by him and corroborated by the testimony of several other victims.

The stories

Unlike the allegations of satanic abuse in the cases of younger children, the accounts associated with older children are less likely to be the constructions of adults. Most of them are told by the teenagers themselves. There are five cases in which the allegation is an adult interpretation. One example is the case of a thirteen-year-old boy who drew pictures of penises shooting at aeroplanes and a strip cartoon of rape which was seen as possible evidence of satanic ritual abuse.[8]

Another concerned a girl in the care of a local authority who was subject to fugue states and 'saw' white hands on the windowsill of her bedroom, then a figure hanging there that vanished when she pushed it off.[9] In the first case the diagnosis of satanic abuse reflected the influence of a social work 'consultant', a firm believer in the menace of satanic abuse, who it seems had encouraged a premature conclusion by the child protection services; in the second it was the girl's own interest in the occult that seems to have invited the label satanic abuse. Three other cases involving adolescents have allegations of satanism that can be shown to be mistaken, all for different reasons.

The accounts of teenagers generally resemble those of adults, some of which have been published in Britain (Harper & Pugh 1990; Boyd 1991), as they have been in north America. Like the adult accounts, adolescent stories may lack the information that is crucial for identifying all the perpetrators and prosecuting them. By contrast with this very general amnesia, the accounts show an apparently good memory for details of the rituals. Most survivors claim that they were forced to participate for years, from early childhood. They may claim to have been born into groups where membership of a satanist group was a family tradition and children were inducted in infancy. Some say they are still members of the group. It seems improbable that frequent participation in these rites would not have resulted in some recollection of participants other than parents, or of the organisation. Where adult survivors or teenagers claim to have held high office in the cult, or to be the children of such officiants (Scott & Wistrich 1994), the failure to remember persons or to identify locations is even more surprising. The ignorance may be explained as the result of the group's concern to protect themselves with secrecy or of the survivor's incomplete separation from the group. Coleman states that two of her patients 'admitted reporting to the cult details of their disclosures and therapy' (Coleman 1994b: 90). One of the three anonymous members of police forces who contributed to a book on survivors of satanist abuse also felt that 'the adult victim may still be involved in some way and can be passing information back and forth to the group without your knowledge' (Anon. 1994: 198). It is not explained why the group should permit this when it might lead to its exposure.

Children may name other children who they allege were also involved, but are vague on the names of adults. The Orkney case was almost entirely concerned with children who had been taken into care on the basis of having been named by some of the children already believed to have been satanically abused (Clyde 1992). Adults, however, say they are afraid to do this. One adult survivor was prepared to describe the

unnamed men she said had participated in the satanic abuse, but after
she had given ten descriptions and shown willingness to continue with
more, her interviewer called a halt because she had said earlier that she
was sure there were only eight people there and he was convinced that
she was just trying to please him. In general, however, survivors seem
able to describe the details of regular and terrifying events, but are
unable to remember the people who were present or officiated in them,
except occasionally for parents and siblings, despite the claims of several
to have been involved in the satanist cult since childhood. This makes
survivors unlike witches in early modern Europe or the Third World
who were prepared to accuse fellow-villagers and even their relatives; it
also makes them quite unlike the survivors of the concentration camps,
with whom the designation invites comparison; the memories of
survivors of the Holocaust do not display a similar distribution of
amnesia as the evidence at the subsequent trials of war criminals attests.

As in most cases of satanic abuse involving children, the central
figures in survivors' allegations are parents. There may also be others,
sometimes many others, who are unnamed, shadowy participants in the
rites. One respondent in the survey answered the question about how
many people were involved with the phrase 'more than 200', but in
most cases only a few adults were said to have been present. Adults are
more inclined to refer to large numbers of participants than teenagers.
It may be said that survivors fear for their lives if they reveal the identity
of leaders of the satanic cults they were abused by, but no survivors have
been killed for talking, unlike fugitives from the Mafia or informers in
the IRA.

The satanic rites

All over the world people perform rituals and the most widespread
feature of them is that they must be done 'right', that is according to
precedent. The believers' claim that 'There's an uncanny similarity.
There are so many threads going though the cases, which are the same
thing' (Core, quoted in Boyd 1991: 54; see also Tate 1991: 2) is
consistent with this and gives the impression that a single religion or
religious group is responsible. In general outline the stories do resemble
one another, being concerned with secret cults that practise human
sacrifice, particularly abortion and infanticide, cannibalism and vampirism (the drinking of blood), and indulge in sexual orgies that include
sadism and every variety of sexual perversion. The frequent appearance
of these features underlie the assertions by believers, like that quoted
above, that the allegations are 'remarkably similar' and therefore show

the same satanic cult or cults at work. However, there are considerable difficulties in seeing the stories as reflecting either a single satanist organisation or related organisations of the same satanist type. When looked at in detail the accounts vary very considerably.

Accounts by survivors may be linked by one feature that they share but differ from one another in others. For example, the book *Michelle Remembers* refers to keeping children in cages, as was noted earlier.[10] Being locked in a 'jail or cage' is the first item on the list of allegations compiled by Pamela Hudson, the former social worker from California who is now regarded as an 'expert' on satanic abuse (Hudson 1988: 27); children in cages appear as one of 'the same threads' referred to by Dianne Core, and form a prominent part of Joan Coleman's account of the case of a teenager (Coleman 1994a: 242)[11] which was also part of my study. Cages are not mentioned in it by any other teenager or survivor. In children's cases the 'standard' elements listed above do not occur in a surprisingly large number of cases (see Chapter 4). The range of variation in cases involving teenagers is equally wide. For example a common feature is blood sacrifice, but four teenagers do not mention it and the others vary as to whether they refer to babies, other teenagers, adults or animals, the last being the most common. In two accounts all three kinds of sacrifice are mentioned; four do not include sacrifice of any kind.

Coleman (1994a) has published an account of satanism that appears to describe groups with similar organisation, regular practices, and identical rituals. However, as she indicates, it is a 'composite of descriptions' from a number of cases. The features she describes do not appear in all, or even some of the cases, since some come from one and some from another. The account in fact fits none of the cases exactly. In the same way, half the cases in my study involve a feature that is found in no other case and some cases show more than one (La Fontaine 1994: 21). Some may include one feature mentioned by Coleman but not others. This variation shows that the assertion of similarity is exaggerated. Only by omitting the differences, or amalgamating the details of one story with those of another could a general account like Coleman's be given of the cases in my study. But the result would be a totally misleading uniformity.

There might be several different reasons for such variation. The differences in descriptions might indicate different branches of satanism or types of cult. It is after all in the detail of practice and belief that religious groups are identified with, or distinguished from, one another; for example, doctrinal differences and sharp differences in the conduct of worship distinguish the churches within Christianity. Robes, incense and chanting are popularly associated with the Roman Catholic Church, while the evangelical churches consider such devices as profaning the worship of Christ. However, the known satanic cults show considerable uniformity in their ritual and the differences in these allegations are greater than those that might occur between sects of the same religion. The differences may even appear in accounts that purport to refer to the same group.

Accounts of a ceremony by different participants can be expected to show some discrepancies: they might have had different view-points, literally or figuratively, or one person might have a better memory for detail or be more interested in the ritual than the other. However where my study has found allegations by more than one person that refer to the same group, the differences are too great to be explained in this way. In each of two cases of teenagers in my study there were two girls, both of whom gave accounts of satanic ritual abuse; in one case they were sisters and in the other friends; in both cases they both provided 'descriptions' of rituals. These two cases are unusual in that, in both cases, the children mainly affected by the allegations were unrelated to the girls whose stories provided the main evidence, and in one case the accused did not include their own parents. In one case the victims were said to be the children of friends of the accusers' mother; in the other case the girls accused a woman who had befriended teenagers in the community, allowing them to use her house for a place to meet, smoke pot and (perhaps) drink alcohol.

It was alleged by social workers in both cases that the girls had no contact with one another and that therefore their accounts were completely independent. However, there was evidence to show that this was not true in either case. Investigation in the file showed that the two girls who were friends had telephoned each other on at least one occasion, and both were in touch with other teenagers who had belonged to the group that used to visit the accused. In both cases the accounts contradict each other on details, and the conclusion must be that these are not the same rituals, although both accuse the same people.

In the first case to be examined the first girl described two rituals, while the other made general comments and described one complete ritual. The girls claimed to have been involved with the same group, but the rituals seem rather different. There are some similarities: counting, Arabic marks, gowns or robes, the sacrificed cat, the 'Jewish star' (though here one child refers to a pentagon, probably meaning a pentagram, which seems to indicate that the 'Jewish star' may be an error made by both of them – the occult symbol is a five-pointed star, not the six-pointed star of David), candles and drinking blood, though they differ as to what blood it was. In this case, the possibility for collusion certainly existed.

Comparison of the stories of two teenage survivors

(Similar features highlighted)

First girl	Second girl
First rite	*Rituals in general*
Counting exercises.	There was **counting in threes and**
Sitting in circle.	**nines** to summon up demons and powers
Chanting in Arabic.	of darkness.
Sipped **goat's blood** from	She has drunk **animal blood** from
a **gold chalice**	**chalice.**
	There was a cat hanging out of a pentagon
	(sic) with six candles (see below).
	Animals were sacrificed.
Second rite (indoors)	*One ritual occasion*
Initiation at full moon.	Place with a sandy beach.
'We took cocaine by	We put on gowns, joined group.
injection' before going	Formed circle; children in groups of three.
M. gave me a black robe.	There was a woman in red.
M. put on white robe.	Pile of wood lit for fire.
People had snakes with them.	First lot of children made to lie
Counting and chanting.	down.
Jewish star on floor; candles were	**Jewish star** in sand.
lit at the six points.	Jewish star in red liquid drawn
Slit throat of cat into	onto each child.
chalice in middle of star.	Man knelt and licked it off,
	especially off star.
	Man had sex with the children. 'This took
	10 mins for each child'. Then Arabic mark
	inscribed onto chest of first child of second
	group of children. It drew blood.
Later meetings	
Chants similar to Christian prayers,	
words inserted to make it worship	
of Satan.	
The Master's Verse was the 'opposite'	
of the Lord's Prayer.	

The possibility of collusion has already been raised as an explanation for the similarities in these accounts. Alternatively the reason for the similarities may have been their source: the house they visited. Books

found there indicate that the girls might have been familiar with runes –
the 'Arabic writing' – and pentagrams from their visits there. The
woman they accused said that she had taught them relaxation exercises,
using numbers, when they had said they could not sleep. She also had a
long robe. Perhaps they had become convinced that these things were
evil and were eager to make them seem more so.

There were also a number of important differences between the girls'
allegations. Apart from the different locations of the rituals, children
figure centrally as victims in the second girl's account; not even their
presence is mentioned in either of the alleged rituals described by the
other. Neither of them mention the children of the woman they are
accusing, whom the social workers claimed were ritually abused; these
children allegedly referred to quite different scenes. Their mother
figures as little more than an onlooker, even though she is said by one of
the girls to have been an important person in the cult.

Some differences between what the girls said also contribute an
insight into how the two accounts might have been matched. During the
investigation, the second girl had run away from home and when she
returned she admitted she had had an abortion. Later the first girl
described it as a ritual abortion, but when the social worker told the
second girl of this[12] she reacted with surprise, saying that it had not
been that bad. Later, however, she acquiesced in the description as a
ritual abortion. A search for the place which she identified as the place
where it had been held revealed nothing. A social worker gave the first
girl's foster-mother a document about ritual abuse. Later she telephoned the social worker saying that she had shown the document to
her foster-daughter, who had then recalled that the group she had
observed used plastic sheets to ensure no traces of the sacrifice would be
left behind. The other girl never mentioned this.

The second case involves a description by each of two sisters of what
was said to be the same occasion; each girl said the other was also there.
The central act was the sacrifice of a baby, said to be their mother's own
son and hence their baby brother. They were accusing their mother and
also a friend of their mother's – a woman with small children – of
sacrificing him. One psychiatrist said that he believed the girls; he felt
their accounts were consistent with each other and therefore reliable.
Another psychiatrist on the case did not find the girls credible and felt
they could have got the stories from the media or from their mother,
who for several years had been describing herself very publicly as a
former satanist who had found Christ. The first foster-mother with
whom they were both placed mentioned that they were in the habit of
taking long walks together, so collusion was not ruled out, although

they were separated before the final interviews when they described the rituals analysed here.

Comparison of girls' descriptions of baby sacrifice

(Similar features highlighted)

First girl	Second girl
Child naked	Child clothed
Child awake, injected, went to sleep	
Curtains drawn	
Candles	**Candles**
Lord's Prayer backwards written on black crosses	No mention of Lord's Prayer Crosses upside down – no mention of writing on them or colour of them
Sweetish, sickly smell	No mention of smell
Mother wore black dress	
Others normal dress	no mention of special dress Decorations: earth stars moon
High pitched **chanting**	**Chanting** to Satan
Child on silver dish, in alcove	Child on table
Mother kneeling	A mother of young children stood She poured hot water
Knife white handle, with three black dots and silver blade	Knife black handle
Hands on knife: second girl's, then first girl's, then mother's	
	Baby marked with satanic symbols, blood drawn, baby beaten; salt rubbed in eyes, and wounds of baby
Cut made in stomach near navel. Saw and felt warm blood	Throat cut, baby slashed with knives, blood saved, put into chalice, flesh cut from baby.
Saw no more	(account stops
Woke when it was all over	no clear end)

These two comparisons show the discrepancies in accounts that allegedly concern rituals of the same cult or even rituals performed on the same occasions.

Discrepancies between survivors or teenagers in different cases show more differences, but there it is still possible that different groups might be involved. The discrepancies consist of omissions of common elements such as human sacrifice or clothing that is popularly associated with satanism, but cases may also include elements that distinguish them clearly from others. Thus only one child in the eighty-four cases refers to the injection of a 'black and white liquid' and only one set of allegations includes that of babies being kept in cages.[13]

The beliefs of any cult group cannot be recognised, let alone understood, from the allegations of teenagers and survivors in these cases. One of them refers to praying to Satan, another to God; in another the leader of the group is said to be called Satan, elsewhere he is the Master. Otherwise little is said of what or whom is being worshipped.

In the accounts of cases published by believers in satanic abuse, there is much more information on the organisation of the groups and their beliefs than in these cases, and much more than in cases where young children are said to be the source of the information. This may be the result of the relative freedom of supporters in these situations to encourage the survivors to talk about such matters. Where the teenagers were concerned, the main interest of their supporters lay in finding the abusers, and their freedom to investigate the alleged cults was curtailed by social services practice. This is not the case where adult survivors are concerned and therefore they can provide a great deal more detail, although they still stop short of identifying the members of the groups whose organisation they describe.

Despite the greater amount of information from survivors, the beliefs or doctrines of satanists that make them a distinctive cult are still not clear. References to indoctrinating children so that they continue the cult (Coleman 1994b: 90) might equally apply to any religion which recruits members for the future. Even the motive of obtaining power over the children is not specific, though it is mentioned in the same account that the children are told that the abuse 'pleases Satan, who is the supreme power and will eventually rule the earth' (ibid.). Even those who claim that they were being prepared for high office within the cult do not give a coherent account of its gods or its theology. The survivors interviewed by Boyd refer to a wide range of names although there is some confusion between alternative names for the devil, the names of other demons and other non-Christian divine figures, such as the Goat of Mendes (Cavendish 1975: 174). (This last may be referred to as a manifestation of the devil and figures in Dennis Wheatley's novel and the film of the same name, *The Devil Rides Out*.) Coleman refers simply to 'transgenerational satanic cults' which seems to mean family-based groups, but then gives a wealth of detail about their organisation, hierarchy of offices and activities which indicates that they are not based on any family organisation (1994a: 243). Apart from an occasional reference to a high priest or priestess, none of these features is replicated in my cases, many of which revolve around large extended families. The teenagers and survivors in my study were remarkably vague on all these points.

It is said to be characteristic of children and survivors that their stories are told piecemeal over what may be a very long series of encounters. This is seen by believers as the natural result of having to reveal such traumatic material and as being the result of the victim's gradually feeling safe enough to talk. Others see the process as paralleling the step-by-step disclosure of sexual abuse by children. However, the detailed cases involving teenagers show that several of them related their stories immediately they went into care or soon after; they seemed not to fit the stereotype. The way the accounts developed is compatible with continued elaboration for the benefit of listeners.

The belief of people who listen to the accounts of teenagers and survivors that for the 'survivor' to bring out all her memories is therapeutic puts pressure on a self-confessed victim of ritual abuse to produce more and more stories. Sympathetic acceptance of a story slides easily into curiosity to learn more. When the listener is eager to hear more, gratitude for support may impel the young person to confirm this and to find ever more dramatic memories to recount. This approach to abuse gives no indication of how to tell when the account has ended; the victim's claim to have no more to tell may not be accepted but be interpreted as refusal to tell something even worse than what has already been recounted. The case of one young woman, Caroline Marchant, allegedly a survivor of satanic abuse, who finally committed suicide, made this clear (Hebditch & Anning 1990). There is some evidence in the cases of adolescents and survivors in this study to confirm the existence of pressure for more information. It was noted earlier in this chapter that the two teenagers who finally had to be hospitalised had been listened to sympathetically.

In the United States the testimonies of adults who claimed to have been ritually abused as children have been an important element in the spread of the epidemic. In Britain, their influence has waxed and waned. To begin with they set the scene, but during the period when cases involving children were receiving publicity, it was said that it was the fact that children were telling these stories that was most significant. Since 1994, with the collapse of a number of cases involving children and the publication of my report to the Department of Health (La Fontaine 1994) which emphasised the lack of corroborative evidence for satanic abuse, adult survivors are once more said to hold the key to the problem in England.

Not surprisingly, teenagers and survivors make allegations of satanic abuse to people who will believe what they say, by whom I mean those who will not query even the most unlikely claim. It is likely that situations in which belief is ensured from the outset are more conducive to such allegations being made than others where there is no such atmosphere. Three of these can be identified as commonly found: groups that advertise their concern with the victims of sexual abuse in childhood or with satanic abuse, such as the Maureen Davies' Beacon Foundation or Dianne Core's ChildWatch, to cite just the best-known; groups for incest survivors or rape victims, which hold it as a central principle that victims must be believed; finally certain psychotherapists, such as Valerie Sinason and Robert Hale, claimed that in these cases the normal rules of psychotherapy must be waived in order to provide what survivors need. Proselytising evangelical Christianity, certain forms of feminism and of psychotherapeutic practice are areas offering support for survivors of satanic abuse; it is here therefore that adult survivors often make their appearance. Their appearance in turn sustains the belief in satanic abuse. The next chapter will consider them in more detail.

9   A modern movement of witch-finders?[1]

The social context for the controversy over satanic abuse is complex, as is to be expected in a late twentieth-century Western society. The allegations that have emerged in cases of children and adults alike are the results of a largely uncoordinated and heterogeneous social movement (cf. Victor 1991: 224). There is a variety of groups involved in promoting the idea that satanic abuse is real and prevalent, but they are not formally linked and the different categories of those who support their views extend well beyond their membership. Like African witch-finding cults, the movement has no single organisational structure (Willis 1970: 129). Moreover, categories of people who take the same anti-satanist stance may be sharply divided on issues other than the main one of belief in the allegations. Christian fundamentalists, for example, hold deeply conservative views on the family and on moral issues such as abortion that are diametrically opposed to those held by radical feminists, but both groups have seen a reason to support the view that satanic abuse is rife and spreading (Jenkins 1992: 175–6).

This chapter will broadly share the conclusions drawn by Jenkins that I quoted earlier (p. 20) about the success of a small network of activists, and will confirm his analysis of the social trends behind the movement. It will also try to go beyond this to show the shifting and broadening definition of the problem over time. As new supporters were recruited they introduced new dimensions of meaning into the issues and mobilised different social interests. The enlargement of the arena in which the growing body of activities operated was the result of media interest that reflected public anxieties over the welfare of children. However, public issues are often contested and leaders may be superseded. The allegations of satanic abuse generated opposition as well as support, and the fight to dominate public thinking itself generated changes in the movement.

To begin with, however, it is important to stress that many of the labels such as fundamentalist, evangelical, feminist, social worker and so on, are classifying terms, not descriptions. A category includes a variety of individuals who may hold only some views in common. In particular they may not share the views of activists referred to in this chapter as promoting belief in satanic abuse. Nevertheless, the labels, as well as being summary descriptions of kinds of person, also refer to elements in their social situation, interests and outlooks that influence their attitude towards anti-satanism. For example, a 1996 conference on women and domestic violence held in Brighton included a section on ritual (i.e. satanic) abuse that seems to indicate compatibility between feminist activism and promoting belief in ritual abuse. The organisers would have rejected an application to hold the workshop if this were not so. Even so, not all feminists will hold the same views on allegations of satanic abuse; some individuals may differ quite sharply from others with whom they share views of the feminist issues. To take another example: there were sceptical foster-mothers in some of the cases where allegations of satanic abuse were made and it was a sceptical social worker who wrote a scathing account of the social work press accounts of the issue (Clapton 1993). It is not my intention to entrench existing stereotypes but to sketch the many different strands of belief and action that supported the anti-satanist movement.

The anti-satanist movement differs from the other moral panics that Jenkins describes as preceding it in that, unlike the concern over sexual abuse, serial murders or paedophile rings, it was a construction with no foundation in actuality; there was no evidence of satanic rituals, while serial murders did take place (however rarely) and paedophile rings were discovered and their members convicted. The anti-satanist movement may have been supported by the other concerns, but it did not take them over or replace them in the public mind. The sexual abuse and murder of children, and the convictions of members of paedophile rings continued to be reported during the years when anti-satanism was at its peak without their being attributed to satanism, although it would be possible to argue that the publicity for them was partly due to the heightened public sensitivity to such matters. The reporting of actual murders and paedophile networks were claimed by believers as 'proof' that satanic acts were real. As this book goes to press (1997) a dreadful Belgian case of the kidnap and murder of children is being claimed as the work of a 'satanic cult'. However, the investigation of the cases of alleged satanic abuse has shown that the allegations were unsupported by material evidence and the last two chapters have shown how doubtful were the grounds for alleging that children, the alleged victims of these atrocities, were the source of the allegations. The analysis of survivors' roles has shown how the relationship between damaged and needy individuals and people convinced of the existence of autonomous forces of evil resulted in accounts that could not be verified. Jenkins remarks that 'there are few contemporary academics who would examine the roots of a "witchcraft problem" in the seventeenth century, except in terms of public reaction to a largely imaginary menace.' The lack of evidence to substantiate the allegations suggests that a similar approach is reasonable.

The last two chapters concerned themselves with the questions: given the lack of corroborating evidence why were the allegations of satanic abuse accepted, and how were particular cases identified as cases of satanic abuse? Now we must pull back from the grass-roots and consider the anti-satanist movement as a whole, the identity and motivations of the categories of persons who are mobilised into giving support, albeit in varying degrees. The analysis confirms Jenkins' account in most respects, although writing four years later, there is some benefit of hindsight and I have taken a different approach.

Although witches, black magic and satanism are part of English popular culture, they have not been regarded as serious threats for two centuries.[2] A genre of thrillers, epitomised by those written by Dennis Wheatley, that have remained popular over forty years have used ideas of the witches' sabbath and the black mass to add a dimension of horror to their stories; some of these elements reappear in the stories told by today's adult survivors. But occultists and witches were not taken seriously right up to the start of the anti-satanist movement (Jenkins 1992: 154–8). In the general attitudes of its members to such phenomena, late twentieth-century England was quite unlike early modern Europe or the societies in which anthropologists have studied witchcraft beliefs and accusations. Why, then, were the allegations successful in starting an epidemic of cases? The answer lies in the processes which shaped British society at the time, that not only influenced the pattern of allegations but produced categories of people that were particularly likely, for very different reasons, to accept the allegations or to hesitate to denounce them as spurious.

The social trends that Jenkins identified as contributory to the phenomenon I am calling a social movement are the economic changes under successive Conservative governments; a sharp growth in the proportion of the population supported by state benefits; increased hostility between classes; a rise in the crime rates and in figures that, to some people, indicated the decline of the traditional family those indicating the increase in the divorce rate and the number of unmarried mothers. One cannot quarrel with his description of an unstable and changing society, in which the majority faced an unpredictable and insecure future, as a source of a movement designed to root out evil.

Such factors have been identified in other societies undergoing witch-cleansing movements, whether in the recent past abroad or in early modern Europe. In addition, Jenkins rightly points out the more frequent resort of both Conservative and Labour politicians to images of conspiracy, remarking that they 'helped disseminate ideas about official cover-ups and upperworld (sic) malfeasance that would permeate the debate over threats to children' (1992: 29). Cases of police corruption and public debate over whether being a Freemason was compatible with holding public office, encouraged these ideas. Since many people might argue that Freemasonry is an occult organisation, the perception that it was rife among police forces could be used to support the idea that they were protecting witches and satanists.

Finally, the accusations were not random. The 'sink estates' where the majority of the adult population had no work, where the level of inter-personal violence was unusually high and the future for any children growing up there was bleak, provided an intractable problem for overstrained social services. As Chapter 4 showed, social rejects and the marginal members of the new society who failed as parents were the most likely to be categorised as evil tools of the satanic organisation. The fact that the wealthy and successful were not accused fuelled the talk of powerful figures behind the scenes, just as the talk of conspiracy encouraged the belief that the 'real satanists' had not been found.

So far, the social phenomenon that we have been examining has been seen as though it were static, an insect pegged on a board for study. This heuristic device has allowed us to consider various aspects of the problem which are not greatly affected by the factor that is omitted: time. Despite some shifts in the nature of cases over the period from which the cases were drawn, they did not differ sufficiently to make the time-factor significant in analysing them. Now, however, in turning to consider the movement as a whole, one can no longer ignore the fact that there has been considerable and continuing change in the formulation of the problem since its inception.

When Jenkins wrote the book I have been quoting, he considered that the ritual abuse scare had ended. He wrote: 'Of the several panics outlined in this book, ritual abuse is the only one that can be said to have effectively ceased and to have been almost entirely discredited among media and policy makers' (1992: 193). While he conceded that 'some of the original claims makers' remained active, he envisaged its essential ideas as merely surviving in the public consciousness to shape a future problem. By 1995, three years later, it had become clear that this judgement was premature. In April 1996 the tabloid *News of the*

World published an allegation by a witness in a notorious serial murder case that she had been raped by the killer in front of several men, and described the incident as a 'satanic ceremony' (*News of the World*, 21 April 1996). The flyer for a conference to be held in September 1996 uses the title 'Better the devil you know?; putting ritual abuse in context.' But the names of participants advertised suggests that although some things have stayed the same, the leadership of the movement and its figureheads have changed.[3]

The movement has shifted ground, bringing adult victims, the survivors, to the fore again, but as patients this time, rather than saved souls. What could have been crudely but accurately described at the outset as an alliance between Christian fundamentalists fighting against the occult, feminists and social workers who had been convinced there was a new threat to children, has become, at least in its public manifestations, a debate over the testimony of survivors and the validity of their memories of abuse, accompanied by the development of a pressure group seeking change in the relations between therapists and patients.[4] Most recently its entrepreneurs have become involved with the recrudescence of the phenomenon of multiple personality and the start of an epidemic of cases of a new disorder, one that is said to be diagnostic of satanic abuse in childhood. The new allegations, being located in the past, are much more difficult to investigate and virtually impossible to disprove. This new phase, like the earlier ones, follows the same line of development as the movement in the United States. As Jenkins points out, each development was shaped by influence from the United States (Jenkins 1992), but I shall argue that this influence was more prominent to begin with than it is now. Now that the movement has taken root in Britain, American experts must compete with their home-grown counter-parts for the positions at conferences and the well-paid consultancies which four years ago brought American 'experts' to Britain.

Public leadership of the movement seems to have passed, particularly as far as the media are concerned, from the Christian fundamentalist evangelicals to professionals in the psychotherapeutic community supported by certain feminist activists. These people, not the evangelical Christian groups, appear as the public supporters of the victims of satanists in the new version of the allegations. Although a number of these therapists are clearly Christian in their beliefs, it is as professionals that they claim the authority to adjudicate on the truth of what their patients tell them of satanic rituals (Mollon 1994: 136; Coleman 1994b: 91–2). New interests and motives can be discerned among the psychotherapists (Sinason 1994: 1–8), but those who say they are not

Christian take the same approach as those who are, like the non-Christian social workers who were involved in the inception of the movement.

In part, the changes are superficial, the result of a constant search by the media for novelty.[5] The old ideas and those who present them do not vanish, although they lose their drawing power. They then need to be presented in different guise. Those who are prominent in the leadership now were unknown to the media to begin with and the first experts, whose names were the attraction at the early conferences, have undoubtedly lost some of their influence. The new ideas, significantly, are psychological rather than religious, and consequently those who are prominent now are therapists. The new public controversies may not bring entirely new ideas into the debate; some that are given prominence now were in circulation earlier in the development of the movement but were unnoticed. The diagnosis of multiple personality disorder is presented as a new development, but seminars were being held on the subject at least five years ago.[6] An adult survivor, 'Helen Chandler', interviewed for a book published in 1991 complained: 'People just won't believe it's happening. They say it's fantasy and imagination, that it's multiple personalities' (Boyd 1991: 377). She had clearly heard a discussion of multiple personality, which did not become part of the public image of the movement until five years later. But whatever the form of the public debate, and its media presentation, allegations of satanic abuse continue to be made.

There has also been genuine change. The changes undergone by the anti-satanist movement since its inception add to its appearance of heterogeneity; and also pose problems of description. A succession of different groups that campaign for the recognition of satanic abuse can be identified as the core of the campaign, but the categories of its supporters extended beyond these groups and the core itself has altered. There are networks of connections among the individuals who have become prominent in the last few years on the issue of satanic abuse and the earlier campaigners, and some, though not all, of these links can be identified. The network is responsible for the spread of information, for invitations to conferences, for case referrals and for support in particular cases. These connections link groups informally and overlap sufficiently for one to be able to speak of a single social movement, but no single organisation or individual controls it.

This situation is not static, just as the witch-hunts in early modern Europe were not; describing the groups, networks and individuals that make up the movement is not enough; groups split or lose influence, networks become the basis of groups or break apart, individuals become linked into networks, and join groups or found new ones. With the change of leadership, the presentation of the allegations changes and so do the supporting arguments. This chapter will try to indicate the fluidity of the movement's public image at the same time as describing its constituent parts. For convenience I distinguish three phases: the initial phase, in which religious activists are dominant and American influence most visible, a second period during which cases involving children are exposed and there is the greatest media interest and public controversy, focusing on social work and, finally, a third phase in which the victims are mainly adults and the public leadership has been taken over by members of the therapeutic professions.

The question of evidence for the allegations showed the existence of two opposed outlooks, the rationalist and the believers. This opposition must also be considered part of the social context of the phenomenon we are considering and one which distinguishes the Western phenomenon from those elsewhere.[7] The conflict between views and the groups holding them provided much of the momentum for change within the movement itself. Scepticism has not been much considered in connection with studies of witch-hunts, and although there clearly were sceptics in early modern Europe, they mostly seem to have been unusually independent-minded individuals. In certain parts of Europe, such as Italy, scepticism was more general, but the ideas that finally and fatally undermined beliefs in witchcraft were new (Levack 1987: 203, 217–24). The twentieth-century social movement differs from the earlier witch-hunts and from African witch-hunts in the nature and strength of the opposition to it. The modern equivalent of the witch-finding already described by anthropologists and historians is a controversy (Beckford 1985: 9), not an unopposed campaign or witch-hunt.

The reason for this difference is that a rational approach to phenomena and an attitude of disbelief in supernatural phenomena which was only just beginning in the seventeenth century is now deeply embedded in Western culture, athough some intellectuals consider reason to be in decline as a presiding genius in Western society.[8] Those who rejected the allegations were not just idiosyncratic individuals, but occupied identifiable social positions or held ideas that encouraged scepticism. They reacted critically to the allegations, rather than elaborating a set of ideas and a campaign of their own, but they did so from a largely consistent standpoint. Perhaps even more important than this, it was opposition that generated changes in the anti-satanist movement itself: changes in leadership as new people supported the allegations in the press, in the visible personnel of the movement as belief spread, and in the issues taken up in the media. However, the surface changes hid a continuity that indicates the tenacity of the campaign and the importance, to both sides, of issues that underlie both the old and the new forms of witch-hunting.

The construction of a campaign

The initial impetus to the anti-satanist movement in Britain was undoubtedly the campaign by fundamentalist evangelicals against new religions, or as they termed them, 'cults'.[9] Like the similar revival in the Church in early modern Europe, the evangelicals were attempting to root out folk superstitions and superstitious practices and to cleanse the church itself from undesirable elements (cf. Ankarloo & Henningsen 1990). In Britain the fundamentalists were fighting the spread of irreligion and the turning away, in the established church, from the fight against sin to social welfare and liberalism (Jenkins 1992: 161–9). The Christian revivalist movement which began in the 1970s and gathered strength in the following decade, emphasised a Christian spiritual war against satanists, a term they defined very inclusively, as we have seen (see pp. 29–30), but which most frequently referred to new religions and 'the occult'. Campaigns such as those against ouija boards, fortune-telling by tarot cards, and the celebration of Hallowe'en, were set in motion. Groups were also founded by individuals to further these aims. Campaigning groups need publicity for their work so they were happy to give the press stories that would achieve it. One such group was the Reachout Trust, founded by Douglas Harris in 1985, with the general aim of missionary work among people involved either in new religious movements or the occult. The Evangelical Alliance provided an umbrella organisation for such groups and its newsletter disseminated their views. It also distributed pamphlets and videos (e.g. 1987) in support of the campaign against satanism.

Another organisation which campaigned against satanism was Child-Watch. Founded by Dianne Core, a former residential care worker, a year before the Reachout Trust,[10] its original aim, as the name indicates, was to help children who were being sexually abused. Core had worked for ChildLine, the telephone helpline for children, and in the early years was interviewed on television about paedophile rings and the existence of snuff movies. Her Christian orientation was clearly shown in her speech to a conference in Rome in 1988 funded by an American far-right organisation. In it she spoke of spiritual warfare against Satan and claimed that at the moment Satan was winning (*New Federalist*, 1988). At the height of her influence Core held a position as an 'agony aunt' on a Hull newspaper, a useful vehicle for her views. During the Rochdale case in 1990 she was strongly criticised by a member of her own organisation who became sceptical about the allegations being made. Her organisation then suffered a number of vicissitudes: there was conflict with Humberside police, who claimed she had coached a witness in a case of sexual abuse, a member of ChildWatch was accused of sexually abusing a child, and finally her association with the newspaper ended in recriminations. Thereafter Core and ChildWatch both disappeared from the national press, although her book, written with a journalist, Fred Harrison, was published in 1991. But in 1993 she collaborated with a Birmingham doctor on a video for television, *Satanism and children – no greater evil*.

Fundamentalist organisations spread the allegations, holding conferences, publishing accounts of abuse and checklists of symptoms, and selling sophisticated videos that warned of the dangers of satanism. When the first cases involving children came to light, journalists took up the story.[11] To begin with, the bias of the press was all towards believing the allegations (cf. Jenkins 1992: 22). The senior social worker concerned in the Nottingham case wrote an article published in 1989, and followed it with another written jointly with her colleague early in 1989. The journalist Bea Campbell was active in her support, writing four articles in 1990 alone. Journalists participated in the writing of two influential books by survivor Audrey Harper (Harper & Pugh 1990) and by Dianne Core (Core and Harrison 1991). Between 1991 and 1993, three other journalists published books on the subject of satanic abuse (Boyd 1991; Tate 1991; Parker 1993); all three of them presented a case for believing the allegations.

The evangelical campaign was also assisted by the use of promotional videos and television programmes. One of the first programmes, transmitted on 27 April 1987 and called *Lucifer over Lancashire* 'focused on a book published by Hyndburn Christian Fellowship (*To God be the Glory*) which highlighted how God had been working in great ways in and around Pendle – the "occult capital of the North" (Logan 1988: 7). It included unnamed survivors of satanism. The same day, the late Geoffrey Dickens MP, a long-term supporter of the campaign, spoke in the House of Commons about the threat of witchcraft. Subsequently there were two television programmes, involving many of the same journalists who were active in the press.

By contrast with the television programmes, which were locally focused and made in England, the first videos were American imports that were merely distributed in this country. One of the earlier ones linked the campaigns in the United States and Britain by including an extended interview with the British evangelical Maureen Davies, referred to as an expert on the subject. The Reachout Trust was responsible for two later videos: *Doorways to danger*, which accompanied a pamphlet with the same title, and *Devil worship – the rise of satanism*. They were advertised in the Evangelical Alliance newsletter and distributed through churches; according to one informant their contents, like those of other dramatic Christian videos warning against the dangers to the faith, were disseminated in school playgrounds to fascinated children whose parents were not evangelicals.

According to Jenkins (1992: 158) the first reference to satanic abuse in Britain was an interiew with Sandi Gallant (Thomas, *Colchester Evening Gazette*, 27 January (1989), a Californian policewoman who was known to be a 'satan-hunter' or 'cult-cop', as they were called there. In it she gave it as her view that there would be similar cases in Britain,[12] and a report issued by the NSPCC shortly afterwards seemed to prove her right. What happened then exemplifies the manner in which the allegations spread in the early period. On 17 July 1989, the charity issued a press release stating that they were becoming increasingly 'anxious about the existence of ritualistic abuse involving children.' (It later turned out that the evidence for this in their report was rather thin.) It referred to a programme on the subject, in the series the *Cook Report*, due to go out the same night. On 18 July, reports of the press release were to be found disseminated throughout Britain. Papers in Aberdeen, Carlisle, Coventry, Edinburgh, Exeter, Kettering, Plymouth, Wolverhampton, Wrexham and York all had items referring to the press release. (The *Lincolnshire Echo* of 20 July used an interview with a local NSPCC worker.) The language in the reports, whether given in full or shortened, was identical, as might be expected if the papers were publishing a syndicated piece. The *Kettering Evening Telegraph* identified the source as the Press Association. However, between the release of the NSPCC statement and the items published in the various newspapers, someone, possibly in the syndicating agency, had altered the description of what the NSPCC was concerned that the public should know, and most articles referred to a 'chilling warning'. The original rather unspecific NSPCC phrase had become 'ritualistic abuse *of youngsters in occult ceremonies* (my italics)', a much more direct reference to satanic abuse, which had the effect of associating a much-respected British charity with the allegations.[13]

This instance of news dissemination shows how quickly the whole nation was made aware of the apparent seriousness of the satanic threat. The details of what was alleged in many cases was available equally quickly and just as widely. Hence the similarities between allegations in different cases could not be considered totally independent right from the beginning. It is also an illustration of how small and interconnected a group was involved in activating the movement. In the very early stages of the anti-satanism movement, the 'experts' to whom the newspapers turned for quotes were drawn from the ranks of the evangelicals, some of whom of course were journalists. There is no doubt that the single most quoted English 'expert' in the first phase was a former nurse, Maureen Davies. She had joined the staff of the Reachout Trust with a brief to focus on victims of the occult generally, but rapidly came to concentrate on satanic abuse. She was regularly interviewed and quoted during the big initial cases in Nottingham and Rochdale and her advice was asked by social workers in those, and many other, cases. In only one of the many cases where I have a record of her involvement, did she fail to confirm the existence of satanic abuse.

Campaigners such as Maureen Davies worked very hard. One record of her speaking engagements between April 1989 and November 1992 shows a formidable load. According to this list, she spoke at thirteen conferences, gave eleven lectures (of which three were a part of training courses), participated in seven seminars and three study groups and another six miscellaneous meetings with police, social services and other interested groups, besides writing an article for the social work magazine *Community Care* and taking part in a programme for television. She also visited the United States where she was filmed for a video made by an evangelical group there. It was a measure of her pre-eminence in the field and that of Reachout, that the first sceptical television programme, a two-part programme by BBC Wales in October 1991, concentrated on her and on Marshall Roland, a solicitor connected to Reachout.

The evangelical associations for Christian psychiatrists, teachers and social workers have not publicly committed themselves, as organisations, to supporting the anti-satanist movement. However, they have undoubtedly provided fora for the discussion and dissemination of ideas, including the controversial indicators, of satanic abuse from the United States. It seems unlikely that it was coincidence that two very early cases diagnosed as satanic abuse both involved officers in the Association for Christian Social Workers. In 1990, the Association for Christian Psychiatrists and Psychologists held a conference in London attended by many believers. The involvement of social workers and then therapists that signalled new phases in the development of the movement almost certainly owed something to conferences held by these Christian organisations.

American influence was very visible during the early stages of the movement. The frequent references to American campaigners and campaign materials in this chapter already make the origin of much of the proselytising efforts clear. In addition, a number of American experts were consulted. Their 'expertise' was based for the most part on religious conviction, since they did not understand the rather different way in which the police and social services work in England and Wales. However, several conferences were organised at Reading by a pair of freelance social workers, one of whom was an American and a campaigner against satanic abuse. Several speakers at the 1989 conference were American, although two English social workers spoke about their case in Nottingham. This conference initiated a second phase: it centred on cases involving children who, it was being alleged, were disclosing that they had been abused in satanic rituals. At this point the differences in the new social context in which the nascent epidemic was being implanted began to influence the direction in which it developed.

Believe the children – the second stage

When the evangelical campaign against evil entered a sphere that entailed legal action, the anti-satanism movement as a social movement gathered momentum. It also, by provoking investigation into the claims, sowed the seeds of controversy that eventually caused a shift back to adult victims. The allegations of survivors like Audrey Harper, however well publicised in the Christian community, had not required action by the authorities against the abusers because those responsible were usually not named. Accusations of witchcraft against unnamed persons may occur like this in Africa (Middleton & Winter 1963) and were recorded in early modern England (Macfarlane 1970). They express the sufferer's sense of threat or, by warning the evil-doers that retaliation will follow further attack, represent action to try to ward off the danger. It is where accusations name particular persons that public action is precipitated. In the United States as in Britain, the allegations that particular children were being abused in satanic rituals required action by the authorities and generated public alarm and media attention. In the United States this was brought about by the children's parents; in Britain social workers triggered the next stage. There were good reasons why this was so.

In the late1980s, social work was a beleaguered occupation and many social workers felt themselves to be misunderstood and unjustly vilified. The publicity that attended failures to protect children and the subsequent judicial inquiries into their deaths had disseminated a negative image of social workers. Since the establishment of the

NSPCC in the late nineteenth century, those who worked in child protection had provoked both hostility and anxiety in the working classes, who were more likely to suffer their professional attentions. A century later, with a professional social work organisation established and paid for out of public funds, the conservative elite came also to view it adversely for its allegedly left-wing views and its manifestation of the spread of state control into family life, which many held should be a private sphere immune from state 'interference'. The discovery that children might be physically damaged, even killed, by their parents and subsequently that fathers might sexually abuse their children, girls and boys, was countered by claims that these were stories invented by social workers to support their claims for increased resources and greater powers.

The controversy surrounding the newest of these issues, the diagnosis of sexual abuse, had been raised to a higher pitch in 1987, when there was a highly publicised and bitter conflict over large numbers of children taken into care in Cleveland, in north-east England because of allegations of sexual abuse (Campbell 1988; La Fontaine 1990).[14] Those responsible for taking this action, including the social workers, were subjected to a hostile national press and television campaign led by the local Member of Parliament. The affair demonstrated a major conflict between the police (largely male) and social workers (largely female) that was not resolved by the government's subsequent issue of revised guidelines on child protection practices called, somewhat optimistically, 'Working together'. One social work view of the outcome of the Cleveland affair was that it had demonstrated the difficulty of convicting the sexual abusers of children, and moreover showed that the perpetrators of abuse had supporters among the elite and in the police. Fear of a repetition of the Cleveland affair was very much in the minds of the social workers in the first few cases of alleged satanic abuse. Moreover, the Cleveland enquiry had pointed to the lack of special training in sexual abuse, the result of a rapid expansion of child protection work (Jenkins 1992: 36, 201). Although funds were subsequently released to deal with this, it took time for the additional training to take place, so that social workers were still aware that they might have to deal with problems for which they were not trained. This can only have heightened the anxieties that have already been shown to lie behind the experiencing of cases as so different or stressful.

As I have already argued earlier, the hypothesis of satanic abuse offered an explanation for what had happened in these cases. In some cases the suggestion seems to have come from foster-mothers who were considered the closest to the children, once they had been taken into care. It accounted for the state the children were in by suggesting a cause that was commensurate with the damage that they displayed in their behaviour and in what they said. Sympathy for these children was a powerful motivator, and may have been quite deliberately used in some cases to encourage belief in the horrors that were being alleged. The difficulty of obtaining foster-parents for these damaged and difficult children may have made social workers more willing to accept ideas that foster-parents found helpful.

Social workers accustomed to working with a rule of optimism about the possibility of changing human behaviour were confronted with what many were quite prepared to call evil (Dawson and Johnston 1989). Anxiety and lack of training motivated some social workers to accept the explanation of satanism with relief; others certainly accepted it through religious motivation. Many were probably prepared to believe members of the profession rather than (potentially critical) outsiders; the social work press showed a distinct bias towards belief (Clapton 1993) and that too may have influenced social workers. Whatever individual social workers may have felt, there was no public dissent from social workers at that stage. At the grassroots, where a whole team, or even a social work department might be convinced of the anti-satanist view, it was difficult for anyone to question the validity of the explanation. In several cases, I heard an account of the extreme social pressure, up to and including complete ostracism, that had been exerted on those who doubted the diagnosis of satanic abuse in a case where their colleagues had accepted it.

The first cases involving allegations of the satanic abuse of children made it clear that social workers in Congleton, Nottingham and Rochdale had transformed the evangelical campaign against satanism by associating it with child protection. Moreover what had been a war of words now became action by the state's employees. Religion is considered a private matter in Britain, a question of individual beliefs. As long as the campaign remained religious it might be a matter of public controversy but it was not a question of public policy. The children's cases transformed what had been an evangelical movement for religious revitalisation into action against the evil manifest in an acute social problem. A pressure group developed in support, which in turn provoked opposition. The religious campaign became a social movement with the aim of influencing the public and, through it, state policy.

The allegations were transformed into a claim to have discovered a new danger to the country's children. The sources for the allegations were, the believers asserted, the children themselves. As we have seen in chapter 7 the allegations were, in fact, 'constructed' by adults. However, citing the children as sources allowed the campaigners to support their assertions with the psychological argument that disbelief was really a reaction to the horror of the discovery, a collective denial of the existence of the problem. The denial of the truth of satanic abuse, they argued, paralleled the reaction to the discovery of sexual abuse, that in turn had reflected the effects of the revelation of physical abuse. This had the effect of deflecting attention from the complete lack of corroborative evidence for the satanic/ritual aspects of the allegations and made disbelief seem a betrayal of children.

Linking satanic abuse with the discovery of other forms of child abuse provided an argument that was convincing, particularly to feminists of many different kinds, who had identified with the sufferings of children since the 1970s, claiming that their abuse represented yet another form of domestic violence, another dimension of the effects of a patriarchal system (Jenkins 1992: 174). Since abused children, like raped women, were victims of it, justice demanded that they too be believed when they revealed what they had suffered. This argument was effective in a wider field than feminism itself. The preponderance of women in social work and men in the police forces allowed conflict between them to be presented as a gender struggle as it had been in the Cleveland affair (Campbell 1988; La Fontaine 1990; Jenkins 1992). Feminist ideas had been accepted in left-wing circles (Jenkins 1992: 35), but the issue of satanic abuse did not take on a party-political flavour, despite this.[15] Like all welfare institutions, social services had ensured that all their staff had been sensitised to issues of gender; believers were presented as dedicated women struggling to protect children against paedophiles. A wide variety of people were prepared to accept the view (originally a feminist one) that refusal to believe victims was hurtful to them. Rape crisis centres attracted women who claimed to be survivors of satanic abuse, and they lent further weight to feminist reasons for accepting the allegations as true. Women police officers, who are more likely to be involved in child protection and may suffer from an institutional chauvinism that I have observed myself (and see Jenkins 1992: 201), were more likely to believe than men, although the numbers of believers in the police force seem rather small. This feminist support of the satanic abuse allegations was felt early in the movement through the involvement of the feminist journalist Bea Campbell, and still retains its influence. The most recent 'training' video, which effectively supports the idea of satanic abuse, has been produced through a feminist network and marketed through Manchester Rape Crisis Centre.

The rise of opposition

The police by their role and training were inclined to be sceptical and less easily influenced by claims of satanism. Their investigations searched for evidence to support allegations and when none was found, they considered the accusations unproven. When the absence of corroborative evidence became known, others began to voice their scepticism. The areas from which dissent most often arose were those in which evidence and the testing of evidence were central to their professional methods: the law and the academy. The claim that the allegations were made by children was considered against a background of changes being made to facilitate children's giving testimony in court. Lawyers who opposed these changes saw the lack of evidence in the satanic abuse cases as validating their stance; one commented to me tartly that the last time children's testimony was considered sufficient evidence of a crime having taken place was during the sixteenth century witch-hunts. Like lawyers, academics were disinclined to believe in events for which there was no material evidence and some social scientists were, like myself, intrigued by the apparent incongruity of such allegations in the late twentieth century.

Difficulties in the relationship between police and social workers helped to strengthen the commitment of each to their opposed views. The charges that they had failed to find the evidence through incompetence, unwillingness or worse, an attempt at cover-up, alienated the police, who had been affected by reading about recent cases of corruption in other police forces and were angry at being accused of it themselves. In some cases the police saw the criticisms of themselves as an attempt by social workers to take over the role of investigators in child protection cases, which the latter were not trained for. The police in many areas had only just begun to accept child protection as an important part of policing. The facts that the police were perceived as being all men (despite the use of women detectives to interview the children in several cases) and that the majority of social workers in the field were women evoked the same gender issues as the Cleveland affair (Campbell 1988; La Fontaine 1990: ch.1). However, the issue of satanic abuse did not just mobilise the same factions as the Cleveland affair, which had not involved Christian groups.

The close association between evangelical fundamentalism and the allegations of satanic abuse became the initial target of the opposition to the anti-satanism movement. According to this view the allegations were the invention of fundamentalist Christians (Waterhouse 1990). As early as 1989, the two senior social workers in Nottingham had made a point of dissociating themselves from the evangelical Reachout and its spokesperson, Maureen Davies, in order to counter criticisms. In writing about the Nottingham case, they denied that they or their team were motivated by their Christian beliefs to find satanic rituals where there were none (Jenkins 1992: 170). The link with the religious formulation remained, however, in that they described the case as a confrontation with 'pure evil'; they also compared themselves, somewhat dramatically, with survivors of the concentration camps (Dawson & Johnston 1989; Jenkins 1992: 170). From then on, others such as the therapist Valerie Sinason, would also declare that they were not Christians in the apparent belief that the statement negated any possibility of being influenced by a Christian culture. This view is characteristic of Western society, where religion is held to be a matter of individual belief rather than communal practice. Yet, all the members of the anti-satanist movement appear to adopt the concepts of good and evil presented in Christian discourse (La Fontaine 1992; Jenkins 1992: Pocock 1985; Victor 1993). As Chapter 3 demonstrated, the image of the secret conspiracy to reverse all that is good is not limited to practising Christians, but has a long history in Western societies.

Another change occurred in the press itself. As might be expected, the social work press largely supported what social workers claimed to be the case, and the various articles it published tended to encourage belief in the existence of satanist cults that abused children. As Clapton pointed out, even where articles were ostensibly neutral the illustrations and even the magazine covers were putting across the horrors of satanism (Clapton 1993). Jenkins described the press in general as having at first supported the idea of satanic abuse, with the exception of the *Independent* and the *Mail on Sunday*, but later, with the collapse of two more large cases, as launching 'an uncompromising attack against the ritual theorists and the police and social workers who had accepted their views' (1992: 187). As the journalist Nick Anning pointed out later in the *Journalist* (Anning 1991/92), the affair proved very lucrative for the media, whichever side of the controversy they supported. A number of television programmes were made, one directly promoting the social workers' view of the Nottingham case, but later another expressed a more sceptical approach.

Adults and therapy – the third stage

The results of large and well-publicised cases, like that in Rochdale which collapsed early in 1991, to be followed by the return to their families of children taken in a similar case in the Orkneys, was to encourage scepticism. The remarks of the judge in the Rochdale case made it clear that he thought the stories were produced by faulty and suggestive interviewing, and a similar conclusion was to be found in the Orkney inquiry report. An experienced child psychiatrist from the Tavistock Clinic, Dr Judith Trowell, was quoted in the report as saying that one interview was 'a superb example of how not to do an investigative interview' (Clyde 1992: 260). These two cases encouraged the scepticism that was beginning to make itself felt. This stimulated further reactions among believers. However, the announcement of a judicial inquiry into the Orkney case produced a relative lull in press attention until late 1992, when it issued a report that was highly critical of almost all the parties to the disputed cases but which made its scepticism clear (Clyde 1992).

A further development was under way within the movement itself. RAINS, the organisation referred to earlier in connection with research on stress among child protection workers, was founded in 1989, but did not begin to displace the original Christian organisations cited in the press until two or three years later. Its aims and composition show very clearly how the main thrust of the anti-satanist movement was no longer religious but led by members of the social services. The founding group consisted of a psychiatrist and her nurse colleague from a psychiatric hospital[16] and the two senior social workers from Nottingham who were then beginning their publicity campaign. The last founder-member was described as lecturing to social workers at Keele University.[17] The most visibly active member, now known as the co-ordinator, is the psychiatrist, Dr Joan Coleman, one of the founders. The aim of the organisation, as its title implies, is to provide and distribute information about what, following Sinason (1994), they now refer to as satanist abuse and to offer support to people dealing with a case. It is oriented to the needs of the professionals rather than those of the victims, but Dr Coleman has also been extensively interviewed as speaking for survivors and for believers generally.

The study of RAINS published in a child protection journal, *Child Abuse Review*, confirms that RAINS has been quite successful in recruiting members from workers in the child protection field (Youngson 1993; see also 1994). In March 1993 its 120 members[18] were 'social workers, psychiatrists, psychologists and foster parents'. Of the seventy-one who returned questionnaires social workers constituted by far the largest group (41 per cent). The other professionals mentioned, clinical psychologists (17 per cent) and independent or voluntary agency counsellors or therapists (27 per cent) together only just outnumber them. Women made up 80 per cent of the respondents

(Youngson 1993: 253). Tate, who is also a member, states that 'there are three professional journalists in RAINS' (Tate 1994: 186) and a few police officers.

Dr Coleman has emerged in public as the leader of this group, although she did not become well-known to the press until 1994. She dates her involvement with self-styled victims of satanic abuse to a case in 1987 (1994a; 1994b). Her second case, a teenager, was referred to her by Dianne Core of ChildWatch, who also knew the journalist she consulted, Tim Tate, but whom Coleman emphasises that she had met independently (Coleman personal communication).[19] Like Core she is a Christian, but her position in RAINS regarding satanic abuse is based on her profession and her role as founder; her religious affiliation is ignored as irrelevant. Although some of the original religious campaigners are said to be members of RAINS, they appear to have had little influence within it. As an organisation RAINS is quite different from the first anti-satanist organisation, the Reachout Trust or its successor, the Beacon Foundation. Its target is the growing community of therapists, social workers and those who train them: the health services in general.

This third stage of the anti-satanist movement has given therapists the expert role. 'Therapist' is a term with a wide range of meaning: from trained clinical psychologists or psychiatrists to self-styled therapists with little or no training. One example of the latter is the American Pamela Klein, whose only training is in 'counsellor education' which 'is designed primarily for public (state) school counsellors. It does not prepare a person to do intensive long-term psychotherapy' (Victor 1993: 242). Many, like Norma Howes, who was her business partner for some time, are experienced social workers. Others have been in therapy themselves, often in a women's group or a 'survivors' group, have graduated to leading the group and then to undertaking therapy with individual clients. Some of them, like Sue Hutchinson and Gillian Burke, advertise that they have had personal experience and are themselves 'survivors'. Most will offer 'training' as well as 'therapy'. Therapists have a higher status in the public estimation than social workers and are not so subject to attack and denigration. They are also very much better paid[20] (cf. Victor 1993). It is small wonder, then, that many social workers aspire to become therapists. Treating survivors of satanist abuse helps them to achieve that aim.

As a very rewarding profession that is easy to enter, therapy has expanded rapidly. The more highly qualified psychiatrists and psychoanalysts appear to accept their untrained colleagues without demur, particularly if they have clinical experience. Beit-Hallahmi, writing of a similar situation in Israel, points out that 'The general blooming of psychotherapy in Israel indeed meant that numerous individuals lacking any formal training have been successful in establishing psychotherapy practices' (1992: 117–18). He goes on to argue that because the demand for psychotherapy was so high that it could not be met by the professionally trained, they did not feel threatened by the activities of the untrained and did not attempt to control them (1992: 127). In Israel there is a licensing system for therapists; in Britain no licences are required and there is no professional body that monitors standards, so that becoming a therapist is even easier than in Israel.

A school of therapy that rejects some of the traditional rules of the established profession appears to be emerging in connection with treating adult survivors. To begin with, it has much in common with the feminists, recognising an obligation to 'believe' their clients. It is considered 'damaging' to the patient to show any scepticism; Sinason refers to it as a 'secondary trauma' (Sinason 1994: 5). When what their patients say is manifestly impossible, the therapists find other explanations, such as the use of drugs or brainwashing, to sustain belief. Thus where patients, like children in the Rochdale case, claim to have been able to fly, it may be assumed that they have been taking drugs, whether or not there is any evidence that they have been doing so.[21] Such secondary rationalisations often require further explanation that results in still more elaboration of the story. In addition, it is not considered adequate to take the traditional approach of distinguishing between internal or emotional reality (true for the patient) and external reality (objectively demonstrated) (Hale & Sinason 1994: 274). They assert: '. . . there is a real objective event that needs to be validated'. There is no room in this scheme for the possibility that the patient may not, for one or another discoverable reason, be telling the truth. Finally they claim, like Hale and Sinason (1994: 278–9), that these patients require the therapist to abandon the notion of a limited period of time per therapeutic session and to forget the usual restriction on touching the patient, who needs to be held and comforted like a child. The contrast with the more orthodox view that is also represented, rather surprisingly, in the Sinason volume (Adshead 1994) is striking.

The increasing role for therapists is linked with the return to prominence of adult survivors. The collapse of cases involving children and the discrediting of the processes by which their 'stories' had been extracted left the sceptics in a dominant position. The newspapers castigated social workers for removing children from their families without cause and for forcing them through endless interviews to confirm their preconceived ideas. By 1993 there was a strong bias in

believers' accounts towards cases involving adults, who far outnum-
bered the child victims. While Valerie Sinason,[22] who has emerged as
one of the leaders of the present phase, made her name working with
children, her first satanic abuse case involved an adult; Dr Coleman, the
other leader, has worked almost exclusively with adults. Only nine
respondents in the Youngson study stated that they were the therapists
of children, while forty-eight were counselling adults. Only ten of the
twenty-nine social workers were concerned with cases involving children. The adult patients of members of RAINS provided detailed
accounts of satanic rituals that were said to 'explain' what the children
had not made clear. These were not publicised as Christians newly
come to Christ but as patients, whose psychological disturbance
testified to their extreme suffering.

In part the emphasis on adult disclosures has been a reaction to my
research. As well as Youngson's study, Coleman published two articles,
one in a collection of articles on satanist abuse and another in *Child
Abuse Review*. The tone of the articles is professional and presents
conclusions based on case material. It was widely known (I had spoken
to RAINS on the subject) that my research was a study of cases
involving children; in response it was stressed that lack of information
from adult 'survivors' invalidated its conclusions. As I am an academic,
clinical experience was stressed as the only legitimate source of
information. A book, *Treating survivors of satanic abuse*, timed to precede
the publication of my research findings was presented as 'the first *clinical*
(as opposed to *research*) book on the subject' (Sinason 1994: 6; my
italics) but has the air of a demonstration of strength, a rallying of
supporters. Sinason writes: 'When I started planning this book as a
result of my first supervision experience, I found only a handful of brave
(sic) contributors. As the book progressed, the number rose and as we
went to press, thirty-five people had wanted to contribute, with many
more in the wings (Neil Frude, Norma Howes *et al.*). The knowledge
that this book was being planned has already changed the environment
(Cooklin & Gorell Barnes 1994: ch.13)' (Sinason 1994: 6). The book is
also a vivid illustration of the altered shape assumed by the anti-satanist
movement by the end of 1993. Over half of the forty-two contributors
(twenty-three or 55 per cent) are psychiatrists, psychotherapists and
clinical psychologists;[23] only four are social workers and two of them are
also described as therapists. The psychologising of the movement
appears complete.

10   Aftermath and conclusions

The changes in the anti-satanist movement have continued to confirm the predominance of therapists. Since the cases that are given prominence now are those of adults rather than children, the focus has altered. In the case of adults there is nothing to require police or legal action unless the victims themselves initiate it, so that the question of material corroboration of the allegations of satanic abuse has gradually become less salient in public. The identities of the satanists are not pursued with such vigour and have faded into the shadows to become figures of evil with no real human identity. Paradoxically however, where extremes of evildoing are demonstrably proven, as in the case of the serial killer Frederick West, or the self-confessed Belgian kidnapper and murderer of young girls, attempts are made to prove a satanic connection retrospectively. Nevertheless the main focus of attention where adult survivors are concerned is on the victims rather than the perpetrators of satanic abuse. The main public debate concerns diagnosis, and the labels given the issues – false memory syndrome and multiple personality disorder – make it clear at once that they are concerned with psychological rather than religious matters. Their potentially divisive nature has made them the subject of concerned discussion within the psychological profession.

The first of these debates focuses on an element in the recounting of satanic abuse in childhood by adults – the nature of memory. Some adult survivors, like the famous Michelle Smith of *Michelle Remembers*, claimed to have started therapy without being aware that they might have been sexually abused or that the abuse had been satanic. Their amnesia was said to have been a reaction to pain or shock (trauma) and under appropriate therapy these memories might be recovered. Before memories were recovered they might show themselves in bodily symptoms and these might be referred to as 'body memories'. The amnesia itself was considered 'proof' of trauma so that the diagnosis was incontestable. As sceptics put it: if you could remember the abuse you had been abused, but if you could not remember being abused you certainly had been. The fact that a wide variety of psychological difficulties might be attributed to sexual abuse by untrained counsellors or therapists generated scepticism that was increased by the results of research on relevant issues. The discovery that particularly suggestible people might recount stories of their involvement in crimes in which they had not been involved was followed by evidence that certain types of therapy, such as hypnosis and regression therapy[1] seemed particularly prone to induce memories of sexual abuse in patients. A study of cases in the United States showed that they related to a small number of therapists, a further suggestion that the diagnosis was being affected by the therapists who made it (Bottoms et al. 1996a). The 'recovered memories' were relabelled 'false memories' by sceptics.

Scepticism about the idea of recovered memories was publicised by a pressure group, the False Memory Society. This was an organisation for parents affected by the recovered memories of their children, mostly daughters. Adult survivors of sexual abuse might break off relations with their parents after the recovery of such memories in therapy, accusing them of sexual abuse; a small number of them also made accusations of satanic abuse. In Britain none of these cases have come to court, but in the United States some parents were successfully sued for damages on the basis of their children's recovered memories. Support groups were founded independently in both countries and grew rapidly. They publicised research on memory and case-histories, and gave advice to accused parents. The most famous case has been the only one known in which a man was convicted of satanic abuse on his own confession. Richard Ofshe, the expert on cults who interviewed him, demonstrated conclusively that the confession had been induced in him by the type of interrogation he had suffered. His 'recovered memory' of perpetrating the abuse faded rapidly once the questioning was over but his appeal against his life sentence failed. On both sides of the Atlantic this case was buttressed by the stories of young women who retracted their accusations, claiming that they had been pressured into making them by their therapists.

The False Memory Society has been accused by believers, particularly therapists and feminists, of giving encouragement to sexual abusers of their children who were seeking support for their denials of guilt. The FMS declares that their own cases are the personal responsibility of members, but continues to claim that research shows that it is possible to generate false memories. The effect of the controversy has been to indicate a potential split among clinicians and therapists on the related issues of memory, forms of therapy and training. An investigation by the

British Psychological Association did not succeed in reconciling the two views.

The second debate concerns the diagnosis of a new psychological disorder, multiple personality disorder (MPD), which is not yet accepted by the regulatory authorities in Britain although it is in the United States. In both countries there are many psychologists and psychiatrists who do not accept it. It is a condition which was once thought to be very rare, in which the patient displays more than one and sometimes many different personalities. One personality may or may not be aware of the others and they represent different aspects of, and or even ages of, the patient. The splitting is said to be due to the patient's dissociating from intolerable pain or stress and creating an 'alter' (another personality). The issue, as the last chapter indicated, is not new but is only just beginning to attract media attention. MPD has close links with the anti-satanism debate because the disorder is now said to originate in satanic abuse and the diagnosis of the disorder is considered an indicator of satanic abuse in childhood. One of the controversial issues concerns the methods and the degree to which this is a condition constructed by therapist and client together. Mulhern's study (1991) comes to the firm conclusion that it is entirely a construct.

MPD patients may use different voices and mannerisms when different personalities are in control; to an observer the effect is not unlike possession by spirits, but in Western culture it is explained as internal fragmentation rather than intrusion by external agents. The anthropologist Erika Bourguignon has considered MPD as an inverted form of possession by spirits or demons (1989), and a connection between witchcraft and spirit possession was postulated long ago by Lewis (1970). In this connection it is interesting to note that Christian psychologists such as Friesen may state that in some cases of MPD, the clinician's task may be to identify which personalities are intrusive demons and which genuine fragments of the patient's own personality (1991: 220–3). In the United States there is an association for people with MPD, who are known as 'multiples'; some of them have become quite well known as media personalities. In the Netherlands I was given a booklet written by a multiple who was handing them out at a conference I attended; it was entitled *All forty-two of us*.

Clearly the topic of MPD falls outside the scope of this book; it merely serves here to illustrate the new directions of the anti-satanist movement. That this still exists, albeit in reduced and less well publicised form is attested by the RAINS conference held in Warwick in September 1996: Better the Devil You Know? The topics listed also suggest an emphasis that turns attention away from the domestic incidence of sexual abuse, still the most common, to the activities of strangers. A new expert, a multiple personality from the United States, signals the introduction of the new topic. The inclusion of 'research' in the advertisement of the perspectives offered in the conference suggests a continuing reaction to my work and that of the psychologists whose survey in the United States supported its conclusions; however, it may also be an attempt to link ritual abuse to the proven activities of criminal organisations, to pornography and prostitution. That is where the movement began: with survivors who were saved from such sins.

Conclusions

This account of the anti-satanist movement in Britain at the end of the twentieth century is intended to contribute a case-history to the study of beliefs in mystical evil. It is my contention that the allegations of which it is composed can be considered to constitute an instance of a general phenomenon that anthropologists have studied in many parts of the world. The terms that are most commonly used to translate the indigenous notions of this kind are 'witchcraft' and 'sorcery', but it has long been recognised that the ideas that are labelled in this way are not identical but vary somewhat from place to place. There are, however, sufficient similarities for them to be considered members of one class of social phenomena. The allegations in the anti-satanist movement indeed referred initially to witchcraft and the term may still be used. There seems little distinction in the popular mind between witchcraft which is equated with black (or evil) magic, and satanism, the worship of the devil. This association has a sound historical basis. In English culture the two are closely linked.

It has been suggested by more than one anthropologist that the term 'witchcraft' is no longer useful in the anthropological task of cross-cultural comparison.[2] It was said to be insufficiently well delimited, as each culture contains too many subtle gradations in its use of the term and too many different associated notions to permit comparison. However, to substitute the term 'evil' is no solution, because this may open the door to even greater indeterminacy and a wider array of questions and categorisations. Moreover 'evil' has the disadvantage of being part of a dualistic morality, of evil contrasted with good, that may not exist elsewhere; using the term 'evil' instead of 'witchcraft' may unwittingly impose this dualism on data to which it is foreign. 'Witch-craft' was used in this study precisely to limit the comparisons to culturally variable concepts in which extreme evil is personified, but endowed with a human form that has inhuman qualities – the night witch – but where this evil is also believed to be used by human beings against each other so that those who use it are also in some sense witches. Witchcraft is thus not simply a matter of belief but is embedded in how events in human lives are evaluated and other human beings are judged; it is a quintessentially social concept.

The approach I have used has been comparative, cross-cultural. Comparison has been one of anthropology's traditional strengths. It not only furthers the aims of understanding humanity in general and identifying the universals in human society, but provides an essential check on the universal habit of viewing the world through the perceptions native to one's own culture. This is particularly necessary when the topic is as emotive and controversial as the subject of this book. The close study of the ideas and behaviour of members of another society reveals the contingent nature of assumptions one always thought were 'natural'. Any discovery of widely distributed similarities is then more reliable because it does not depend on prior assumptions about 'human nature'. The comparisons here are not as detailed as a fully comparative account would require because the main aim is to document the ethnography of one particular instance, but attention has been drawn to similarities in other societies that stimulate thinking about the problem in hand or provide a check on groundless speculation.

Studies of witch beliefs in modern times still mostly use data drawn from outside Europe. Starting with Evans-Pritchard, the founder of the anthropology of witchcraft, it has long been assumed that such ideas are extinct in Europe. The assumption may even be quite explicit: in 1993 an American historian wrote of the 'disappearance of witchcraft concerns' in Europe (Austen 1993: 97). One reason for this was exemplified very clearly in Trevor-Roper's account of the witch-hunts; he argued that the triumph of rationality in different forms – intellectual, administrative and political – spelt the end of beliefs in witches (see also Macfarlane 1985). Even critics of this particular explanation find a variety of other reasons, such as a different intellectual structure, the development of medicine and of a national legal system or the successful establishment of capitalism to account for the demise of these beliefs. In addition the persistent ethnocentricity that divides the world into what has been called 'the West' and 'the rest' continues to prevent the assumption being called into question. The anti-satanism movement provides a refutation of these theories, an example of such beliefs in an age dominated by the most sophisticated technologies and some of the most complex and powerful bureaucratic organisations in human history.[3]

Historians have found that treating the past as 'another country', using anthropology's findings to do so, has been a fruitful method of understanding it. In return, the modern historiography of the European witch-hunts has stimulated me to make cross-temporal as well as cross-cultural comparisons and to draw on the insights of historians as well as on those of other anthropologists to explain the phenomenon. A consideration of the most recent historiography of the European witch-hunts of the sixteenth and seventeenth centuries has shown that the allegations of satanic ritual can be understood as historical developments from the earlier notion of the witches' sabbath. Historians distinguish between the belief in harm caused by mystical means that formed the substance of common accusations of using witchcraft, and the image of the witches' sabbath, the ritual of devil-worship. An important distinction between them lay in the fact that the people who used witchcraft to cause harm remained human beings but the new doctrine turned them into inhuman figures of evil, like the night-witches of the Third World. The ideas that animated the witch-hunts were not the folk beliefs, but the link between the evil figures of folk belief, witches, and the Christian Devil, that was provided by the theologians of the Church. The witch-hunts were, in effect hunts of devil-worshippers, of satanists.

Beliefs in the existence of a secret and wicked conspiracy to destroy society, which formed the core of the idea of the witches' sabbath, were not new among the upper reaches of early modern European societies. Nor did they have a fixed form. They had developed slowly from their origin in pre-Christian times. New elements were added to the picture and changes of emphasis occurred with innovations in Christian dogma and the shifts in the identity of their perceived enemies. Witches were not unique, merely the latest in a series of demonised opponents of the Church. There was thus no reason for the idea to disappear abruptly when the witch-hunts ended. It continued to persist as an imagined threat expressed in different ways and strengthened periodically in periods of perceived danger to the body politic. Its most recent expression before the allegations of satanic abuse was, of course, the anti-semitism of Europe which reached its peak in Nazi Germany.

Historians have argued that the effect of the witch-hunts in early modern Europe was to impose the Church's idea of witchcraft on the people. This imposition was also a process of bringing two distinct class and sub-cultures together, and subordinating the popular to the central, elite one. It was also a conscious missionary endeavour, aiming to Christianise the margins of society and the peripheries of the emerging states. Something similar on a smaller and milder scale happened in

Africa, when Christian missionaries in Africa in the nineteenth and early twentieth centuries engaged in vigorous extirpation of pagan super-stitions by encouraging communities to burn the objects associated with their pagan beliefs. The central African witch-cleansing movements of the 1930s used the same techniques, forcing villagers to jettison any charms or medicines they possessed. Still later, witchcraft was linked with satanism and in post-independence countries the use of evil mystical powers can take either form. The connection between pentecostalism and belief in 'satanic riches' in Ghana, with its public confessions of former involvement (Meyer 1995), invites comparison with the fundamentalist churches in Britain and north America and their allegations of satanic abuse based on the confessions of its 'survivors'.

Changes in Britain have almost dispensed with the idea of witchcraft. The idea of witches flying to their sabbath has not endured as a serious belief; it survives in popular culture today only in the images associated with Hallowe'en, which has become a children's festival. However, the remnant of the former clerical concept, the concept of a ritual focused on the worship of Satan is still taken seriously, and, as we have seen, literally, within certain quite large sections of the Christian church. It is significant that one element of the fundamentalist attack on occultism was to attempt to prevent schools celebrating Hallowe'en by restoring its sinister connotations. The allegations of secret rites no longer emphasise acts of fealty to Satan that mock subordination to the high officers of the Church, Christ's servants. They make the central element the participants' belief in, and subjection to, the devil and it is this that is reflected in their ritual of worship. It is characteristic of the twentieth century that religion is seen as a matter of individual belief rather than a duty to the creator and ruler of the universe, but in this case such a perspective also widens the constituency of support for the campaigners by allowing those who claim no Christian allegiance to profess belief in the allegations, since it is others who believe in the reality of Satan and who worship him.

To discover continuity with the past is thus not to claim that cultural concepts of evil have not changed. That would require explaining why a long historical process of change stopped. Beliefs in witchcraft as *maleficium* have indeed faded, although there are still people who believe in the efficacy of black magic. The means by which evil is manifest, and thus the contents of the secret rites, owe more to the twentieth century than to the sixteenth or seventeenth. The perverse sexual acts are those which cause horror and disgust in contemporary society, not those that aroused similar feelings in early modern Europe. The appearance of forced abortions and aborted foetuses in modern allegations about satanic rituals reflect contemporary moral controversies; these have not displaced the sacrificial slaughter of human beings, frequently including babies, and the consumption of human flesh and blood as the ritual's core acts. The changes leave the fundamental principles of meaning in the allegations unchanged. We shall come back to their elucidation later.

Given the similarities between the two movements, the work of the historians of early modern Europe in documenting the role of the Church in the witch-hunts can also shed light on the anti-satanist movement. The early modern witch-hunts were both religious and political: they aimed to banish heresy and superstition and to bring marginal communities more firmly under the control of the central authorities. A view that society was being fatally undermined reflected clerical concerns about opposition within the church and superstition outside it. Today the Church is weaker and no longer established in the centres of power, but the rise of fundamentalism is a remarkably similar missionary effort. It, too, aims to Christianise the population and re-establish a Christian morality in all walks of life. To the campaigning Christian fundamentalists in the late twentieth century the work of the devil is exemplified, much as it was three or four centuries ago, in the immoral condition of society and in the practice of magic and concern with the occult. Sexual permissiveness, the prevalence of divorce and the rise in cohabitation rather than formal marriage, abortion, divorce and single-parent families are all seen as destroying (Christian ideals of) the family. For a whole conservative section of society and for those to the right of the political spectrum 'the family' is seen as the basis of society; like the fundamentalists they regard any attack on the family as undermining the whole of social life. The future is represented by the nation's children and parenthood is natural and/or a God-given duty. The picture of children sexually abused, tortured and murdered condenses into a single image the horrors of social breakdown, whether in secular or Christian terms.

While adult converts to fundamentalist Christianity had long followed a tradition of describing their former lives in terms of both witchcraft and satanism, the anti-satanism movement proper consisted of a rash of cases in which children, many of whom had already been taken into care, were said to have described having been abused in satanic rituals. An almost universal feature of the cases was that there was no evidence to support the allegations that rituals had taken place. In addition to the perverse acts that were said to have taken place, animal and human sacrifice were said to have occurred without leaving any traces that even the sophisticated technology of the late twentieth century could pick up.

In a few cases that might have been credible, but when the cases without corroboration grew to include every case in which there had been allegations of satanic abuse the conclusion that the allegations were not true was inescapable. However, to those for whom the status of the accuser allowed of no doubt, evidence was irrelevant, although there was faith that it would be forthcoming. To show scepticism was to be accused of supporting paedophiles; to try and explain was seen as an attempt to excuse. The claim that satanic abuse was the cause of serious psychic damage to children and adults was a moral judgement, not a rational argument from the facts.

It is this belief in unverified and unverifiable mystical evil that, par excellence, classes belief in satanic abuse with belief in witchcraft, whether in the European distant past or in the recent past and the present of many other societies. The allegations have to be understood differently from references to actual events, their meaning construed as symbolic. Dundes takes the view that the witches' sabbath constitutes a reverse image of the central rite of the Christian Church, the Mass or Holy Communion (1989). His argument is attractive, but it is the Protestant churches that have been most receptive to the idea of the witches' sabbath in recent times and their rituals have diverged considerably from the original Christian mass. Many fundamentalist churches whose beliefs in witchcraft and satanism were a motivating force in the current anti-satanist movement do not perform this symbolic enactment of the sacrifice of Jesus, and regard the Roman Catholic mass itself as satanic. In their case the sabbath would merely be an exaggerated version of older Christian ritual. However, the resolution of a long debate over sectarian responsibility for the witch-hunts, was to show that in effect there was broad agreement between Protestants and Catholics over witchcraft and satanism. The symbolism of the witches' sabbath ritual appealed across sectarian divides as emblematic of evil. Today, however, many people who are not Christians, although they are full members of a society which has a largely Christian culture, also find its meaning compelling. This would seem to indicate that the symbolism has a more secular, perhaps a deeper, cultural, significance in Western society than its apparent Christian associations would lead one to conclude.

The symbolism of the allegations can be understood by analogy with the acts that define the night-witch: these constitute 'what human beings are not' (Pocock 1985: 48; La Fontaine 1992). Human beings are part of the natural order and their identity is established in no small measure by what they do not do. Satanic ritual violates what European culture constitutes as the natural order in several ways: by denying the categorical distinction between animal flesh, which may be eaten, and human flesh which may not; by indulging in perverse sexual acts that are incapable of creating life and are performed with 'unnatural' partners. The image of the witches' sabbath had the effect of identifying all who were guilty of *maleficium* as night-witches, non-human beings.

The satanist of the modern allegations, in addition to representing the inhuman quality of the night-witch, also combines in this image the attributes of two other personifications of the illegitimate and the anti-social: the terrorist and the paedophile. Both are dificult to identify and their activities are criminal. Their secret organisations, masked features and readiness to kill and torture make terrorists figures of violence and destruction, representing the antithesis of orderly government and the rule of law. Paedophiles, who are also shadowy figures, abuse and kill other people's children for their selfish pleasure, the vicious mirror image of parental care and altruism. Both these figures are represented as unknown outsiders (only one's opponents are terrorists and inces-tuous fathers are not called paedophiles). Their combined character-istics added to their inhuman acts make the satanists the essence of the monstrous stranger, a serious threat to children and to order in society.

So far we have considered belief in satanic rituals in which children are abused as a set of meanings, but to restrict the analysis entirely to an examination of meanings without taking into account their relation to actions carries some risk. The French historian, Robert Muchembled, has described the risk as the likelihood 'that the investigator will describe his own mental processes rather than the subject of his research, by imposing an arbitrary significance on his collection of brief, out-of-context citations . . . ' (1990: 141). This danger has not always been avoided in anthropology, when the analysis of meaning has been based on concepts taken out of their social context.[4] Considering ideas in relation to the behaviour in which they are both realised and embedded provides a check on the spinning of webs of meaning rather than the analysis of the meanings of others.

The essence of both the historical and the cross-cultural comparisons that I have been making is that belief in a secret conspiracy of great evil, the 'night-witches' of African witchcraft beliefs, were related to actions against human beings. Witch-hunts were actions taken to cleanse a whole community of evil and to identify the witches in order to prevent them from doing further harm; the anti-satanist campaign was a similar attempt to instigate communal action. It is impossible to ignore the fact that many children were taken into care and large amounts of public money were spent on investigations and on subsequent inquiries; it has been said that the Orkney inquiry cost over £6 million. However, accusations of witchcraft and, by analogy, allegations of satanism, are not epiphenomena of beliefs but add another, essential, dimension of meaning. It has been shown in several, justly famous monographs, how the deployment of accusations of witchcraft in contested social situations illuminate their significance. Similarly, a study of the ideas manifest in the allegations of satanic abuse would be incomplete without an analysis of cases that were said to be instances of it. The first question one must ask is: who were actually accused?

If the allegations of satanic abuse are to be taken literally they are directed very specifically at practitioners of certain types of occultism, that are singled out from among other opponents of Christianity. The historian Keith Thomas has argued that there was an element of self-interest in the Church's drive to eliminate magic, for at the time when the Church was engaged in suppressing the activities of the cunning folk, it also dispensed, in return for monetary gifts, very similar charms and nostrums for healing and protection. Within the religious revival of the late twentieth century one can see the alternative religions and occult groups as competing with evangelistic Christianity for adherents. The trappings of occultism in general are implicated in descriptions of satanic ritual by believers. They may be referred to as satanist, since by impeding the spread of Christianity they do the work of Satan against God. For these reasons it is not surprising that the anti-satanist campaigners of the present day should have viewed their competitors as a threat to Christian society. But it is the actual existence of witches and satanists who practise ritual magic which may also be cited by believers in satanic abuse as evidence that Satan is a real force in contemporary society; it is witchcraft and satanism that are implicated as a threat to children. The idea mobilises the force of longstanding fears of evil.

Twentieth-century occultism is built up from traditions that overlap substantially with Christian folklore concerning witches. The occultists' adoption of dress and ceremonial from these sources accounts for some of the similarities with Christian ideas of witches, for example their appearance or the ceremonial use of circles. Some of its practitioners deliberately choose to reflect the satanic image in their appearance and take delight in provoking public scandal with exaggerated claims to wickedness. The founders of the Wiccan tradition took the witch-hunt mythology as a major source and, following the misguided Margaret Murray (1921), have claimed witches as their forebears, seeing them as dedicated pagans keeping the pre-Christian religion alive in spite of the Christian Church's persecution. Playing on many of the same images as the Church, but giving them the opposite connotations and moral values, the very few satanists and the more numerous Wiccans, pagans and magicians seemed tailor-made to be targets of the allegations of satanism.

The pattern of accusations in actual cases shows something rather different. Despite the public statements and sermons of campaigners occultists were not the majority of those accused. There was undoubtedly an increase in public prejudice against them; I was told of several cases where the children of occultists were taken into care for no other apparent reason than their parents' beliefs. But the accused in these 'satanic' cases did not reflect the expressed beliefs of the campaigners. Almost none of those accused of satanic abuse in the cases studied could be said to be occultists. (The educated men who were suspected of dabbling in demonic magic do not seem to have been accused in the early modern witch-hunts either.) In the very few cases in my study in which some occult practices were described, they consisted of holding seances and telling fortunes with tarot cards, pursuits which are much older than the new occult movement and can almost be considered folk practices like those of the earlier cunning folk. In three cases where the sexual abuse of children occurred in conjunction with some ritual activities, the rituals represented a ragbag of elements invented to further the abuse, having no similarity either to occultism or, indeed, to the allegations of satanic abuse.

Those actually accused in cases of alleged satanic abuse were mostly the parents and neighbours of the children, and in nearly half the cases it was clear that the children had been maltreated, sometimes grossly (see pp. 132–3; 153–5). Moreover, in a large proportion of the cases those accused could be described as society's rejects. Not only were they deprived economically, their behaviour and their treatment of their children deviated from all acceptable practice so greatly that it could be characterised as inhuman. The allegations thus follow the pattern of witchcraft accusations in many other societies past and present: the accused are those who violate basic premises about human nature or who are socially marginal in other ways. In particular, and most damning to believers, their children had been seriously damaged by their parenting. Charity or sympathy may be withdrawn, without guilt or fear of reprisal, from those who are designated as evil.

The social differences between those accused in fact and the witches and satanists who appear in the accounts by believers or by adult survivors of satanic abuse, are crucial to understanding the anti-satanist movement. All accounts of modern occultists show them to be educated; while a non-rational approach to causation and influencing the world is fundamental to their practice, it also includes a lively interest in symbolic systems, folklore and other religions. This interest is

an early symptom of being drawn into satanism, according to campaigners. The growth of occult book-shops is a clear indication of
intellectual interests that would be most unusual in the communities
from which the accused came. The accused therefore were unlikely to
include modern occultists, simply because of the communities from
which they were mostly drawn.

An examination of the cases involving children thus shows a
considerable lack of fit between the Christian image of satanic abuse
involving occultists from all walks of life and the actual situations in
which satanic abuse was alleged. This discrepancy was partly removed
by postulating the existence of unidentified participants who could fulfil
the roles designed for them. Moreover, as we have seen, the belief in
rich and powerful satanists who were clever enough to ensure the
absence of all material evidence of their crimes and who were also being
protected from prosecution served other purposes as well. It explained
the lack of proof and also associated satanic abuse with the known
activities of paedophile networks. Satanic abuse in the context of cases
of child protection became a metaphorical representation of all that was
not being done to protect children from serious harm by identifying the
source of it.

According to Rowlands the link between the clerical notion of the
witch as Satan's follower and the peasant notion of the witch as guilty of
maleficium was provided by the confessions of accused witches in the
European witch-hunts. They confessed, in the anthropological idiom
we both use, to being night-witches, not merely to using witchcraft. The
stories of adolescent and adult survivors are not confessions in quite the
same sense as those told by accused witches, in that they are seen as
accusations and not confessions, made by the victims of satanists rather
than satanists themselves,[5] but they have a similar format and effect.
They translate the abstract image of devil-worshipping satanists into the
experiences of real people whose existence guarantees the truth of these
ideas. Unlike the young children, adolescent and adult survivors
produce a narrative shaped by their awareness of their own culture, the
ideas that make up the current epidemic and their own particular
concerns, experiences and knowledge and those of their supporters.
The discrepancies between these accounts and the paradigmatic ones of
the campaigners reflect the variability of social knowledge and sensitiv-
ities of different individuals. The stories they tell transform their
sufferings through the paradigm of inhuman evil from being the mark of
their personal experiences into something of cosmic significance. These
vulnerable individuals, with deep needs for approval, relief from pain or
explanation of their unhappiness become living proofs of satanism, just

as the imprisoned witches in Essex or the Basque country testified to the reality of the witches' sabbath. They are witnesses, not to what happened, but to the truth of the Church's perception of evil.

Despite the established status of survivors, young children were given a special status in the anti-satanism movement that reflected the symbolic value of childhood in the late twentieth century. During most of the period of the allegations of satanism, the cases that were given media publicity concerned young children. Campaigners themselves emphasised that it was the children who were telling of such enormities. The impact of child victims, who, the public were given to understand, rarely lied about being abused, was a powerful force convincing people that the allegations must be true. When the movement began believers were insisting that the children's stories were the key to what was happening. This is one element that marks out the modern anti-satanism movement from other similar phenomena.[6] Children's testimonies in the witch trials do not seem to have been given a different weight from those of adults, except in some mentions of the effectiveness of using children as informants because they would be unable to withstand pressure. Except for the instructive case of child-witches among the Bangwa, children hardly figure in the anthropological record of witchcraft or witch-hunts. The prominence of children is a characteristic of late twentieth-century Western culture.

In the cases of young children, the attempt to translate ideal concepts into reality was a failure. The picture of the modern witches' sabbath, reinforced by the accounts of adults detailing the sufferings of children at satanic rituals, seems to offer an explanation of the extreme state of children who had been taken into care. The description of misinterpretation and pressure on children both in and outside interviews, together with the distortion of the results given in Chapter 7 all represent attempts to transform an icon of evil into a diagnosis. The efforts failed in most cases because child protection is not an independent activity. It is an integral part of a legal system to which the diagnosis had to be submitted for testing, as evidence of a crime. Since different rules of argument and proof apply in the legal world, the 'evidence' submitted was found wanting. Psychotherapy, by contrast, has a special status which is protected from such confrontations so that the accounts of patients and of adult survivors face no such tests of reality. It is hardly surprising that by the end of the period accounts by adult survivors came once more to be the means by which the reality of evil was made manifest.

The question remaining to be considered is why the satanic abuse epidemic should have appeared at this point in history. This is not really a question on which an anthropologist should offer an answer but there are several suggestions that might be made, none of which alone is wholly satisfactory. The first is that the movement represents the effect on the religious community of the end of the second millennium, which is easily associated with the Second Coming. The Second Coming, it is believed, will be preceded by a period of anarchy when Satan's servants will attempt to dominate the world. The perception of widespread satanism thus encourages hope of a glorious aftermath to the struggle. The number of New Christians is growing rapidly, and their crusade to regain the central place for Christian morality that it is believed to have had in the past is openly acknowledged. In this the influence of the United States can be identified in the new churches established in Britain and the regular, and successful, visits of American preachers.

However, neither the influence of the United States, dominant though it is, nor evangelical Christianity exhaust the cultural changes that can be perceived in Britain in the second half of the century. The 'New Age', following on the era of 'flower power' and the hippies and encouraging the development of a wide range of mystical beliefs and religious practices was a significant development, not least in the alarm it raised in the Church and even among people who would not call themselves Christians. The development of occultism, although much less visible than the other religious movements, was reaching the point where a sizeable minority of people were involved. The effect of all these developments was to encourage a widespread reliance on empathy rather than reasoning and belief in persons rather than in academic knowledge or training. Charismatic and fundamentalist Christianity resemble the New Age subculture in this respect. Science appeared to have failed and environmental campaigners argued that technology had endangered the whole planet. The rationalist enthusiasm of the Enlightenment appears finally to have run out.

The role of part of the psychotherapeutic community in the antisatanism movement has become a public and powerful one. The growth of individualism and its attendant psychological strains has been accompanied by a great increase in the kinds and varieties of solutions, that is of therapy, offered and the numbers of persons offering them. The culture of therapy places a great deal of weight on the charismatic authority of the clinician. This is expressed by some as an ability to judge the truth of what the patient is saying; evidence is less important than clinical experience. What is relevant here is that some therapy displays an approach to allegations of satanic abuse that encourages belief and discourages scepticism in a manner similar to that of fundamentalists.

However, the anti-satanist movement was not just a current of thought within a favourable climate of mental culture; it mobilised several networks of people in actions that were designed to influence public policy. Widespread concern with the prevalence of evil can be seen to reflect mundane and secular concerns. The analysis of early witch-cleansing movements in Africa claimed that they reflected under-lying efforts to restore a social and moral order that was perceived as destroyed by rapid and uncontrollable change. Similar ideas are reflected in explanations of the witch-hunts. On a very much larger scale, the late twentieth century is a period of rapid social change that has generated widespread anxiety and malaise. Economic developments have threatened gender roles and family structures, while the widening gulf between rich and poor has been accompanied by a fundamental undermining of respect for all authority. Nostalgia for the past, which is represented as an ideal of which present society falls far short, and disenchantment with the present support the revival of the traditional idea that the good society is being undermined by a secret conspiracy of its enemies.

Notes

1 INTRODUCTION: THE PROBLEM

1 *Independent on Sunday* August 12th 1988

2 Gordon Thomas, *Colchester Evening Gazette*, 27 January 1989. Dr W. Thomson in his manuscript written in 1990, 'The origins of the allegations concerning satanic child abuse in Britain', refers to similar estimates.

3 See Jenkins 1992: 224–5, and Ellis 1993; see also Victor 1990, for the United States.

4 The analogy is emotive rather than exact because sexual abuse is not a policy of extermination nor a method of carrying it out.

5 A research team from the Social Policy Department of Manchester University collaborated with me in a postal survey of police, social services and the National Society for the Prevention of Cruelty to Children in England and Wales; this resulted in reports of sixty-two cases. In addition I read files held in the Official Solicitor's office. The total number of cases considered in my study is eighty-four. See La Fontaine 1994 for details of how data were collected.

6 The anthropology of witchcraft is largely focused on the local, community, level but for a broader perspective, that still uses local studies, see Comaroff & Comaroff, 1994.

7 Semantic anthropology in the 1970s aimed to give beliefs priority and denigrated the study of behaviour (Crick 1970); later American post-modernism substituted the study of cultural concepts for the traditional focus on human behaviour. In Britain, where 'culture' did replace the more traditional concept of 'society' as a basis for analysis (which was not everywhere), the political and economic dimensions of the phenomenon of witchcraft were ignored in favour of a discussion, that was often very ethnocentric, of the 'meaning' of more inclusive notions with fewer behavioural connotations.

2 THE PERSONIFICATION OF EVIL

1 Boyd works for Christian newspapers such as the *Christian New Herald* and *Prophecy Today*, both newspapers of the new fundamentalist Christian movement.

2 This is not to say that nothing had happened to the children in many cases, but it was not what was alleged.

3 The Cathars, Albigensians and other heretics were pursued for a variety of doctrinal disagreements with Christian orthodoxy; their views were much closer to those of Calvin and the later Protestants than to satanism in any form. The stories circulated about them by the Church, which are presented as accounts of actual events, are the distortions of the Church's propaganda against them. The charges against the wealthy Templars made by the megalomanic but financially embarassed King Philip of France, were self-interested and their contradictory confessions extracted under torture. The idol of Baphomet that they were alleged to have worshipped seems likely to have represented their lack of fervour in pursuit of followers of Mahomet (Cohn 1975: 75–98, 87). They were rumoured to be sympathetic to their Muslim opponents, from long familiarity with the near East, and Philip needed to smash this rival religion to satisfy his aspiration to become King of Jersualem. Gilles de Rais confessed under torture and at his trial only evidence for the prosecution was heard. The courts who tried him stood to benefit from the confiscation of his property and the verdict of the courts, according to Lamb, 'was almost a foregone conclusion' (1977: 139).

4 For example, Ginzburg (1983 [1966]) has described the beliefs of villagers in the north Italian region of Friuli, which differ markedly from those of Essex villagers of roughly the same period (Macfarlane 1970). See also Kiekhefer (1976: 48–56) for a description of the varied folk beliefs of early modern Europe.

5 An exception to this generalisation is apparently provided by recent events in certain parts of South Africa, Vendaland for example, where mobs have attacked and killed persons suspected of being witches, both men and women. Others have been driven into refuges that have been sent up specially for them and their families (Ralushai 1996). But this is actually very different from the judicially sanctioned execution of witches that took place in sixteenth and seventeenth century Europe. The South African authorities are making efforts to understand and to stop these lynchings. As this book nears publication that have also been reports in Britain of mobs attacking suspected paedophiles, who seem to have acquired a similar status as witches.

3 WITCHES, SATANISTS AND THE OCCULT

1 The Beacon Foundation is an offshoot of the Reachout Trust, which was founded to help former members of cults, but became increasingly focused on the campaign against satanic abuse. It was founded by Maureen Davies, a former employee of the Reachout Trust, to concentrate on satanism.

2 Irvine was later quoted as saying that she had omitted details of the satanic rites she had been involved in, as people were not able to deal with them at the time she wrote her book.

3 A footnote in *Michelle Remembers* relates the fact that Michelle's story includes an episode of being shut in a cage according to notions of pagan rituals. 'Hearing about the cage, Dr Pazder was reminded of the dreaded Ekpe Society of West Africa. Kidnapped children were raised by its members in small, low cages like animals. These 'leopard children' could not stand but ran on all fours. Their teeth were filed to points and they were used as assassins. Of course (sic), Dr Pazder never told Michelle about the correspondences he

sometimes saw between her experiences and the things he had studied' (Pazder & Smith 1980: 140). The relevant literature on West Africa (e.g. Ruel 1970; Jackson 1990) does not mention 'leopard children', who are likely to be a product of European fantasies, although the leopard is a common symbol of power in some societies in the region. Nwaka, who describes a mysterious outbreak of murders in Nigeria in the 1940s, refers to 'vague rumours . . . especially in missionary circles' about 'leopard cults' (1986: 417). The Ekpe society to which Pazder refers was accused of implication in the murders that Nwaka discusses, but for purely secular reasons, as it was the traditional group that enforced law and order and its symbol was the leopard. The mere fact of secrecy seems to attract myths of evil-doing.

4 *Satan's Underground* is still cited as genuine by psychiatrists who appear not to know that the author has admitted it to be a fake (see Katchen & Sakheim 1992; Coleman 1994).

5 Margot Adler, in a comprehensive survey of paganism in the United States, *Drawing Down the Moon*, refers to 'a probable murder' (1986: 133).

6 The organisation of different groups, their beliefs and practices and the terminology they use are laid out in various books on the subject, both by occultists and, less frequently, by interested observers. They show that many Wiccan rituals are celebratory and have no magical aim. Tanya Luhrmann's book on witchcraft and ritual magick is so far the only study of this community in Britain (Luhrmann 1989).

7 Sinason adopts the term 'satanist' abuse in order to emphasise this distinction (1994: 4).

8 Elen Williams, a former president of the Pagan Federation, pointed out to me that since most groups do not admit members who are under eighteen there would have been fewer questionnaires distributed to younger people.

9 According to C. Bray, proprietor of the Sorcerer's Apprentice bookshop, 'warlock' is 'common currency in the United States and quite a few American occultists use it as a title' (private communication). He argues that 'wizard' has a quite different etymology, coming from the same root as 'wisdom'.

10 Ritual magicians may use a circle to protect themselves from the forces they raise. Satanists by contrast do not use a circle at all (Harvey 1995a).

11 There is material from the United States on the Church of Satan and a full-scale study of the Process Church by a participant observer (Bainbridge 1978). Moody, who studied the Church of Satan over twenty years ago, reported the beneficial effect of membership on young and inhibited men, arguing that it increased their self-confidence (Moody 1974). The Church of Satan seems to be the best-known satanist group, probably because its founder has never minded publicity and has written a good deal about his church.

12 Interview with the manager, Mysteries bookshop, London, October 1990.

13 It should be remembered too that many fundamentalist or charismatic Christians regard the Roman Catholic Church as satanic (Davies 1989); its plainsong and the intonation of Latin prayers, that were part of the traditional Roman Catholic mass, may be regarded as satanic chants.

14 There are two main traditions in modern witchcraft: the Gardnerian and Alexandrian, named after the founders of modern Wicca, Gerald Gardner and Alex Sanders. The Gardnerian is the older.

15 Adam and Eve were traditionally depicted naked, displaying their innocence. However, the choice of the female body alone as a symbol must raise some further questions about the group's general attitudes to women.

16 There is no indication that LaVey knew of the Church tradition that associated satanism with the learned magic of the clergy, or the folk fears of the monk turned devil-worshipper.

4 THE EXTENT OF THE ALLEGATIONS

1 Nathan refers to her under her real name of Wilson.

2 In fact, by the time this book went to press (1997) no such video had been discovered.

3 Objections to the use of the term epidemic have been raised by Ankarloo in relation to the early modern witch-craze (1990: 301). While I see his point, I use 'epidemic' metaphorically in preference to 'moral panic' to underline the spreading nature of the phenomenon.

4 Defined as cases involving multiple perpetrators collaborating to abuse children. See Belanger et al. 1994 and Bibby 1996 for other definitions. An estimated national incidence rate for organised abuse is 278 cases per year. This is roughly between 1 and 3 per cent of all the cases of child protection in the areas studied (Gallagher, Parker & Hughes 1994: 7). As the Department of Health has commented, this means a very small minority of social workers were involved in these cases.

5 The equivalent table in La Fontaine 1994 is arranged according to different regional divisions, but although there are minor differences in the figures, the main clusters are the same.

6 There have been changes of personnel in the social services department since then and the compiler of the list has left it.

7 The police reported twenty-one cases but the survey counted only eighteen: two related reports were merged to form one case, and in two others the allegation had ended in a retraction or proved to have no substance, so the reports were not included. In the discussion of the Nottingham situation I have added some cases from the period that came to light outside the survey, so the figure of twenty-four does not represent the survey figure.

8 I first heard them speak in 1991 at a conference in Cardiff organised by the evangelical campaigner Maureen Davies.

9 On a video made in 1996 by Manchester Rape Crisis, which is being sold as a training tape. In it, Judith Dawson, now Judith Jones, formerly a senior social worker in Nottingham, repeats some of her criticisms of the police.

10 This traditional phrase indicated the poor who deserved help, because of their attempts to keep up standards and their godliness. The respectable poor took great pains to distinguish themselves from those whose manifest moral failings, like drunkenness and criminal activities, showed they deserved their sordid lives. The research of a more compassionate age showed that these failings can be the results rather than the causes of poverty, but late twentieth-century England appears to be returning to Victorian judgements.

5 THE QUESTION OF PROOF

1 It may be forgotten that cruelty and what is now defined as sexual abuse are not the discoveries of the late twentieth century but were recognised a century earlier in the founding of children's charities such as the NSPCC (Ferguson 1994).

2 This was despite a forensic psychologist's writing: 'I am at a complete loss as to how these injuries could be interpreted as being ritualistic burns.'

3 It probably also symbolised forbidden sexual activities: anal intercourse and homosexuality. The Cathars and the Templars were accused of these satanic activities.

4 Tate (1994: 191–4) cites seven cases which he refers to as successful prosecutions of satanists. I have seen files on these cases: four involved abuse by men acting alone who used pretended evil mystical powers (not usually referred to as satanic) to intimidate their victims. In another one the participants had been using a ouija board before interrogating the victim sadistically about some missing money, using actual violence as well as threats; the last two were part of my study and will be discussed in more detail below. Only two of the seven involved abuse during rituals.

5 Tate in *Children for the Devil* stated that the name indicated profound knowledge of the occult; however, occultists say that this is not so and I found the name in occult dictionaries that are easily obtainable, so his view seems unjustified.

6 The husband of the second woman was not involved in the ritual (contrary to Tate 1994: 191), although he had committed incest with his daughters. The little girls were also sexually abused by their uncle, with, in one instance, the active assistance of their mother; their baby cousin had been involved in some token sexual ritual by his father but had not been abused.

7 Unfortunately, none of the written material found in the perpetrator's house was available at the time of the study for me to see.

8 After his release from prison the main perpetrator was arrested for another act of sexual abuse, this time without ritual. Soon afterwards he committed suicide.

9 There were several instances in these cases where adults seemed to find it amusing to frighten children. In another case a young woman and her boyfriend dressed in sheets and climbed to a window to frighten her much younger brother who was already terrified of ghosts.

10 It is possible that in common with many victims of sexual abuse these children felt humiliated by being watched by others during the abuse and expressed it in exaggerated form by claiming to have been filmed. Alternatively the idea was suggested to them by adults; this is not uncommon, as Chapter 7 will show.

11 I have been unable to find a copy of this book.

12 The whole issue of the validity of so-called recovered memories hinges on this view of the clinician (Ofshe & Watters 1994). But see Adshead for a more traditional view denying the ability of a therapist to determine the truth of an account (1994: 61–3).

6 EXPLAINING BELIEF

1 The fact that it happened over Christmas partly explained the failure to call for help. However, very little significance seemed to be placed on the incident in the case records, as symptomatic of the child's health, mental or physical. The foster-mother told me merely how disappointed she had been that the child had missed the Christmas she had planned to compensate her for her former 'troubles'.

2 The phrase 'skinning alive' is an old-fashioned metaphorical phrase for peeling clothes off someone; it seems to have been taken literally by the child's social worker. Philippa Youngman tells me that it might also be used as a heavily jocular threat to children, but not one to be taken literally. In this case it is not clear whether it was the child or her social worker who took the phrase as a serious threat.

3 The group uses the term 'ritual abuse', but includes the cases I have been discussing under the label satanic abuse. The question of whether workers were members of RAINS did not arise at the time when the case files were compiled, so it has been impossible to tell how many of the social workers in those cases were, or became members. However at a meeting of RAINS that I attended I noted workers concerned with at least five of the cases. Some of those present did not give their names, having said they were too afraid to. I had been told that others might not attend the meeting for the same reason.

4 Put in this leading form, the question was more likely to be answered 'Yes'.

5 One day she had seen its ghost, which came right up to her in a friendly fashion before vanishing. Thereafter things had improved.

6 Further evidence of the mental disturbance of survivors is given in Coleman's description of her patients, aged between fifteen and forty (Coleman 1994: 83–93).

7 This refers to the period 1988–92 and even then did not apply to all areas.

8 A good deal of publicity was generated by the claim that the social workers in the Nottingham case had got their ideas of satanic abuse at the 1989 Reading Conference. They rightly argued that this was after they had reported satanic elements in the case. However, the c.v. of Pamela Klein, who helped organise that conference, indicates that similar conferences had been held in 1988 and 1987. Satanic abuse was not among topics listed, but Pamela Klein had been an expert on it for some years. The site of the 1990 conference was changed because, according to the organisers, the original choice, a university, could not guarantee the safety of participants. According to my informant at the university in question, the change was the result of the university's deciding that they did not wish to be associated with what they had found out about the purpose of the conference. The two or three protestors at the gate of the new location, handing out leaflets on behalf of occultists, were somewhat of an anti-climax after the initial build-up.

9 Hudson is a licensed social worker in California. From her own clinical work with twenty-four children in a single case in California she selected a list of twenty-eight symptoms and allegations. Each item was confirmed by 'at least eleven children independently'. As these children were all allegedly involved in the same case, this is a surprisingly low level of agreement. Hudson then

telephoned a parent of one child involved in each of ten other cases of alleged ritual abuse in day-care (all but one in California), asking them whether the child had symptoms to match the list. They might say 'yes', 'no' or 'not stated'. Symptoms not on the list either were not asked about or were not recorded, their absence thus creating an apparent confirmation that the features chosen were all there were. It is not made clear how she chose the cases or how comparable they are, although one apparently involved only one child. Nor is it clear why she did not cover all the children in the eleven cases, as she had done in her own cases, or how having decided to choose one parent to talk to, she made that choice. Even in this case, then, the basis for the list is weak. Hudson has lectured more than once at the Tavistock Clinic and an article by her is included in the volume by Valerie Sinason, who introduced her at the talk I heard.

10 Chanting is a regular feature of satanic abuse allegations that recalls the fundamentalist view of Catholic and high-church singing of parts of their services, such as the psalms and the credo.

11 See Graham Johnson in the *News of the World*, 21 April 1996. I was twice telephoned from the area with questions about satanism.

12 I may have been guilty of underestimating this difficulty myself, although the questionable nature of some disclosures does not alter the fact that children can and do make clear statements that they have been sexually abused and by whom (La Fontaine 1990).

7 CHILDREN'S STORIES

1 In distinguishing childhood as a category, early modern society must also have invented the category of 'adulthood' with which it was, implicitly, contrasted, but Western concepts of adulthood have received virtually no attention, although anthropologists have considered the assumption of adult status in other soceties. Boas' linking of childhood and primitivism suggests one reason for its greater importance in the West; another might be that adulthood was and is so fundamentally constituted by class and gender that a single adult identity was meaningless.

2 It has been argued that, in the late twentieth century when the idea of progress has generally been seen as an empty promise, childhood represents, not so much a future potential as a golden past (Jenks 1994: 116). The prevailing attitude of adults to childhood has come to be one of nostalgia for a period of innocence and happiness. One example of this attitude is to be found in the idea that the abuse of children is 'stealing their childhood', a phrase often used by survivors of sexual abuse to describe the damage done to them.

3 An exception to this was the practice of early infant betrothals and child marriages which the elite contracted for political reasons, but the whole notion of there being a single version of 'childhood' in any society where socio-economic class was (and is) of such importance is clearly more symbolic than realistic.

4 The idea that it is strangers who are a danger to children seems to reflect the notion that while home and school are safe places for children the world outside is dangerous. The emphasis on strangers also distracts attention

from the possibility that parents and teachers – familiar adults placed in authority over children – will abuse their positions.

5 Until recently social science has not queried this view and has studied the process of socialisation/education as though children were unthinking lumps of clay to be moulded, rather than social actors in their own right (see James 1993: 76–80).

6 Brain takes a similar view, stating that in the early modern period children's views were accepted 'as gospel' (Brain 1970: 161). Both he and Robbins imply that the view of children as liars was not general in those communities, although Walinski-Kiehl shows that there were other, harsher views of them (1996: 174–5).

7 Advertising has been sharply criticised for sexualising the image of children (see Ennew 1986: 134–5 & figs. 4, 6, 7).

8 It seems to be commonly thought that the abuse of children was only discovered in the mid-twentieth century. In fact the maltreatment of children had been the concern of philanthropists a century earlier. It was less publicised in England after the First World War, but the NSPCC which had been founded in the late nineteenth century, and other similar children's charities continued to raise funds by publicising the necessity of their work.

9 At the time the article was published, the fifteen children in the case ranged in age from four to fourteen; half of them were nine and over. There had been most activity in the case between one and two years earlier.

10 Jenkins has pointed out that by writing of the 'oppression of children' Campbell, whom he describes as writing 'from a "red-feminist" perspective' (1992: 147, 175), can reconcile her views with those of the conservative evangelical Christians and promote belief in satanic abuse.

11 Her foster-mother finally resolved the question, for me at least, when she told me that they had gone to a farm and when the car had stopped beside a bank, a goat had put its head up close to the window.

12 The origin of the reference is not clear, but might be the film *The Sound of Music* shown on television.

13 In three cases there was no suggestion that the allegations had come from the child, which was very young; it was the parent who had made them. A social worker in one case complained that the children were prompted by their mother when she interviewed them.

14 In this case there were no disclosures of sexual abuse and most of the children were returned to their parents, although after a considerable delay.

8 CONFESSIONS AND TALES OF HORROR

1 Dr Henningsen also kindly showed me some transcripts of the documents in the case, one of which was the source for his account in the book.

2 Finkelhor et al., in their study of cases of sexual abuse in nursery schools, make a very young age one of the defining characteristics of ritual abuse (Finkelhor et al. 1988). This feature appears to have been missed or ignored by the many English people who quote this study and claim to use the definition.

3 They were known as 'breeders' in the United States. Larry Jones, the 'cult cop', writing in his newsletter, *File 18*, remarks that he thought the British

term referred to animal mutilation at first, until it was explained to him by Maureen Davies. 'Cult cop' was the term coined in the United States to refer to a policeman or woman who was an 'expert' on satanic abuse, who were also known as 'satanhunters'. Some of them, like Larry Jones or Jerry Simandl, even resigned from the police to carry out their activities full time.

4 The figures were greeted with scepticism by some of those mentioned as Boyd's sources when I discussed them with them.

5 'Irrational disbelief' suggests an (implicit) contrast with 'rational disbelief', but this is not discussed further.

6 This man was in a secure mental hospital. The police, who somewhat reluctantly filled in a survey form for him, were sceptical about his allegations.

7 I owe this point to Fiona Dunne, who did an analysis of the survivors' reports for me.

8 The cartoon strip ended with the execution of the rapist so that it could be said to tell a moral story, not a satanist one. The advice of a Christian psychiatrist, with experience of satanic abuse cases, was sought. He reported that the boy had probably been sexually abused by his half-brother, concluding: 'From my investigation of these matters, the small disclosure amounts to little more than common public knowledge about such things; Mrs C. (his mother)'s involvement in palmistry and tarot cards seems to have been a passing interest in amateur clairvoyancy.'

9 The girl ran away from the children's home to her father in another town, where a social worker subsequently considered her case as one of satanic abuse, noting that her father (whom no one, according to the original case file, had accused of either occultism or sexual abuse of his daughter) was 'steeped in satanism'.

10 Of course the cage motif might have other sources: in the folk-tale 'Hansel and Gretel' the witch keeps the children in a cage to fatten them for eating.

11 According to Dr Colman (personal communication) Dianne Core, the Christian campaigner and founder of ChildWatch, referred the case to her.

12 It seems just as likely that the social workers in the case kept each girl aware of what the other was saying, either by their questions or by the conversations they had with the foster-mothers, who clearly told everything to the girls.

13 See note 10.

9 A MODERN MOVEMENT OF WITCH-FINDERS

1 Audrey Richards' article with this title (1935) is one of a handful of early accounts of African witch-finding movements.

2 Some residual beliefs may have remained; there was a case of 'swimming a witch' in the nineteenth century (Nice; unpublished ms.). Moreover the idea of the flying witch and the witches' sabbath have remained part of folklore.

3 Those listed were a Dutch couple (both doctors), a psychotherapist, the astrologer for a tabloid newspaper, an American psychologist prominent in the early part of the campaign, and a survivor with multiple personalities. All have given evidence of their commitment to belief in satanic abuse.

4 An anthropologist, Sherrill Mulhern, who has studied survivors and their therapists, predicted this and has proved to be right (private communication). See Mulhern 1994 for the historical connection between allegations of satanic abuse and multiple personality disorder.

5 Observers who rely on the press for data may be misled into thinking an issue is dead when it is merely no longer newsworthy, but see the reference above to the item in the *News of the World* in 1996.

6 Dr R. Aldridge-Morris, personal communication.

7 Evans-Pritchard discussed the scepticism showed by some Zande in relation to the powers claimed by witch-doctors to seek out witches, but he also showed why their belief in witchcraft in general was unchallenged by doubts (1937). Henningsen (1980) documents the career of a Spanish sceptic and see Levack (1987: 55–7, 203).

8 The doyen of British social anthropology, Sir Raymond Firth, is cited as saying that he characterises the twentieth century as 'in terms of ideas, the change from a relatively rational and scientific view of things to a non-rational and less scientific one' (Hobsbawm 1994: 2). See also Gellner 1992.

9 Jenkins 1992: 161–9; see Henningsen 1980: 206 for a similar religious campaign that sparked off a wave of accusations against witches in the Basque country in 1610.

10 Jenkins records it as 1985 but the flyleaf of Core's book, *Chasing Satan*, shows the earlier date.

11 Tate's allegation that the social workers in Nottingham were prevented from putting their case (Tate 1991: 190) seems exaggerated. He himself talked to them on the telephone and met them on at least one occasion while the case was going on. He refers in footnote 3. to his introduction in *Children for the Devil* to interviews with Judith Dawson that took place from October 1988 to December 1990 (1991: 357). The social workers published two articles in 1989 and 1990 and Beatrix Campbell wrote at least four articles putting their views in 1990 alone.

12 Sandi Gallant worked in the San Francisco police force, developing an expertise in occult crime (see also Jenkins 1992: 158). She did not figure largely in the movement subsequently and was said to have changed her views radically. Another journalist, Tim Tate, active in the anti-satanist movement also used interviews with her in his book on satanic abuse (1991: 3–4).

13 It was suggested by critics that the NSPCC was using this to create a high profile for itself and help in its vital funding campaign (see Jenkins 1992: 197). Perhaps this was so, but their profile was pushed up even higher through no fault of theirs.

14 These were not allegations of satanic abuse, but gender stereotypes were mobilised on both sides in the subsequent dispute.

15 In 1994 MPs of the three main parties, who were also members of the Movement for Christian Democracy, were able to put their common cause as Christians before their party alignments in order to support and publicise an anti-satanist book.

16 This person is something of a mystery. As far as I know, she has given no interviews, written nothing about satanic abuse, and appeared in no case I

have studied. She is not mentioned by name in the Youngson articles and her existence is only revealed in the mention made of her by Dr Coleman (Coleman 1994a).

17 He was also involved in a consultancy offering support services to social work staff and has not taken a public role as a leader of RAINS.

18 At the time of Youngson's survey there were only 120 members (1993: 252). Coleman refers to the membership at July 1993 as numbering 150 (Coleman 1994a: 243).

19 Tate writes that his involvement with satanic abuse began in 1987 when he was consulted by a Dr C. He was then writing a book on child pornography (Tate 1991: xi–xii; 357 fn. 1). He subsequently made inquiries in the United States, where he had contacts.

20 In the case of Sue Hutchinson, as advertised by Manchester Rape Crisis papers, the fee for 'training' is £250 a day. One therapist was said to have doubled her fee to £400 a day after having established herself as an expert on satanic abuse.

21 Drugs have been advanced as an explanation of the confessions of witches during the witch-hunts (Harner, cited in Levack 1987: 16). The views of specialists that it is impossible to ensure the same effect each time the drug is taken would cast doubt on the explanation here too. In the cases I examined it was the adults who thought of drugs as an explanation, not the children who described taking them; in one case the child was complying with a request to describe her dream.

22 Valerie Sinason of the Tavistock Clinic acted as hostess for Pamela Hudson on two lecture tours in Britain. In 1990 she supervised her first case of satanic abuse – in Sweden and by telephone (Sinason 1994: 13). This case has subsequently been investigated by the police and the idea of any cult involvement discredited. In 1994 she edited a book of articles, largely by committed believers, that gave her a great deal of publicity; like Maureen Davies in the first stage, she has subsequently taken on a large number of speaking engagements.

23 They were described in a letter to the *Independent* as 'forty trained health service contributors'. But of the nineteen (nearly half of them) who are not referred to in the text five are teachers of psychiatry or social work in an educational institution, three are journalists, one is a foster-mother, one is a 'survivor', two are untrained counsellors, three are anonymous sources in the police, three are doctors and one is the social work director of an independent charity. Three of the psychological professionals are not British residents and presumably do not contribute to the British health service. Such hyperbole is consistent with a political campaign rather than a professional debate.

10 AFTERMATH AND CONCLUSIONS

1 In regression therapy the patient tries to go back in time to recover the sensations and emotions of being a child or a baby or even of being born. The aim is to discover the earlier incidents that have caused present distress in the adult.

2 Crick claims that 'the gulf between the intellectual structures of seventeenth-century England and Zande society, for instance, is vast. Moreover, Evans-Pritchard himself emphasized that our historical witchcraft was not like anything we so label in primitive cultures' (1937: 64). In fact, Evans-Pritchard said nothing of the sort. In emphasising the place of witchcraft in Zande society he wrote: 'When a Zande speaks of witchcraft he does not speak of it as we speak of the weird witchcraft of our own history. Witchcraft is to him a commonplace happening,' and some lines later: 'To us witchcraft is something which haunted and disgusted our credulous forefathers. But the Zande expects to come across witchcraft at any time of the day or night' (1937: 64). This says more about the views of the past held by British people in the 1930s than it contributes to a discussion of the possibilities of comparing beliefs across time.

3 Were it not for China, one might say *the* most complex and powerful bureaucratic organisations.

4 For example, the attempt to analyse social meaning in terms of binary classifications led to Needham's analysing some East African material in terms that were quite inconsistent with the social context portrayed in the ethnographic data.

5 Although some survivors confess to having killed victims or otherwise participating in the rituals. In some circles of believers, it is now believed that all victims became perpetrators of abuse in this way.

6 There are several others, of course, of which the two most important are the absence of torture to induce confessions, and the death of those convicted. It may not be realised that even suspected witches are still being killed in some parts of the world.

Bibliography

Adler, M. 1986. *Drawing Down the Moon*. Boston: Beacon.

Adshead, G. 1994. 'Looking for Clues: a Review of the Literature on False Allegations of Sexual Abuse in Childhool'. In V. Sinason (ed.), *Treating Survivors of Satanist Abuse*. London: Routledge.

Anderson, P. 1988. *Satan's Snare;The influence of the Occult*. Reading: Cox & Wyman Evangelical Press.

Ankarloo, B. 1993 (1990). 'Sweden: the Mass Burnings 1668–76'. In B. Ankarloo & G. Henningsen (eds.), *Early Modern Witchcraft: Centres and Peripheries*. Oxford: Clarendon Press.

Ankarloo, B. & Henningsen, G. (eds.) 1993 (1990). *Early Modern European Witchcraft; Centres and Peripheries*. Oxford: Clarendon Press.

Anning, N. 1991. 'How Satan Sold his Story to the Pops', *Journalist*, December 1991/January 1992.

Anon. 1974 (1970). *A Hundred Questions on Witchcraft answered by a Member of the Craft*. London Quest.

Anon. 1994. 'Questions Survivors and Professionals Ask the Police'. In V. Sinason (ed.), *Treating Survivors of Satanist Abuse*. London: Routledge.

Aronsson, K. & Nilholm, C. 1992. 'Story-telling as Collaborative Reasoning: Co-Narratives in Incest Case Accounts'. in M. L. McLaughlin, M. J. Cody & S. J. Read (eds.), *Explaining Oneself to Others: Reason-giving in a social context*. New Jersey: Lawrence Erlbaum.

Austen, R. 1993. 'The Moral Economy of Witchcraft: an essay in Comparative History'. In J. Comaroff & J. Comaroff, J. (eds.), *Modernity and its Malcontents*. University of Chicago Press.

Bainbridge, W. S. 1978. *Satan's Power*. California: University of California Press.

Balch, R. & Gilliam, M. 1991. 'Devil Worship in Western Montana: a Case Study in Rumor Construction'. In J. T. Richardson, J. Best & D. Bromley (eds.), *The Satanism Scare*. New York: Aldine de Gruyter.

Barker, E. 1989. *New Religious Movements; a Practical Introduction*. London: HMSO.

Barnes, J. A. 1994. *A Pack of Lies; Towards a Sociology of Lying*. Cambridge University Press.

Barth, F. 1975. *Ritual and Knowledge among the Baktaman of New Guinea*. Oslo: Universitetsforlaget; New Haven: Yale University Press.

Barton, B. 1990. *The Church of Satan*. New York: Hell Kitchen Productions Inc.

Baskin, W. 1972. *Satanism: A Guide to the Awesome Power of Satan*. New Jersey: Citadel Press.

Beacon Foundation 1991. *The Rehabilitation of Satanic Cult Members*. Rhyl: Beacon Foundation.

Beail, N. 1994. 'Fire, Coffins and Skeletons'. In V. Sinason (ed.), *Treating Survivors of Satanist Abuse*. London: Routledge.

Beckford, J. 1985. *Cult Controversies*. London: Tavistock.

Beit-Hallahmi, B. 1992. *Despair and Deliverance: Private Salvation in Contemporary Israel*. State University of New York Press.

Belanger, A. et al. 1984. 'Typology of Sex Rings Exploiting Children'. In A. W. Burgess, (ed.), *Child Pornography and Sex Rings*. Massachusetts: Lexington Books.

Bennett, C. 1994. 'In Search of Satan'. *Guardian*, 10 Sept.

Bentovim, A. et al. 1988. *Child Sexual Abuse within the Family – Assessment and Treatment. The work of the Great Ormond Street Team*. London: Wright.

Best, J. 1991. 'Endangered Children and Antisatanist Rhetoric'. In J. Richardson, J. Best & D. Bromley (eds.), *The Satanism Scare*. New York: Aldine de Gruyter.

Bibby, P. 1994. 'Definition of Organised Abuse'. In *Child Abuse Review*, 3 (3).

Bibby, P. (ed.) 1996. *Organised Abuse – The Current Debate*. Aldershot: Ashgate Publishing.

Boas, G. 1966. *The Cult of Childhood*. London: Warburg Institution.

Bohannan, P. 1958. 'Extra-Processual Events in Tiv Political Institutions'. *American Anthropologist*, 60 (1).

Bottoms, B. L., Diviak K. R., Goodman G. S. & Shaver P. R. 1996a. 'Individual Differences in Therapists' Experiences with Ritual Abuse Allegations'. Poster presented at the Conference of the American Psychology-Law Society, February.

Bottoms, B. Shaver, P. & Goodman, G. 1996b. 'An Analysis of Ritualistic and Religion-Related Child Abuse Allegations'. In *Law and Human Behaviour*, 20 (1).

Bourguignon, E. 1989. 'Multiple Personality, Possession Trance, and the Psychic Unity of Mankind'. *Ethos*, 17 (3).

Boyd, A. 1991. *Blasphemous Rumours: Is Satanic Ritual Abuse Fact or Fantasy? An Investigation*. London: Fount Paperbacks.

Brain, J. L. 1989. 'An Anthropological Perspective on the Witchcraze'. In J. R. Brink, A. P. Coudert & M. C. Horowitz (eds.), 'The Politics of Gender in Early Modern Europe'. *Sixteenth Century Essays and Studies* II.

Brain, R. 1970. 'Child-Witches.' In M. Douglas (ed.), *Witchcraft Confessions and Accusations*. ASA Monographs No. 9. London: Tavistock.

Brierley, P. & Hiscock, V. (eds.) 1994/5. *UK Christian Handbook*. The Christian. Research Association, Evangelical Alliance & British & Foreign Bible Society.

Bromley, D. 1991. 'Satanism: The New Cult Scare'. In J. Richardson, J. Best and D. Bromley (eds.), *The Satanism Scare*. New York: Aldine de Gruyter.

Butler-Sloss, E. 1988. *Report of the Inquiry into Child Abuse in Cleveland 1987*. London: HMSO.

Buxton, J. 1963. 'Mandari Witchcraft'. In J. Middleton & E. Winter (eds.), *Witchcraft and Sorcery in East Africa*. London: Routledge & Kegan Paul.

Campbell, B. 1988. *Unofficial Secrets*. London: Virago.

1990a. 'Children's Stories', *New Statesman and Society*, 5 October.

1990b. 'Hear No Evil'. *New Statesman and Society*, 19 October.

1990c. 'Satanic Claims Vindicated', *New Statesman and Society*, 9 November.

1990d. 'Seen But Not Heard'. *Marxism Today*, November.

Carlson, S., Larue, G. et al. 1989. *Satanism in America: How the devil Got Much More Than His Due*. Committee for the Scientific Examination of Religion.

Cavarola, A. A. & Scheff, M. 1988. 'Behavioural sequelae of physical and/or sexual abuse'. *Child Abuse and Neglect*, Vol 12: pp 181–8.

Cavendish, R. 1975. *The Powers of Evil in Western Religion, Magic and Folk Belief*. London: Routledge & Kegan Paul.

Ceci, S. & Bruck, M. 1993. 'Suggestibility of the Child Witness: A Historical Review and Synthesis'. *Psychological Bulletin*, 113.

Ceci, S. J., Ross, D. F. & Toglia, M. P. 1987. 'Suggestibility of Children's Memory: Psycho-legal Implications'. *Journal of Experimental Psychology: General*, 116.

Charleson, N. & Corbett, A. 1994. 'A Birthday to Remember'. In V. Sinason (ed.), *Treating Survivors of Satanist Abuse*. London: Routledge.

Clapton, G. 1993. *The Satanic Abuse Controversy: Social Workers and the Social Work Press*. London: University of North London Press.

Clark, S. 1993 (1990). 'Protestant Demonology: Sin, Superstition, and Society (c.1520–c.1630)'. In B. Ankarloo & G.Henningsen (eds.)*Early Modern European Witchcraft: Centres and Peripheries*. Oxford: Clarendon Press.

Clyde, J. J. 1992. *The Report of the Inquiry of the Removal of Children from Orkney in February 1991*. Edinburgh: HMSO.

Cohn, N. 1970. 'The Myth of Satan and his Human Servants'. In M. Douglas (ed.), *Witchcraft: Confessions and Accusations*. London: Tavistock.

1975. *Europe's Inner Demons*. St Albans: Paladin.

Colchester Evening News, 27 January 1989.

Coleman, J. 1994a. 'Satanic Cult Practices', in V. Sinason (ed.), *Treating survivors of satanist abuse*. London: Routledge.

1994b. 'Presenting Features in Adult Victims of Satanist Ritual Abuse'. *Child Abuse Review*, 3 (2 June).

Colver, S. 1994. 'Cutting the Cord: the Resolution of a Symbiotic Relationship and the Untwisting of Desire'. In V. Sinason (ed.), *Treating Survivors of Satanist Abuse*. London: Routledge.

Comaroff, J. 1994. 'Contentious Subjects: Moral Being in the Modern World' – The eleventh Westermarck Memorial Lecture Suomen Antropologi, *Journal of the Finnish Anthropological Society* (2).

Comaroff, J. & Comaroff, J. (eds.) 1993. *Modernity and its Malcontents: Ritual and Power in Postcolonial Africa*. Chicago: University of Chicago Press.

Cooklin, A. & Gorell Barnes, G. 1994. 'The Shattered Picture of the Family: Encountering New Dimensions of Human Relations, of the Family and of Therapy'. In V. Sinason (ed.), *Treating Survivors of Satanist Abuse*. London: Routledge.

Core, D. & Harrison, F. 1991. *Chasing Satan*. London: Gunter Books.

Core, D. 1988. Speech reported in *The New Federalist*, 15 November.

Cotton, I. 1995. *The Hallelujah Revolution*. London: Little, Brown & Co.

Crick, M. 1976. *Semantic Anthropology*. London: Malaby Press.

Culling, L. T. 1971. *Sex Magick*. Minnesota: Llewellyn Publications.

Cunningham, H. 1996. 'The History of Childhood'. In C. P. Hwang, M. E. Lamb & I. E. Sigel (eds.), *Images of Childhood*. New Jersey: Lawrence Erlbaum.

Davies, M. 1989. 'Satanic Ritual Abuse'. Reachout Trust. Transcript of audiotape recording of lecture and newsletter (Winter).

Dawson, J. 1990. 'Vortex of Evil', *New Statesman and Society*, 5 October.

Dawson, J. 1991. 'Confronting Disbelief'. *Social Work Today*, 9 May.

Dawson, J. & Johnston, C. 1989. 'When the Truth Hurts', *Community Care*, 30 March.

Douglas, M. 1963. 'Techniques of Sorcery Control in Central Africa', in J. Middleton & E. Winter (eds.), *Witchcraft and Sorcery in East Africa*, London: Routledge & Kegan Paul.

Douglas, M. (ed.) 1970. *Witchcraft: Confessions and Accusations*. London: Tavistock.

Dundes, A. 1989. 'The Ritual Murder or Blood Libel Legend: a study of Anti-Semitic Victimization through Projective Inversion'. *Temenos: Studies in Comparative Religion*, Vol. 25. Helsinki.

Dundes, A. (ed.) 1991. *The Blood Libel Legend: a Casebook in Anti-Semitic Folklore*. University of Wisconsin Press.

Ellis, B. 1991. 'Legend Trips and Satanism: Adolescents' Ostensive Traditions as "Cult" Activity. In J. T. Richardson, J. Best & D. Bromley (eds.), *The Satanism Scare*. New York: Aldine de Gruyter.

1993. 'The Highgate Cemetery Vampire Hunt: the Anglo-American Connection in Satanic Cult Lore', *Folklore*, 104.

Ennew, J. 1986. *The Sexual Exploitation of Children*. Cambridge: Polity Press, in association with Blackwell (Oxford): Chapter 8.

Evangelical Alliance 1987. *Doorways to Danger*. Worthing CPO.

Evans-Pritchard, E. E. 1937. *Witchcraft, Oracles and Magic among the Azande*. Oxford: Clarendon Press.

Eve, R. A. & Roy, L. n. d. 'Satanism and the Decline of Morality. An Investigation into a Moral Panic and the Mental Health of Texans'. Unpublished MS, the Centre for Social Research, University of Texas at Arlington, in collaboration with The Cult Awareness Council and the North Texas Skeptics.

Feldman, M. D., Ford C. V. with Reinhold, T. 1994. *Patient or Pretender: Inside the Strange World of Factitious Disorders*. USA and Canada: John Wiley.

Ferguson, H. 1994. 'Protecting Children in Time: a Historical Sociological Study of the Abused Child and Child Protection in Cleveland from 1880 to the "Cleveland Affair"'. Ph. D. thesis, Cambridge University.

Finkelhor, D. 1984. *Child Sexual Abuse: New Theory and Research*. New York: Free Press.

Finkelhor, D., Williams, L. M. & Burns, N. 1988. *Nursery Crimes*. New York: Sage Publications.

Frazer, Sir J. G. 1922. *The Golden Bough*, abridged edition. London: Macmillan.

1936. *Aftermath: A Supplement to the Golden Bough*. London: Macmillan.

Friesen, J. G. 1991. *Uncovering the Mystery of MPD; Its Shocking Origins, Its Surprising Cure*. California: Here's Life.

Gallagher, B., Parker, H. & Hughes, B. 1994. Report to the Department of Health. MS.

1996. 'The Nature and Extent of Known Cases of Organised Child Sexual Abuse in England and Wales'. In P. Bibby (ed.), *Organised Abuse: the Current Debate*. Aldershot: Ashgate Publishing.

Gellner, E. 1992. *Reason and Culture: The Historical Role of Rationalism and Rationality*. Oxford: Blackwell.

Ginzburg, C. 1976. 'High and Low: the Theme of Forbidden Knowledge in the Sixteenth and Seventeenth Centuries'. *Past and Present*, 73.

1983 (1966). J. & A.Tedeschi (trans.), *The Night Battles*. London: Routledge & Kegan Paul.

1993 (1990). '"The Ladies from Outside": an Archaic Pattern of the Witches Sabbath', in B. Ankerloo & G. Henningsen (eds.), *Early Modern Witchcraft: Centres and Peripheries* Oxford: Clarendon Press.

1993 (1990). 'Deciphering the Sabbath'. In B. Ankarloo & G. Henningsen (eds.), *Early Modern Witchcraft: Centres and Peripheries*. Oxford: Clarendon Press.

Gledhill, R. 1990. Report in *The Times*, 7 November.

Goody, J. 1957. 'Anomie in Ashanti'. *Africa*, 27 (4).

Gordon Melton, J. 1986. 'The Evidences of Satan in Contemporary America. Paper to the American Philosophical Society, Pacific Division, Los Angeles, March.

1989. *Encyclopaedia of American Religions* 3rd edn. Detroit: Gale.

Guardian, 10 September 1990.

20 September 1990.

3 October 1990.

Gudjonsson, G. 1992. *The Psychology of Interrogations, Confessions and Testimony*. New York: John Wiley and Sons.

Hale, R. & Sinason, V. 1994. 'Internal and External Reality: Establishing Parameters'. In V. Sinason (ed.), *Treating Survivors of Satanist Abuse*. London: Routledge.

Hames, M. 1993. 'Child Pornography: A Secret Web of Exploitation'. *Child Abuse Review*, 2: 223–231.

1996. 'A Police View of Pornographic Links'. In P. Bibby (ed.), *Organised Abuse – The Current Debate*. Aldershot: Ashgate Publishing.

Harper, A. with Pugh, H. 1990. *Dance with the devil*. Eastbourne: Kingsway.

Harvey, G. 1995a. 'Satanism in Britain Today', *Journal of Contemporary Religion*, 10 (3).

1995b. 'Ritual Abuse Accusations and Incitement to Religious Hatred: Pagans and Christians in Court'. In R. Towler (ed.), *New Religions and the New Europe*. Aarhus: University Press.

Hebditch, D. & Anning, N. 1990. 'A Ritual Fabrication.' *Independent on Sunday*, 30 December.

Henningsen, G. 1980. *The Witches' Advocate: Basque Witchcraft and the Spanish Inquisition 1609–1614*. Nevada: University of Nevada Press.

Hevey, D. and Kenward, H. 1989. 'The Effects of Child Sexual Abuse'. In W.

Stainton Rogers, D. Hevey & E. Ash (eds.) *Child Abuse and Neglect: Facing the Challenge*. London: The Open University.

Hicks, R. D. 1990. 'Police Pursuit of Satanic Crime' (two parts), *Skeptical Enquirer*, 14 (3 & 4).

1991. *In Pursuit of Satan*. New York: Prometheus Books.

Hill, S. and Goodwin, J. 1989. 'Satanism: Similarities between Patient Accounts and Pre-Inquisition Historical Sources', *Dissociation 2*.

Hobsbawm, E. 1994. *The Age of Extremes: The Short Twentieth Century 1914–1991*. London: Michael Joseph.

Hollingsworth, J. 1986. *Unspeakable Acts*. New York: Congdon and Weed.

Holzer, H. 1971. *The Truth about Witchcraft*. London: Jarrolds, Arrow Books.

House of the Goddess 1991. *Guidebook*. London: House of the Goddess.

Howard League for Penal Reform 1985. *Unlawful Sex: Offences, Victims and offenders in the Criminal Justice System of England and Wales*. London: Waterlow.

Hudson, P. 1991. *Ritual Child Abuse: Discovery, Diagnosis and Treatment*. California: R & E Publisher.

Independent on Sunday, 12 August 1990.

19 August 1990.

Irvine, D. 1973. *From Witchcraft to Christ*. Cambridge: Concordia.

Jackson, M. 1990. 'The Man who could Turn into an Elephant: Shape-Shifting among the Kuranko of Sierra Leone'. In M. Jackson & I. Karp (eds.), *Personhood and Agency: The Experience of Self and Other in African Cultures*. Uppsala Studies in Cultural Anthropology No.14; Washington: Smithsonian Institute Press; Stockholm: Almqvist & Wiksell Int.

Jahoda, G. 1970 (1969). *The Psychology of Superstition*. Harmondsworth: The Penguin Press and Pelican Books.

James, A. 1993. *Childhood Identities: Self and Social Relationships in the Experience of the Child*. Edinburgh University Press.

Jenks, C. 1994. 'Child Abuse in the Postmodern Context: an Issue of Identity', *Childhood*, 2: 111–121.

Jenkins, P. 1992. *Intimate Enemies: Moral Panics in Contemporary Great Britain*. New York: Aldine de Gruyter.

Jenkins, P. & Maier-Katkin, D. 1991. 'Occult Survivors: the Making of a Myth'. In J. T. Richardson, J. Best & D. Bromley (eds.), *The Satanism Scare*. New York: Aldine de Gruyter.

Jones, D. & Seig, A. 1988. 'Child Sexual Abuse Allegations in Custody or Visitation Disputes'. In E. B. Nicholson (ed.), *Sexual Abuse Allegations in Custody and Visitation Cases*. Washington DC: American Bar Association.

Jones, D. & McCraw, E. M. 1987. 'Reliable and Fictitious Accounts of Sexual Abuse to Children' *Journal of Interpersonal Violence*, 2 (1).

Jordanova, L. 1989. 'Children in History: Concepts of Nature and Society' in G. Scarre (ed), *Children, Parents and Politics*. Cambridge University Press.

Kahaner, L. 1988. *Cults That Kill*. New York: Warner Books Inc.

Katchen, M. H. & Sakheim, D. K. 1992. 'Satanic Beliefs and Practices'. In D. K. Sakheim & S. E. Devine (eds.), *Out of Darkness: Exploring Satanism and Ritual Abuse*. New York: Lexington Books.

Kelley, S. J. 1993. 'Ritualistic Abuse of Children', Bailliere's Clinical Paediatrics, 1 (1).

Kelsall, M. 1994. 'Fostering a Ritually Abused Child'. In V. Sinason (ed.), *Treating Survivors of Satanist Abuse*. London: Routledge.

Kieckhefer, R. 1976. *European Witch Trials: Their Foundations in Popular and Learned Culture, 1300–1550* London: Routledge & Kegan Paul

1989. *Magic in the Middle Ages*. Cambridge University Press.

King, F. 1970. *Ritual Magic in England 1887 to the Present Day*. London: New English Library, Barnard's Inn.

La Fontaine, J. S. 1963. 'Witchcraft in Bugisu' in J. Middleton & E. Winter (eds), *Witchcraft and Sorcery in East Africa*. London: Routledge & Kegan Paul.

1985. *Initiation*. Harmondsworth: Penguin Books.

1986. 'An Anthropological Perspective on Children in Social Worlds'. In *Children of Social Worlds*. M. Richards & P. Light eds. Cambridge: Polity Press; Oxford: Blackwell.

1990. *Child Sexual Abuse*. Cambridge: Polity.

1992. 'Concepts of Evil, Witchcraft and the Sexual Abuse of Children in Modern England'. *Etnofoor*, 1/2.

1993. 'Defining Organised Abuse'. *Child Abuse Review*, 2: 223–31.

1994. *The Extent and Nature of Organised and Ritual Abuse*: Research Findings. London: HMSO.

1996. 'Ritual Abuse: Research Findings', in P. Bibby (ed.), *Organised Abuse – The Current Debate*. Aldershot: Ashgate Publishing.

Lamb, G. 1977. *Magic, Witchcraft and the Occult*. New York: Hippocrene Books; Newton Abbot: David & Charles.

Lane Fox, R. 1986. *Pagans and Christians*. Harmondsworth: Penguin Books.

Langone, M. D. & Blood, L. O. 1990. *Satanism and Occult-Related Violence: What You Should Know*. Massachusetts: American Family Foundation.

Lanning, K. 1989. 'Satanic, Occult, Ritualistic Crime: A Law-enforcement Perspective'. *Police Chief*, 56 (10).

Larner, C. 1981. *Enemies of God: the Witch-hunt in Scotland*. London: Chatto & Windus.

1984. *Witchcraft and Religion: the Politics of Popular Belief*. Oxford and New York: Blackwell.

LaVey, A. S. 1972. *The Satanic Rituals*. New York: Avon Books.

Levack, B. P. 1987. *The Witch-Hunt in Early Modern Europe*. London and New York: Longman.

Lewis, I. M. 1970. *Ecstatic Religion*. Harmondsworth: Penguin Books.

Lewis, J. 1986. 'Anxieties About the Family and the Relationships Between Parents, Children and the State in Twentieth-century England', in M. Richards and P. Light (eds.), *Children of Social Worlds*. Cambridge: Polity Press, Blackwell.

Logan, K. 1988. *Paganism and the Occult*. Eastbourne: Kingsway.

1994. *Satanism and the Occult*. Eastbourne: Kingsway.

Luhrmann, T. 1986. 'Witchcraft, Morality and Magic in contemporary London'. *International Journal of Moral and Social Studies*, 1 (1).

1989. *Persuasions of the Witch's Craft*. Oxford: Blackwell.

McFadyen, A., Hanks, H. & James, C. 1993. 'Ritual Abuse: A Definition'. *Child Abuse Review* 2 (1) March.

Macfarlane, A. 1970. *Witchcraft in Tudor and Stuart England: a regional and comparative study.* London: Routledge & Kegan Paul.

    1985. 'The root of all evil'. In *The Anthropology of Evil.* D. Parkin (ed.), Oxford: Blackwell.

MacGaffey, W. 1994. *The Eyes of Understanding.* Kongo Minkisi Washington Smithsonian Institution Press for National Museum of African Art.

Mackay, Charles 1841. *Extraordinary Popular Delusions and the Madness of Crowds.* London: Richard Bentley (2nd edn. 1852; republished 1932, New York: The Noonday Press).

Mair, L. P. 1969. *Witchcraft.* London: Weidenfeld and Nicholson, World University Library.

Mail on Sunday, 21 October 1990

Marrs, T. 1989. *Satan's Plan to Destroy Our Kids: Ravaged by the New Age.* Texas: Living Truth.

Meyer, B. 1995. '"Delivered from the Powers of darkness": Confessions of Satanic Riches in Christian Ghana'. *Africa,* 65 (2).

Middleton, J. 1960. *Lugbara Religion.* London: Oxford University Press for the International African Institute.

    1963. 'Witchcraft and Sorcery in Lugbara'. In J. Middleton & E. Winter (eds.), *Witchcraft and Sorcery in East Africa.* London: Routledge & Kegan Paul.

Middleton, J. & Winter, E. (eds.) 1963. *Witchcraft and Sorcery in East Africa.* London: Routledge & Kegan Paul.

Mitchell, J. 1956. *The Yao Village.* Manchester University Press.

Mollon, P. 1994. 'The impact of evil'. In V. Sinason (ed.), *Treating Survivors of Satanist Abuse.* London: Routledge.

Moody, E. 1974. 'Magical Therapy: Contemporary Satanism'. In I. I. Zaretsky & M. Leone (eds.), *Religious Movements in Contemporary America.* Princeton University Press.

Morris, S. 1994. 'You will only hear half of it and you won't believe it: counselling with a woman with a mild learning disability'. In V. Sinason (ed.), *Treating Survivors of Satanist Abuse.* London: Routledge.

Morton-Williams, P. 1956. 'The Atinga Cult among the South-Western Yoruba: a Sociological Analysis of a Witch-finding Movement'. *Bulletin de l'Institut français d'Afrique noire,* 18 (3–4).

Moston, S. 1987. 'The Suggestibility of Children in Interview Studies'. *First Language,* 7.

    1990a. 'How Children Interpret and Respond to Questions: Situational Sources of Suggestibility in Eyewitness Interviews'. *Social Behaviour,* 5: 155–67.

    1990b. 'The Effects of Social Support on Children's Eyewitness Testimony'. *Applied Cognitive Psychology,* 4.

Muchembled, R. 1993 (1990). 'Satanic Myths and Cultural Reality'. in B. Ankarloo & G. Henningsen (eds.), *Early Modern Witchcraft: Centres & Peripheries.* Oxford: Clarendon Press.

Mulhern, S. 1991. 'Satanism and Psychotherapy: A Rumour in Search of an

Inquisition', in J. Richardson, J. Best & D. Bromley (eds.), *The Satanism Scare*. New York: Aldine de Gruyter.

1994. 'Satanism, Ritual Abuse, and Multiple Personality Disorder: a Sociohistorical Perspective', *The International Journal of Clinical and Experimental Hypnosis*, XLII (4).

Murray, M. A. 1921. *The Witch-Cult in Western Europe*. Oxford University Press.

Nathan, D. 1991. 'Satanism and Child Molestation: Constructing the Ritual Abuse Scare'. In J. T. Richardson, J. Best & D. Bromley (eds.), *The Satanism Scare*. New York: Aldine de Gruyter.

Nathan, D. & Snedeker, M. 1995. *Satan's Silence; Ritual Abuse and the Making of a Modern American Witchhunt*. New York: Basic Books.

Newall, V. 1973. 'The Jew as Witch Figure', in V. Newall (ed.), *The Witch in History*. London: Routledge & Kegan Paul.

New Federalist, 15 November 1988.

News of the World, 21 April 1996.

Nice, J. *The Law and the Occult*. Unpublished manuscript.

Norton, K. 1994. 'In-patient Psychotherapy at the Henderson Hospital' in V. Sinason (ed.), *Treating Survivors of Satanist Abuse*. London: Routledge.

Nwaka, G. T. 1986. '"Leopard" killings in Annang, Nigeria'. *Africa*, 56 (4).

Occult Census 1989. *The Occult Census*. Leeds Sorcerer's Apprentice.

Ofshe, R. 1992. 'Inadvertent Hypnosis During Interrogation: False Confession Due to Dissociative State; Misidentified Multiple Personality and the Satanic Cult Hypothesis'. *International Journal of Clinical and Experimental Hypnosis*. July 1992.

Ofshe, R. & Watters, E. 1994. *Making Monsters*. New York: Scribner.

Opie, P. & I. 1967 (1959). *The Lore and Language of Schoolchildren*. Oxford: Oxford University Press.

ORCRO 1990. *The Occult Response to the Christian Response to the Occult*, 6.

Parker, J. 1993. *At the Heart of Darkness*. London: Sidgwick and Jackson.

Parker, R. 1989. *The occult: Deliverance from Evil*. Leicester: Inter-Varsity Press.

Parkin, D. (ed) 1985. *The Anthropology of Evil*. Oxford: Blackwell.

Pazder, L. & Smith, M. 1980. *Michelle Remembers*. New York: Pocket Books.

Pengelly, J. & Waredale, D. 1992. *Something out of Nothing; The Myth of 'Satanic Ritual Abuse' and the Truth about Paganism and Witchcraft*. Great Britain: The Pagan Federation.

Pocock, D. 1986 (1985). 'Unruly Evil', in D. Parkin (ed.), *The Anthropology of Evil*. Oxford: Blackwell.

Pollock, L. 1983. *Forgotten Children: Parent-child relations from 1500 to 1900*. Cambridge University Press.

Ralushai, N. V. 1996. *Report of the Commission of Inquiry into Witchcraft, Violence and Ritual Murders in the Northern Province of the Republic of South Africa*. Unpublished manuscript.

ReachOut News 1991. Newsletter of the ReachOut Trust, No. 24 (October).

Redmayne, A. 1970. 'Chikanga: An African Diviner with an International Reputation. In M. Douglas (ed.) *Witchcraft Confessions and Accusations*. London: Tavistock.

Richards, A. I. 1935. 'A Modern Movement of Witchfinders'. *Africa*, 8 (4).

Richardson, J. T. 1991. 'Satanism in the Courts: from Murder to Heavy Metal'.

in J. T. Richardson, J. Best & D. Bromley (eds.), *The Satanism Scare*. New York: Aldine de Gruyter.

Richardson, J. 1991. 'Satanism as a Social Problem'. In J. Richardson, J. Best, D. Bromley (eds.). *The Satanism Scare*. New York: Aldine de Gruyter.

Robbins, R. H. 1959. *The Encyclopaedia of Witchcraft and Demonology*. New York: Crown.

Robertson, A. F. 1991. *Beyond the Family: the Social Organisation of Human Reproduction*. Cambridge: Polity Press, in association with Blackwell (Oxford).

Roper, L. 1991. 'Witchcraft in Early Modern Germany'. *History Workshop: A Journal of Socialist and Feminist Historians*, Issue 32 (Autumn).

Rose, E. 1989 (1962). *A Razor for a Goat: Problems in the History of Witchcraft and Diabolism*. Toronto: University of Toronto Press, Scholarly Reprint Series.

Rowland, R. 1993 (1990). 'Fantasticall and Devilishe Persons': European Witch-Beliefs in Comparative Perspective', in B. Ankarloo & G. Henningsen (eds.), *Early Modern Witchcraft: Centres and Peripheries*. Oxford: Clarendon Press.

Ruel, M. J. 1970. 'Were-Animals and the Introverted Witch', in M. Douglas (ed.), *Witchcraft Confessions and Accusations*. London: Tavistock.

Sakheim, K. & Devine, S. 1992. *Out of Darkness: Exploring Satanism and Ritual Abuse*. New York: Lexington Books.

Schapera, I. 1969. 'The Crime of Sorcery'. The Huxley Memorial Lecture, Proceedings of the Royal Anthropological Institute of Great Britain and Ireland.

Schneider, D. M. 1976. 'The Meaning of Incest'. *Journal of the Polynesian Society*, 85.

Scott, S. & Wistrich, H. n. d. *Supporting Survivors of Ritual Abuse*. Video distributed by Manchester Rape Crisis Centre.

Shan 1986. *Which Craft: an Introduction to the Craft*. London: House of the Goddess.

Sinason, V. (ed.) 1994. *Treating Survivors of Satanist Abuse*. London: Routledge.

Sjoberg, R. L. 1995. 'Child Testimonies During an Outbreak of Witch Hysteria: Sweden 1670–1671'. *Journal of Child Psychology and Psychiatry*, 36 (6).

Spencer, J. & Flin, R. 1993 (1990). *The Evidence of Children: the Law and the Psychology*. London: Blackstone.

Stainton Rogers, R. 1989. 'The Social Construction of Childhood'. In W. Stainton Rogers, D. Hevey & E. Ash (eds.) *Child Abuse and Neglect: Facing the Challenge*. London: Open University.

Steadman, L. 1985–6 'The killing of witches'. *Oceania*, LVI.

Stratford, L. 1988. *Satan's Underground*. Oregon: Harvest House.

Summers, Rev. M. 1926. *A Popular History of Witchcraft and Demonology*. London: Routledge & Kegan Paul.

Summit, R. C. 1983. 'The Child Abuse Accommodation Syndrome'. *Child-Abuse and Neglect*, 7.

Tait, D. 1963. 'A Sorcery Hunt in Dagomba'. *Africa*, 33 (2).

Tate, T. 1991. *Children for the Devil: Ritual Abuse and Satanic Crime*. London: Methuen.

1994. 'Press, Politics and Paedophilia: a Practitioner's Guide to the Media'. In V. Sinason (ed.), *Treating Survivors of Satanist Abuse*. London: Routledge.

Tattum, D. & Lane, D. 1988. *Bullying in Schools*. Stoke-on-Trent: Trentham Books.

The Times , 7 November 1990.

Thomas, K. 1970. 'The Relevance of Social Anthropology to the Historical Study of English Witchcraft'. In M. Douglas (ed.), *Witchcraft: Confessions and Accusations*. London: Tavistock.

1973 (1971) *Religion and the Decline of Magic*. Harmondsworth: Penguin Books.

Thomson, W. 1990. 'The Origins of the Allegations Concerning Satanic Child Abuse in Britain'. Unpublished ms.

Thornley, M. 1989. 'Fostering an Abused Child.' In W. Stainton Rogers, D. Hevey & E. Ash (eds.), *Child Abuse and Neglect: Facing the Challenge*. London: Open University.

Time Out, 24–31 October 1990.

Trevor-Roper, H. R. 1990 (1967). *The European Witch-Craze of the Sixteenth and Seventeenth Centuries*. Harmondsworth: Penguin Books.

Trinkle, G. 1986. *Delivered to Declare*. London: Hodder & Stoughton.

Trowell, J. 1994. 'Ritual Organised Abuse: Management Issues'. In V. Sinason (ed.), *Treating Survivors of Satanist Abuse*. London: Routledge.

Truzzi, M. 1974. 'Towards a Sociology of the Occult: Notes on Modern Witchcraft'. In I. I. Zaretsky & M. Leone (eds.), *Religious Movements in Contemporary America*. Princeton University Press.

Turner, V. W. 1957. *Schism and Continuity in African Society*. Manchester University Press.

Victor, J. S. 1990. 'The Spread of Satanic Cult Rumours', *Skeptical Enquirer*, 14 (3).

1991. 'The Dynamics of Rumor – Panics about Satanic Cults'. In J. T. Richardson, J. Best & D. Bromley (eds.), *The Satanism Scare*. New York: Aldine de Gruyter.

1993. *Satanic Panic: The Creation of a Contemporary Legend*. Chicago & LaSalle: Open Court.

Vizard, E. & Tranter, M. 1988. 'Helping Children to Describe Experiences of Child Sexual Abuse – A Guide to Practice'. In A. Bentovim et al., *Child Sexual Abuse Within the Family*. Kent: John Wright.

Walinski-Kiehl, R. A. 1996. 'The Devil's Children: Child Witch-trials in Early Modern Germany'. *Continuity and Change*, 11 (2).

Ward, P. 1995. 'The Satanic and Ritual Abuse of Children'. MS.

Warnke, M.with. Balsiger D. & Jones L. 1972. *The Satan-Seller*. New Jersey: Logos.

Waterhouse, R. 1990. *The Independent on Sunday*, 12 August.

Weir, I. K. & Wheatcroft, M. S. 1995. 'Allegations of Children's Involvement in Ritual Sexual Abuse: Clinical Experience of 20 cases'. *Child Abuse and Neglect*, 19 (4).

Willis, R. 1968. 'Kamcape: An Anti-Sorcery Movement in South-West Tanzania'. *Africa*. 38 (1).

1970. 'Instant Millennium: the Sociology of African Witch-cleansing cults'. In M. Douglas (ed.), *Witchcraft: Confessions and Accusations*. London: Tavistock, ASA Monographs No 9.

Youngson, S. 1993. 'Ritual Abuse: Consequences for Professionals'. *Child Abuse Review*, December.

1994. 'Ritual Abuse: the Personal and Professional Cost for Workers'. In V. Sinason (ed.), *Treating Survivors of Satanist Abuse*. London: Routledge.

Index

Lightning Source UK Ltd.
Milton Keynes UK

173010UK00001B/199/A